Skim Milk Yankees Fighting

Skim Milk Yankees Fighting

The Battle of Athens, Missouri
August 5, 1861

Jonathan K. Cooper-Wiele

Camp Pope Bookshop
2007

Press of the Camp Pope Bookshop
PO Box 2232
Iowa City, Iowa 52244
www.camppope.com

Cover illustrations:
The Athens Battle Flag, courtesy of the Harlan-Lincoln House
at Iowa Wesleyan College, Mt. Pleasant, Iowa

Croton, Iowa, ca. 1857, courtesy of the Battle of Athens State Historic Site

Dedicated to the memory
of my great-grandfathers

Captain William Jackson
Private Elkanah Franklin Scott

First Northeast Missouri Home Guard

CONTENTS

ILLUSTRATIONS AND MAPS

Illustrations

Maps

Acknowledgements

My passion for the American Civil War seems to have preceded my awareness of it. Those who maintain that such an intense, primordial affinity indicates a previous life as, perhaps in my case, a Union soldier, may be right. Or, the fact that I was inundated in Civil War books and toys at an impressionable age, during the war's centennial, may explain my seduction. Whatever the reason, I owe a great debt of gratitude in this and all else to my parents, Laura and Lester Wiele. They, above all others, are responsible for my interest in this period of history as well as for my love of learning generally. They read to me, listened while I read to them, they entertained and encouraged my questions. Their child was the father of the man I am.

Of course, it didn't hurt, and endlessly fascinated me, that my mother had known a living, breathing Civil War veteran, her grandfather, George Kearns, once a boy in the Indiana Volunteers. (After the war, George's family moved west to Missouri and there, in Kahoka, he married Martha Jackson, daughter of Captain William Jackson, to whom this book is dedicated.)

It was also my parents who hauled me to the site of the Battle of Athens when they heard about it from friends. Once my passion was kindled, they did whatever they could to fuel its fire.

I shall never forget one exciting Sunday afternoon as a child in the home of local historian Kenneth Doud. Mr. Doud's enthusiasm proved infectious, and for it I remain indebted.

Owner and editor of the Press of the Camp Pope Bookshop, Clark Kenyon, has done yeoman's work in kindly but straightforwardly encouraging improvements in the text and its format over several years. His unfailingly rapid responses to my queries, particularly close reading of the text, questions both of detail and logic, to say nothing of relentless checking of sources, sleuthing to uncover new ones (including an array of wonderful photos included in the book and the battle flag featured on its cover), precision, and unfailing helpfulness, have expedited the process of publication and witness to why his press has become highly respected for both its republication of classics and publication of contemporary works on the Trans-Mississippi theatre of the American Civil War.

Junior High School Civil War buddy, Dick Howard, generously renewed the colloquia on the war he and I used to hold under a large spreading tree behind Oak Street Junior High School in Burlington, Iowa, in the late 1960s. More than thirty years later Dick assiduously read the manuscript and made keen observations, worthy of his lawyer's eye, on how I might enable the reader better to visualize the field of Athens on August 5, 1861. Burlington attorneys and Civil War buffs, Jim Miller, and Gerry Goddard also generously read and annotated the manuscript with lawyerly eyes, providing helpful advice both on content and style.

Roger Boyd, Site Administrator of the Battle of Athens State Historic Site, has been most generous with his time and insights during my visits to the battlefield. The volunteers at the Clark County Historical Society in Kahoka, Missouri, where George Kearns lived and my mother grew up, were wonderful hosts during a visit there in the summer of 1995. Steve Murphy called home to have his wife fax a brief article of his on the battle which contained a source I had not yet encountered.

Roger F. Harris, former principal of the middle school where I teach, related stories of his experiences as a combat marine in Viet Nam, affording me vicarious insight into a world of battle which, while a century and many miles removed from the American Civil War, still has certain analogies with that earlier conflict.

Roger caused me to reflect on "the telling," the narrative of battle, all we non-participants have. The backbone of my book, a letter by Home Guardsman John Hiller written a few hours after the battle, is almost immediate, yet a medium nevertheless. At such times, some Civil War soldiers emphasized to folks back home, pressing to hear what battle was like, that the experience resisted capture with pen and ink. They would have agreed wholeheartedly with their contemporary master of the pen, Walt Whitman, who cautioned that the "real war" would never make it into the books. The historian then and now has narrative, narrated memory, oral or written, with its defining moments of clarity, obscurity, and obscurantism.

This study is deeply indebted to those passionate local historians like Ben Dixon, Kenny Doud, Patricia Mullenix, Jan Gross, Steve Murphy, and others who have worked away in the vineyard of the Battle of Athens for years, some long before I was born. Without their collecting a plethora of obscure documents pertaining to this event, my work would have been impossible.

There is one other. In my first book, on the philosophy of mathematics, I acknowledged her for typing, editing, and general intellectual stimulation and inspiration. Her direct contribution to this book consists mainly in suffering a summer in which I was virtually missing in the action of writing its first draft, and in indulging my unceasing chatter about the Battle of Athens and the Civil War in general. However, she—my wife, Beverly—remains the encompassing, faithful presence reminding me that love means not reflecting the other like a mirror. She provides my joy in living, in coming home, and in being at home that made this effort possible and worthwhile. Having now closed the Civil War chapter of my life and reopened an earlier one—not only attempting to understand the historical Jesus but to reenact his embrace to the expendables of today—I see how her sustaining, sometimes long-suffering, love helped bring me to myself and to my—*our*—time.

While also not directly responsible for this book, members of the Civil War collecting community purveyed objects for my collection of the effects of the Union Infantry Private which were great sources of inspiration. Taking turns sitting with me as I worked, these survivors functioned for me somewhere between those unforgettable animate-inanimates of Robbins's *Skinny Legs and All* and the mirror in *The House of Seven Gables* in which, according to Hawthorne, one could view all the scenes ever reflected in it. Hopefully they now reflect their scenes for others.

While this book is not dedicated to him, I think it just to acknowledge Joseph Kearns, my great-grandfather George's big brother. Enlisting in the Indiana Volunteers in 1861, reenlisting as a Veteran Volunteer in 1864, he was captured in Arkansas and imprisoned at Tyler, Texas. Paroled, his health apparently broken, he returned home to Indiana in March 1865 and died at the end of that month. A brief two weeks later, Robert E. Lee surrendered the Army of Northern Virginia, effectively ending the northern war for Union and Emancipation.

I never heard of Joe Kearns when I was growing up. My mother naturally spoke of her grandfather, George, whom she had known and loved as a little girl, and of his musket, carefully preserved in a corner of the house he built. George, I always heard, had run away three times to join up as a drummer; pursued by his father and brought home twice, his third attempt proved the charm. Whatever the veracity of this anecdote, the patriotic fervor of Unionists surrounding that 4th of July of 1863 apparently overwhelmed sixteen-year-old George, who enrolled in the 115th Ohio, a six month regiment. He was safely discharged the following February at the expiration of his enlistment. Ironically, his older brother, Joe, who had given, in the words of his president, "the last full measure of devotion," became forgotten in a generation.

Eli Wiesel, chronicler of the Holocaust, reminds us that there is no history without memory. In *Pickett's Charge in History and Memory*, Carol Reardon affirms Wiesel's point, but demonstrates that memory—especially of battle—is almost by definition flawed and that the historian must subject all such memories to the fire of critical scrutiny, skim the dross, and fashion what seems to be the relatively pure remainder into a reasonable representation of "the battle." This little book seeks to fashion for this generation the most reasonable representation possible of the Battle of Athens, Missouri.

If I were to dedicate this book to one other, it would be my mother, Laura Elizabeth Scott Wiele, who read and, I think, approved the manuscript but who died before its publication. In retrospect, I see that her, and my dad's, unfailing support of my interests as a child and an adult were really specifications of a broader, deeper, indeed unqualified and limitless love extending well beyond the boundaries of home and family.

Like the above-mentioned love of my wife, I find in my mom's love inspiration to hope, and even believe, that the stories of such battles as I tell here will one day pale beside tales of those who love their enemies and die before taking another life.

Jonathan K. Cooper-Wiele
Jamaica Plain, Massachusetts
September 30, 2007

It had it all: Cemetery Hill, the Cornfield, a cannonade, ignominious skedaddles, valorous stands, backs to a river, a numerically inferior force triumphing, neighbors firing upon neighbors, refugees, a bayonet charge, an arms differential, entrenching, casualties, death, bloated corpses, and the wonder and terror of volunteers "seeing the elephant." Evoking such epic engagements as Shiloh, Antietam, or Gettysburg, these characteristics belong to the nearly unknown Trans-Mississippi Civil War Battle of Athens (pronounced "Aythens"), Missouri. Commencing around 5:30 a.m. on the sultry morning[1] of August 5, 1861, in Clark County, in the far northeast corner of Missouri near the Iowa border, it was over in a couple of hours. Like many of their counterparts at the Battle of Bull Run fought just two weeks earlier in the east, the combatants were state militias—the Home Guard (for the North) and the State Guard (for the South).

The battle first presented itself to me (an eight-year-old, self-proclaimed "Civil War Nut," hauled to its site in 1962 by indulgent parents) through its fields, its leaning, dilapidated houses and overgrown stone foundations, and through the infectious missionary zeal of an elderly man, Kenneth Doud, who literally ran out to greet any passerby who pulled up his lane.

Descended from Southern sympathizing Athenians, of whom there were more than a few in 1861, Mr. Doud eagerly narrated the battle from the standpoint of his house, riddled with minie balls,[2] many still embedded in its siding. He was one of those myriad "local historians" across the country, exhibiting his collection of artifacts from the battle gratis in his own home—his bat-

Kenneth Doud (Author's collection)

tlefield museum. Here one could view minie balls, ersatz canister shot made from chain links, and the anvil on which they had been cut, and one could purchase pamphlets on the battle by another local historian, Ben Dixon.

Athens was virtually a ghost town a century after the battle, inhabited by one or two mortals like Mr. Doud. Their sole purpose seemed to be to speak for the dead and conscientiously to guard the few enfeebled remnants of the once thriving town.

The Thome-Benning "mansion," known in local lore as the "Cannonball House," crowned a steep bluff descending to the Des Moines River. Visitors approached it cautiously through overgrown Virginia Street, having navigated the glares and "Whaddaya want here's?" of the residents of the house up the road where Susan Clark Anthony lived at the time of the battle. Vacant and defenseless before the ravages of time, vandals, and partiers, the Thome-Benning House was falling down and

Author's parents at the Thome-Benning
House in 1964. (Author's collection)

in upon itself. Yet there, against its kitchen wall through which a solid cannon shot crashed a century before, stood Susan Benning's wounded cupboard, its upper left corner torn away by the intruding ball.

We made pilgrimages periodically to the field of Athens as I grew, my interest in the Civil War outstripping my size, imagination, and budget for a nascent collection of sacred relics from the conflict. My connection to the place and the events that occurred there was strengthened by the knowledge that two of my ancestors served in the First Northeast Missouri Home Guard, one of the two regiments engaged there. For years local preservationists lobbied the State of Missouri to make Athens a state historic site, raised money, bought land, and finally, in 1975, triumphed.

Today the "Cannonball House" is beautifully restored, its wounds still visible through protective plexiglass coverings. Many of its original furnishings have returned, but Susan Benning's cupboard is not yet among them. The McKee House, site of Home Guard Colonel David Moore's headquarters, is being restored. Triennial August reenactments of the battle attract increasing numbers of visitors to the site, archaeological investigations are conducted, and further preservation and restoration under the expert eye of Site Manager Roger Boyd are always in the works.

"So little is known as to what actually took place at Athens that day" of battle on August 5, 1861, lamented J. W. Murphy, a local newspaper editor, in 1913.[3] It is true. There are no official battle reports, just a few newspaper stories, but one contemporary description by a participant, a lot of old-timers' recollections stretching into the 20th century, and a smattering of secondary studies. Revisiting Athens years after those boyhood excursions, I realized that my familiarity with the site, while breeding the opposite of contempt, had not bred commensurate insight into "what actually took place" there. So, I assembled sources I had collected over the years, beginning with those bought from Mr. Doud, purchased others, spoke to local historians who shared their writings, xeroxed documents at the Kahoka, Missouri, Historical Society and plats of Athens at the Clark County Court House, and began trying to induce from these materials some coherent picture of the battle.

What began as an article burgeoned and became weighted with notes. The result is, I believe, the most comprehensive, systematic, original, and well-documented study of the Battle of Athens to date. I have not simply patched together various accounts of the battle, but juxtaposed and critically evaluated them (usually in the endnotes so as not to encumber the narrative) in order to paint as accurate a picture as possible of what transpired. A two hour battle, especially one so poorly documented, is an immensely complicated event to understand and to portray. How to present

Thome-Benning House today. (Author's collection)

simultaneous episodes so that the reader will experience them as such while reading about them successively? It is tough to convey the timing of individual events in a battle—when they occurred, their duration, and their temporal relations to other events. Participants are not always accurate sources, not simply because memory is fallible but because, even in the midst of battle, the soldier's experience of time is often far different than that ticked off by his watch. When I draw an educated, though incompletely documented, conclusion about what was happening at a particular time, I make that clear and attempt always to provide the basis for my conclusions in the endnotes.

In the course of writing I have had that most gratifying experience of gradually constructing the outlines of some missing piece of the puzzle with other pieces, knowing that it must have been as its outlines suggest, only to find some new, or reread some old, source that suddenly provides the missing piece itself, looking quite like I knew it must! It is in such moments that one knows that the past, while not a simple set of pre-established facts to be collected, does possess a certain incoercible shape and form discoverable through inference, hypothesis, theory, and the various forms of documentary and physical evidence.

An example of this experience was my piecing together in Chapter 4, "Our Boys Stood Fire!," of the role of a small group of Farmington, Iowa, men in the initial stages of the fight near a cornfield below the town on the Des Moines River. Most sources recount a rout of Home Guard cavalry starting almost immediately after they came under fire from State Guardsmen in the cornfield. The cavalrymen bolted to the left and ran their horses across the Des Moines to Iowa, panicking a few men on foot who abandoned the field with them. Some became easy targets in the river for the State Guard.

Stationmaster D. C. Beaman at Croton, Iowa, just across the river from Athens, described in a 1905 article a rout of the "union outpost," on the heels of which arrived a "union reinforcement" from David Moore, the Home Guard Colonel. Beaman claims to have witnessed a small party come under fire, retreat, and then to have seen a larger reinforcement arrive.[4]

Almost all accounts agree that a Home Guard skedaddle occurred in the face of the State Guard onslaught from the cornfield. All ascribe it to Home Guard cavalry and almost all concur that it was led either by one "Captain Spellman…with his colors flying," as Colonel Moore later sarcastically recalled, or a Lieutenant-Colonel Callihan, who shouted "Come on, men! We'll never stop 'em!" Some accounts say that a Home Guard infantry unit under gargantuan Captain Ellsberry Small held their ground, thereby playing a major role in stemming the State Guard tide in the cornfield and preventing it from overwhelming the Home Guard center up on the hill. Here, therefore, is a two-part scenario: cavalry retreat and infantry stand.

I hypothesized early on that Spellman's cavalry, being mounted, probably arrived at the edge of the cornfield before Small's infantry. However, I had a hard time connecting or equating this cavalry company with the "small outpost" mentioned by D. C. Beaman. After my manuscript was virtually complete, I came across a source by another Croton Beaman, this one the Reverend G. C. Beaman.[5] Reverend Beaman wrote that the State Guard troops advancing through the cornfield "attacked our picket guards and forty men sent from Farmington to aid us." Here, it seemed, was the "union outpost" mentioned by D.C. Beaman. Farmington men retreating across the Des Moines are mentioned as casualties in other sources.

My reconstruction of this part of the battle is that a Home Guard outpost of Farmington men down near Jackson Street, at the bottom of Athens hill, are surprised by "brisk fire" from hidden State Guardsmen advancing through the tall August corn.[6] Panicked, the Farmington men break for the river on their left under fire from State Guardsmen taking position in the Jane Gray house at the edge of the corn. Some Farmington men run back up the hill at their rear toward Athens where the Home Guard center is forming under fire from State Guard artillery.

At the sound of gunfire on the Home Guard left, Spellman's cavalry pound down the hill toward the cornfield, catch the panic underway, and spur across the river to safety in Iowa. On Spellman's heels comes Small's infantry, perhaps slowed and unnerved by Farmington men running back through their ranks up the hill. At the edge of the cornfield, the giant Small rallies his men into a line of battle waving his musket over his head and they open on the advancing State Guard. Iowa militia across the river enfilade the State Guard right in the cornfield, concentrating fire on the Gray house. The State Guard advance falters. Those holed up in the house abandon it, and the State Guard right retreats.

And then, after my manuscript was complete, my editor discovered a letter written by one F. M. Tate in the August 13, 1861, *Keokuk Daily Gate City,* which purports to tell the correct record of the service of "Captain Scott's company of this place" (Farmington). Apparently, this company of 100 men was called to Croton the night before the battle by Colonel Moore. Eight or ten of them crossed over the next morning to have breakfast and to confer with Moore. "As these men were returning to join their company, having arrived at the ford a short distance below town, the right flank of the enemy numbering some three hundred suddenly emerged from the corn in which they were concealed, and at a distance of not more than thirty yards poured a heavy volley of shot at them."[7] The Farmington men fired back three or four rounds (all the ammunition they had), then retreated across the river. In their retreat, two of their number were injured. The rest of their company plus men from the Keokuk militia covered their retreat from the Iowa side and engaged the State Guard in the cornfield. It seems there was not a Farmington outpost as such, but a small group of men fording the river back to Croton at the very moment the State Guard right opened their attack. This is basically the same information reported the day after the battle in the *Keokuk Daily Gate City,* the difference being that the breakfasting Iowa troops were identified as Keokuk militia.[8]

It was probably not exactly like this in the cornfield and it may even have been significantly different. But based on hints and indications from my sources to date, I believe that it makes sense to argue that something like this occurred, all the while remembering J. W. Murphy's dictum fifty-two years after the battle: "so little is known as to what actually took place at Athens that day."

As my manuscript expanded it became clear that I needed to provide an idea of the larger context of the Battle of Athens. I have tried to do this, but I did not intend to give, nor do I pretend to have given, a comprehensive treatment of the events in Missouri, or even those in Clark County, surrounding and leading up to the battle.

The title, *Skim Milk Yankees Fighting,* and the respective chapter titles are taken from a letter written later on the day of the battle by Home Guardsman John Hiller. Running through and uniting these chapters is the theme of ambivalence. While ambivalent attempts to navigate between the extremes of Unconditional Unionism and secession may not have been peculiar to Missourians, having been shared by citizens in all of the "border states" which eventually sup-

John Hiller, ca. 1870s.
(Hiller Family Papers, 1785-1993, C3856, Western Historical Manuscript Collection-Columbia, MO)

plied troops to both Confederate and United States armies, I have found it to be a dominant, recurring theme expressed in a variety of forms in my work on the Battle of Athens. This ambivalence toward extremes is expressed in the fact that the majority of Missourians adhered to centrist, compromising, and neutralist options from the presidential campaign of 1860 through the secession of one southern state after another, to the first summer of the Civil War in 1861. It is expressed as well by local Clark County persons who played roles in events culminating in cannon and musket fire in the streets of Athens.

The reader first encounters this theme in Chapter 1, "Scouts and Other Sources," in the story of the Harrison family divided by politics, but united to warn the Home Guard commander, David Moore, of an impending State Guard attack. The Reverend Jabez Harrison was serving Moore's regiment as chaplain. His daughter, Drucilla, vociferously pro-Confederate, was being courted by a State Guard lieutenant whose Colonel was planning an attack on the Athens camp. Blood proved thicker than politics for Drucilla and her sister, but Harrison blood spilled at Athens nevertheless.

Drucilla Harrison's ambivalence is contextualized, in Chapter 2, "Our Neighbors Against Us," as a case of a wider-spread Missourian quest for compromise, for some tenable middle ground between secession and Unconditional Unionism. The political, economic, and social-psychological context of Missouri as ambivalent is outlined, as well as the gradual shift of some of her citizens from positions of compromise and ambivalence to more clearly defined allegiance to either the United or Confederate States of America.

Illustrative of this shift is the first treatment of a clandestine meeting at the little Highland Schoolhouse in Clark County in March of 1861. Many of the anxious Union men who here formed a secret protection society, drafting an oath which they signed, went on to become very public soldiers of the First Northeast Missouri Home Guard. One could well regard this meeting as the genesis of that Home Guard, the initial purpose of which was to secure the lives and property of its members against neighbors seeking to bring Missouri into the Confederacy. A close reading of the document these men produced suggests that far from being extremists, they were ideologically very close to, if not recent adherents of, the compromising Constitutional Union Party of John Bell, which ran a close second to Stephen Douglas in Missouri in the presidential election of 1860.

Returning to the biographical, Chapter 2 concludes by providing an original analysis of the political development of the Union Home Guard commander, David Moore, in the context

David Moore
(Courtesy of Battle of Athens State Historic Site)

of the perceived options of the day. Reconstructing these options is a daunting hermeneutic task. In the course and wake of the war which followed, both the early options and the decision-making processes of those confronting them, were probably recalled as being more definite than they were. That is, if David Moore emerged by the summer of 1861 as an "Unconditional Union man," and if he fought valorously and faithfully for the Union thereafter, as he did, then it was likely that his adherents would project this "conclusion" backwards, minimizing or denying any indications of early ambivalence or centrism on his part. On the other hand, Moore's detractors would probably tend to construe early ambivalence as evidence of crypto-sympathy for the opposite cause than that Moore ultimately chose, or to interpret his ultimate decision as opportunistic in light of earlier ambivalence.

I interpret David Moore both as exemplifying the ambivalence of most Missourians in the midst of the burgeoning sectional conflict, and as moving with measured tread toward a commitment inexorably shaped by events beyond his control in the nation and in his state. I take the view that there is no real evidence that Moore flirted with Confederate sympathies or that he was an unprincipled opportunist seeking military command regardless of allegiance, a myth the origins of which are examined and which, I hope, is laid to rest once and for all, despite at least one recent repetition of it.[9]

Moore's personal journey to alignment with the United States in order to oppose Sterling Price's State Guard was not necessarily shared so unconditionally by some of his Home Guard rank and file. In Chapter 3, "Rebels and Patriots," I argue that Moore's reduced ranks at Athens just before the battle were due not only to his furlough system, the traditional explanation, but also to ambivalence on the part of many Home Guardsmen toward what appeared to be imminent bloodletting—ambivalence not acknowledged by most sources at the time or since. It seems likely that the combined effects of a disarmament meeting, a proclamation by the State Guard commander, Martin Green, and a State Guard victory at Troublesome Creek served to convince many of the Home Guard rank and file that a chance still existed to remain neutral in the national conflict and to compromise at home, thus avoiding the bloodying of themselves and/or their neighbors.

Also in Chapter 3, I begin to examine the view on both sides that Moore's low numbers (approximately three to four hundred men, compared to some fifteen hundred State Guard troops) were offset by a technological differential in his favor. While there is some confusion as to when and where the Home Guard received some of their U.S. issue rifle-muskets, I present the most complete and systematic discussion yet of the arming of the Home Guard, the net effect of which seems to have been a surfeit of primary

Martin Green
(Courtesy of Arthur W. Green, Jr.)

issue long arms and ammunition. The past is hard to predict. One current dogma is that our forebears were armed to the teeth, especially in areas like Missouri which were battle zones before the onset of formal hostilities in April 1861. Evidence cited in Chapter 3 indicates, to the contrary, that neither side came to the fight well-armed, both with respect to the quantity and quality of small arms. Consequently, I believe that the outcome of the Battle of Athens, as well as the fight for northern Missouri—and southern Iowa—would have been significantly different had the Home Guardsmen not received issue rifle-muskets, bayonets, ammunition, and, presumably, accoutrements, in time before the battle.

Chapter 4, "Our Boys Stood Fire!," presents the most critical, thorough, systematic, and original reconstruction of the battle to date. Recognizing its inexorable and reciprocal bond with tactics, I continue to examine the role of superior Home Guard weaponry acknowledged by both sides.

At the same time, I try to avoid the frequent and facile conclusion that possession of military grade weapons by Moore's Home Guard made victory inevitable. Historians such as Joseph Bilby have exhaustively demonstrated how cautious one should be in drawing such conclusions. As he and others document, casualties in Napoleonic battles fought with smoothbore muskets were higher than those in the American Civil War. Most firefights in the latter occurred well within smoothbore range, and in many instances smoothbore weapons, including shotguns, inflicted devastating losses and were even weapons of choice.

There is, of course, no doubt that rifling increased velocity and, hence, range. There are also examples of infantrymen, from British in the Crimea to New Jerseymen in Virginia, consciously employing this salient advantage of rifle-muskets. Bilby cites the case of the 9th New Jersey effectively neutralizing a Confederate battery at New Bern, North Carolina, through concentrated rifle-musket fire at 200 yards.[10]

I estimate the distance between the Home and State Guard centers at the beginning of the Battle of Athens as some 450 yards. Even if we halve that distance, the squirrel rifles and shotguns of the State Guard were pretty much out of their range, whereas Home Guard minie balls from U.S. issue rifle-muskets (whether Model 1861s or rebored earlier models) had no trouble spanning this distance. This does not, of course, mean that the majority of Home Guardsmen could hit their mark at this range. But it is entirely possible that their sustained and concentrated fire at this or even greater range pinned down their opponents. There is credible testimony from the State Guard side that this is precisely what happened and that more than a few Home Guard bullets found their mark as well.

Rifle-muskets in the hands of Iowa militia across the Des Moines River may also have served not only to enfilade the State Guard right in the cornfield fight, but also to help drive State Guardsmen from a house in that position at the edge of the cornfield.

One State Guardsman insisted that his side had sufficient strength to overwhelm the Home Guard center. Had he and his comrades been able to close the distance rapidly between the lines under fire with loaded weapons, and then open on the Home Guard line at less than 100 yards, the result would probably have been devastating. There is evidence that State Guardsmen attempted at least once to advance beyond their barricades of fence rails behind which they were pinned by Home Guard fire. It was this fire from a significant distance which discouraged their advance.

At the Battle of Fair Oaks or Seven Pines, Virginia, in 1862, the 104th Pennsylvania was wreaking havoc with their Austrian Lorenz rifle-muskets on Confederates armed with smoothbores well over 100 yards distant. General Silas Casey, author of a book on tactics, ordered the 104th to advance, along with other Federal regiments. As they closed to within 50 yards, the smoothbore-armed Confederate opened with a volley of buck-and-ball which drove the Yankee attackers from the field.[11]

David Moore did not make the mistake at Athens that Silas Casey made at Seven Pines. Moore did, however, avail his men of another advantage of their U.S. issue muskets in the face of a faltering State Guard advance—the bayonet. No doubt cognizant of the psychological effect of a bayonet charge, perhaps anticipating that his men could not stand up to a State Guard advance resulting in effective massed fire on them, Moore ordered his command to fix bayonets and to move forward in common time. Instead of advancing deliberately as ordered, his Home Guardsman broke into a run for the State Guard center, yelling at the tops of their lungs. Moore, it seems, could only follow along, ordering the charge already in progress. The sight and sound of screaming men bearing down with fixed bayonets was more than the hesitating State Guardsmen out in front of their barricades could bear. They broke and ran.[12]

The Home Guard victory at Athens was not, Chapter 4 demonstrates, a foregone conclusion. Rifle-muskets played a pivotal role, but that role was inseparable from the competence of the men using them, the crucial positioning of the State Guard center behind barricades at a distance which gave the range advantage to the Home Guard, and, also, from the miscalculations of State Guard artillerists.

The latter opened the battle with a barrage of solid shot and ersatz canister. It seems likely that their intent was to disperse the Home Guard center with these missiles and then to sweep it from the field with a rapid advance of infantry, cavalry, or both (the distinction is not clear-cut, as many, if not most, of the State Guard appear to have been mounted). Like Robert E. Lee's much more experienced artillerists firing on the Union center on the third day at Gettysburg, Martin Green's overshot their marks. David Moore had the good sense to order his men to lie down during the barrage to steady their nerves. However, if Green's artillery commander, James W. Kneisley, had depressed his guns, the fact that the Home Guardsmen were clutching rifle-muskets might have been irrelevant. There is also evidence that two of Kneisley's guns were disabled early.

So, the technology differential played a major role at Athens, Missouri, on August 5, 1861, but it was a role, like that of all technology, defined by and embedded in tactical decisions and calculations made by human beings.

Once begun, a Civil War battle left little room for the ambivalent thoughts and emotions which might have preceded it. Braggarts, bullies, and street toughs frequently fled in terror once the "ball opened," as the soldiers put it. Average men, anxiously fretting that they would turn tail and run, often fought coolly, even heroically. According to James M. McPherson, adrenalin removed both fight and flight from the realm of rational deliberation.[13] It is interesting to note, however, that some, if not all, of Moore's officers who abandoned the field with their men were those who had exhibited dissatisfaction with Moore and the Home Guards for one reason or another prior to the fight.[14] Having left the field of battle at Athens, they did not recast their lots with David Moore.

The concluding Chapter 5, "Rejoiced Over Victory," details the inexorable ambivalence of the Home Guard survivors. On the one hand, as the title suggests, there was joy that victory was theirs, perhaps, it seemed, snatched from the jaws of almost certain defeat. While casualties at Athens were few compared to the coming carnage many of them would experience at such places as Shiloh Church in Tennessee, joy was no doubt tempered by grief at the death of comrades, by a certain queer fascination with some wounds, and by revulsion at the sight of amputated limbs and corpses bloating under the August sun.

For John Hiller, writing to his brother on the afternoon of that battle day, the fight proved one thing for certain. He and his Home Guard comrades were Yankees made of sterner stuff than that suggested by the anemic liquid of the metaphor pinned on them by their foes: "Skim Milk Yankees."

I have loved Athens, Missouri, since childhood. It was here that I first walked a Civil War battlefield. It was here that I learned that all of the profound lessons of being human can be learned anywhere; out-of-the-way places are no less pregnant with possibility than those at the crossroads of history. David Moore became Colonel of the 21st Missouri Volunteers, lost a leg at Shiloh, fought at Corinth, was brevetted a brigadier general, and became a Radical Republican in the years following the war. Martin Green became a Confederate general beloved of his men, also fought at Corinth, Mississippi, just across the lines from his old antagonist, David Moore, and was killed at Vicksburg. William McKee, one of Moore's captains who abandoned the field at Athens, continued as a cavalryman and was killed fighting his way out of an ambush at Prairie Grove, Arkansas. When the Kahoka, Missouri, Union veterans sought a name for their Grand Army of the Republic post, they chose William McKee's.

Two of my forebears were Home Guardsmen. Ambivalence was in the bones of at least one of them. Great-great grandfather Captain William Jackson, one of David Moore's officers, was both a Union man and a slaveholder—one of those whose "property" his president believed was protected by the Constitution. Exempted from the Emancipation Proclamation of 1863 along with such property in the other "border states," those Captain Jackson enslaved waited another long two years for the 13th Amendment and freedom.

A story handed down through our family has it that the Captain, returning home unexpectedly one night from "the army," happened upon a slave taking flour from the pantry and, firing at the man's feet with his revolver, "only to scare him," blew the man's toe off. Perhaps fearing that young listeners would disown their ancestor at this juncture, the storyteller would apologetically interject: "Grandpa always said that he would have given them the flour if they had only asked." Immediately upon the heels of this exculpatory move came the punch line of this benevolent master/thieving slave anecdote—the man exclaimed that he wished his rudely-amputated toe be preserved and buried with him at his death.

I last looked out over what had been Captain Jackson's land in rural Clark County, Missouri, from the front yard of Ira Hall, an elderly black man. Ira's grandparents, I have always understood, were enslaved by my great-great grandfather. Like so many former slaves, they became tenant farmers on his land thereafter. Ultimately they owned the land themselves.

Sitting alongside Ira in a rusty lawn chair under a tall shade tree in 1987, surveying the acres of corn rustling in the hot August breeze, taking in his encyclopedic renditions of Jackson family history, I wondered if Home Guard Captain Jackson would have concurred with his colonel, David Moore, who, twenty-five years after that August battle morning at Athens, observed:

"How changed is Missouri since that time…those who bartered in human flesh have lost their occupation. The world moves."[15]

A note on the sources:

Ben F. Dixon, the indefatigable chronicler of the Battle of Athens often noted that one could look, but would not find information about the battle in the *Official Records* of the Civil War or in the National Archives. There were no official reports of the battle (none found to date, anyway). Contemporary eyewitness descriptions are nearly non-existent. And newspaper reports have to be taken with the proverbial grain of salt (even more so with the recollections of veterans published for years afterward in the regional papers). In this study, I have used original contemporary sources whenever possible, such as the reports published in the *Keokuk Daily Gate City* and the *Chicago Tribune*. Most of the newspaper articles published in Missouri and Iowa immediately after the battle merely rework the original pieces in the *Gate City*. Otherwise, I have relied on Dixon's anthologies of sources published in his three booklets on the battle (as reprinted in 1991 by Dixon protégé Patricia M. Mullenix, who added her own anthology of miscellaneous newspaper articles by Dixon). The two *Last Reunion* books published by Mullenix and Jan Gross have been an indispensable source for facsimiles of archival materials, postwar recollections, and participants' obituaries, which often contain excellent insights on the battle and the wartime situation in northeast Missouri in general. The publications of the State Historical Society of Iowa have provided several recollections of participants and observers of the battle. Two scholarly studies by preeminent Missouri historian Leslie Anders and a comprehensive overview of the battle in the massive *History of Lewis, Clark, Knox and Scotland Counties, Missouri* have proven indispensable. Finally, this work owes a tremendous amount to Roger Boyd, Site Administrator of the Battle of Athens State Historic Site, for his detailed study of the battle,[16] his encyclopedic understanding of the people, places, and events of Athens, and his ever-present willingness to share his knowledge.

Appended to the book is a roster of men who joined the Home Guard in northeast Missouri. This list was compiled in 1863 by the Hawkins Taylor Commission, three citizens of Iowa and Missouri, who were appointed by President Lincoln to report on the claims of soldiers who had served in these units. Many of these soldiers would have been with David Moore at Athens.

Chapter 1

At six p.m., Saturday night, August 3, 1861, forty Keokuk Rangers—Home Guard cavalry—boarded a special train for Croton, Iowa, 25 miles distant, with their captain, Hugh Sample. Steaming northwest on the Keokuk & Des Moines Valley Railroad, the train clanged into the Croton depot along the Des Moines River an hour and a half later.[1]

Colonel David Moore's First Northeast Missouri Home Guard was camped directly across the Des Moines on the Missouri side, atop a bluff in the town of Athens. Sample brought his Rangers up that evening in response to rumors that droves of Moore's men were decamping in the face of an imminent Missouri State Guard attack. If Moore could not hold, then only the river, running low this August, stood between Colonel Martin Green's pro-Confederate State Guard and southeast Iowa. Sample meant to make sure that Moore could keep Green on his side of the Des Moines.

The Iowa captain splashed toward a stone mill looming on the opposite shore. Met by Home Guardsmen, Sample was no doubt surprised to hear that they supposed he came seeking their help. Assured that the four hundred men Moore currently fielded at Athens, reinforced by some two hundred said to be within easy call, could repel the advancing State Guard, the Iowans crossed back to Croton, boarded their train, and were home in Keokuk by 11:00 p.m.[2]

Sample's Rangers might have saved themselves the return trip had Moore possessed better intelligence that night. For throughout the next day of Sunday, August 4, the Home Guard Colonel was deluged with reports that a large force of Green's State Guard was on his doorstep. Home Guard soldier and Athens resident John Hiller noted in a letter he wrote to his brother on the day of the battle "we learned from scouts and other sources that a large force was hovering on us and would probably attack" by nightfall.[3]

That Sunday morning Moore ordered William McKee "to take four or five men and go out near Chambersburg on picket duty," some eight miles southwest. McKee picked "William Ferguson, Wash Collins, Henry McKee, John Schee and one or two more." He did not take his son, Private John McKee, nineteen, and just a month and half in Captain Daniel Hull's company. The elder McKee sent John "across the river to Squire Harland's," ordering him to "report at camp at Athens that night."[4]

Reconnoitering "many miles in the front," McKee's pickets (or other Home Guard scouts) reported Green to be "advancing in strong force from the direction of Edina," thirty-five or forty miles southwest of Athens. A second State Guard force under Colonel Cyrus Franklin was on the march from Lancaster, a little more than forty miles

west. Later reports had Green and Franklin concentrating their "estimated from nine to fifteen
hundred men" at or near Etna, some eighteen
miles southwest of Athens, then coming on and
bivouacking in the timber along Fox River, only
a four short miles southwest.[5]

Moore had little doubt that he was to be attacked soon by a force outnumbering his at
least two to one. He dispatched messengers to
Keokuk again for reinforcements late that afternoon, among them John Hiller. Fording the Des
Moines and securing a handcar at the Croton
depot, they pumped hurriedly down the tracks,
reaching Keokuk about 8:00 p.m.[6]

Although the impending attack "was meant by
the rebels to be a surprise"—and, at least until
that Sunday, it seemed to be to the Home Guard

Aaron W. Harlan,
Quartermaster Sergeant. (Courtesy of
Battle of Athens State Historic Site)

colonel—Moore was "kept constantly apprised of the formation of the rebel camp
on Fox River, near Chambersburg." His ex officio "other sources" of intelligence, as
Hiller called them, included "a couple of boys" who "ran barefoot a distance of sixteen miles across the fields of Luray" carrying the news of "the approach of a large
rebel force." One of them, Samuel Sackett, had a father who was a Home Guard
captain at Athens.[7]

Almost an entire family served as yet another source of intelligence for Moore.
Frederick H. Boone farmed two miles northeast of Kahoka, a small town some ten
miles south of Athens. That same Sunday his fiancée, Charlotte Harrison, wanted to
visit her sister, Drucilla, who was working in Memphis for the Busey family. Slightly
north and mostly west from Kahoka, Memphis was more than a twenty-five mile
drive. Frederick harnessed his team and they set out.

Upon their arrival, Drucilla shared some startling news gleaned from her State
Guard suitor, a Lieutenant Wiley. Green had moved the date of his attack on Moore
up from Thursday, August 8, to Monday, August 5, hoping to catch the Athens Home
Guardsmen napping.

The Harrisons came from Virginia, and Drucilla was an unabashed supporter of
the new Confederate nation. However, her and Charlotte's father, the Reverend Jabez Harrison, was now serving as Moore's chaplain at Athens. Placing concern for
her father's safety above politics, Drucilla had penned a warning to Moore of the
impending attack, but until Charlotte and Fred arrived she had found no way to
get it to him. The sisters slit a seam in Charlotte's slat bonnet and inserted the note
along one of the slats, then re-sewed the seam. Frederick prepared his team and he
and Charlotte hastily took their leave.

Pushing his horses hard a few miles east of Memphis, Frederick managed to drive
directly into the State Guard camp along a creek (probably the North Wyaconda
River just northeast of Etna, or a small tributary of it).[8] Ordered down from his seat,
Boone was unceremoniously stripped and searched by State Guardsmen. John Kim-

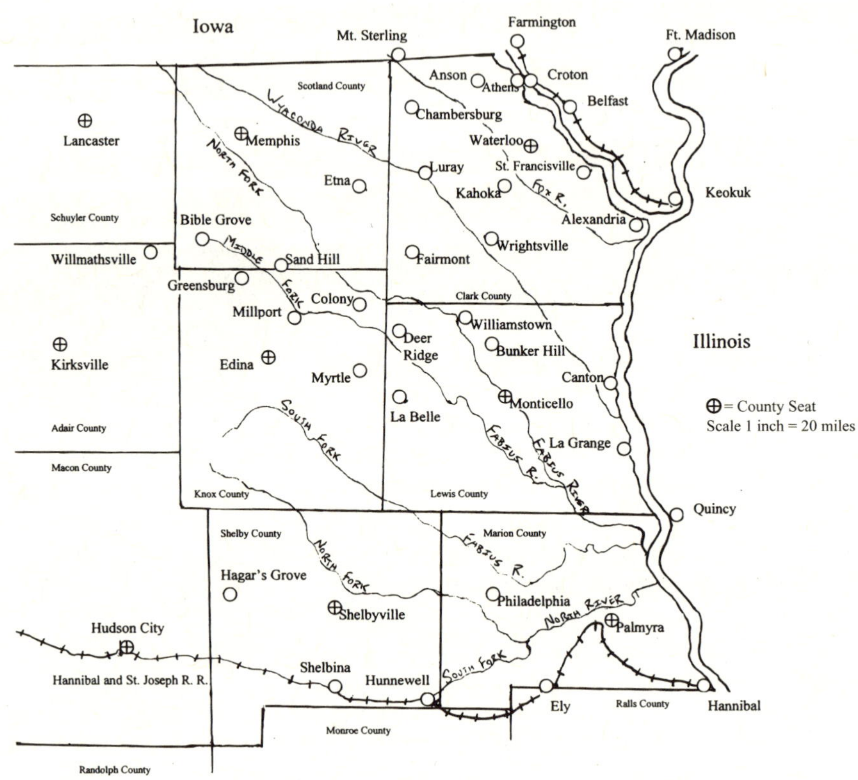

Northeast Missouri in 1861
(Map drawn by Matt Kantola)

brough, an officer who knew Frederick, happened by and vouched for him. Dressed and back at the reins, Boone hurriedly drove his horses east to Kahoka, overheating them.[9]

He and Charlotte passed Drucilla's message to the sisters' brother, John Harrison, who lived just across the road from them north of Kahoka. John pounded into the Home Guard camp at Athens by Sunday evening with the information gleaned directly from one of Green's men.[10]

Moore's intelligence from his own scouts, barefoot boys, and the Boone and Harrison families, corroborated wildfire rumors spreading from northeast Missouri and into southeast Iowa. One Belfast, Iowa, farmwife, Julia McCormack, wrote her father that "the secessionists kept sending word for several days that they were coming to Athens for dinner on the 5th."[11]

Moore's handcar messengers arrived in Keokuk around 8:00 p.m. Sunday night. The Keokuk men had "frequently been alarmed on false reports" such as the one just the night before, so Hiller and company "succeeded only in getting some 75 or 80 men, Home Guards and volunteers" to return with them. This time Captain

W. W. Belknap's City Rifles accompanied Hugh Sample's men. Well-armed with "U.S. rifles and muskets," the Rifles, Rangers, and volunteers boarded one more special train to Croton, arriving at 10:00 p.m.[12]

Belknap and Sample didn't bother to cross the Des Moines this time, but hailed Moore from the Croton side, asking whether he indeed needed assistance. Moore shouted back that Green was advancing in force, that he expected to be attacked on the morrow, and that he would be most obliged if the Iowa men would reinforce him. The Keokuk captains promised to bring their men over at daylight.[13] The Iowans threw out pickets at the fords of the Des Moines and passed an uneventful night guarding "a large quantity of army supplies" at the Croton depot.[14]

Home Guard private John McKee reported back to the Athens camp that night where "old man Sullivan" told him to fetch his "old double

William Belknap
(Library of Congress
LC-DIG-cwpb-06122)

barrel shot gun." According to Private McKee, "old man Heaton" of Big Mound, Iowa, had armed his company "with anything from a corn knife to any old kind of shooting iron. My old gun was in bad shape, one barrel would not shoot at all and the other only part time." John exchanged his almost worthless shotgun for a musket, one of a shipment of such that had recently arrived.[15]

As night descended on the Athens bivouac of citizen soldiers, young John McKee bedded down with the "cavalry camped across the street from the schoolhouse" on Virginia Street.[16] Before sleep overtook him, perhaps he examined and tried his new issue musket, speculating on how it—and he—would perform on the morrow.

The First Northeast Missouri Home Guard:

A Gallery

George P. Washburn, son of Captain Peter Washburn, 14 years old in 1861, too young for service, but, according to Leslie Anders, he was allowed to "come along as general roustabout." He later joined the 21st Missouri. (Courtesy of Battle of Athens State Historic Site)

Joseph Best, Private Co B, brother of Captain James Best, later became colonel of the 21st Missouri and married David Moore's daughter. (Courtesy of Battle of Athens State Historic Site)

The Greenslate Brothers of Adair County. John Mason Greenslate, second from left, joined Col. Moore in August 1861, later was in the 21ˢᵗ Missouri with his brother Carlyle, third from left. (Courtesy of Battle of Athens State Historic Site)

Harrison Toops, 2ⁿᵈ Lieutenant, Co F, injured by a falling tree in Waterloo, MO, August 1861, later joined the 2ⁿᵈ Missouri Cavalry. (Courtesy of Battle of Athens State Historic Site)

Thomas H. "Hughes" Roseberry of the musical Roseberry family, which according to one account entertained with drum and bugle at the July 4, 1861, rally at Kahoka. (Courtesy of Dan Furtak)

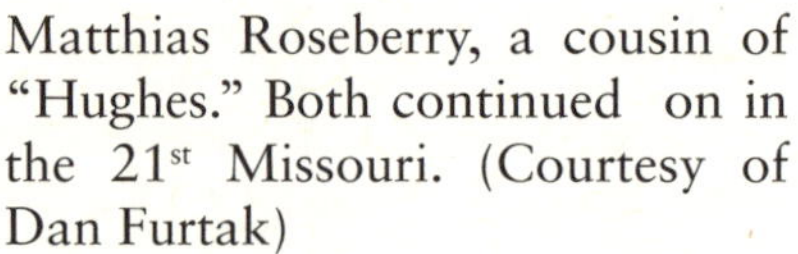

Matthias Roseberry, a cousin of "Hughes." Both continued on in the 21st Missouri. (Courtesy of Dan Furtak)

Aaron Brokaw, Private, Co K, enlisted at age 51, later served as color bearer of the 21st Missouri. (Courtesy of Battle of Athens State Historic Site)

James P. Smith, Private, Co F, 15 years old in 1861, was "ordered to leave Missouri, on account of my abolition principles." Later joined the 21st Missouri (Courtesy Suzanne K. Krogh)

Hiram Hiller, ca. 1862–1863. Home Guard recruiter, Peace Commissioner, David Moore's Adjutant and the brother of John Hiller. (Hiller Family Papers, 1785-1993, C3856, Western Historical Manuscript Collection-Columbia, MO)

Chapter 2

What brought John McKee, his father, John Cox, Bart Hackney, Wash Collins, Bill Ferguson, and their Colonel, David Moore, to Athens in August 1861, waiting to be attacked by fellow Missourians, some of whom were neighbors?

The crisis came the previous March for some of these men. Feeling threatened by talk of secession, they met clandestinely at the little clapboard Highland Schoolhouse between Chambersburg and Athens. There they drafted and signed an oath pledging fidelity to the United States, its constitution and laws, and to each other.

David Moore's signature is not among those who took the oath at the Highland School. In the 1860 presidential race the previous fall, Moore captained the "Hickories," the local northern Democratic organization in Alexandria. His son, William, served in the group as a musician. The Hickories backed Senator Stephen Douglas of Illinois, the famous advocate of Popular Sovereignty, the doctrine that settlers in new territories should be permitted to vote slavery up or down. Popular Sovereignty provided the ideological underpinning for the Compromise of 1850 and Douglas's own Kansas-Nebraska Act of 1854. However, the Supreme Court rendered it irrelevant in its landmark 1857 Dred Scott decision, ruling that slaveholders could take their "property" wherever they pleased, regardless of the preferences of settlers in a given state. Undaunted, Douglas reinvented Popular Sovereignty as the "Freeport doctrine" in his 1858 debate with Abraham Lincoln in Freeport, Illinois.

On Election Day, November 6, 1860, the majority of Missourians—no doubt David Moore among them—cast votes either for Douglas or the other compromising candidate of the upper south, John Bell, who ran on the new National Constitutional Union party ticket.

When his candidate lost to Abraham Lincoln, the path David Moore took from that November to the morning of August 5, 1861, at Athens was most likely a tentative, compromising path. It was that trod by most Missourians. There is no evidence of sudden turns for Moore either in the direction of "Black Republicanism" or pro-southern sympathy. Moore's probable course can be discerned by allowing developments in

Stephen Douglas (Library of Congress LC-DIG-cwpbh-00882)

Missouri and the nation to cast as much light as possible on the views of Missourians like him in the crucial four months between Abraham Lincoln's election in November 1860 and his inauguration in early March 1861.[1]

"As long as there was a sectional fence to straddle prior to 1861, most Missourians kept their perch on it," and most attempted to maintain that perch well into 1861.[2] Probably many of the men who would later join the First Northeast Missouri Home Guard were among them. Missouri, like the other border states of Kentucky, Maryland, Delaware, and even Virginia, straddled the fence in a variety of ways.

Yet Missouri was unique in that north, south, east, and west intersected in it. The state was the resultant hybrid of these regions, exhibiting the contradictions and tensions, but also the continuities, between them. Geographically transitional from north to south, east to west, free to slave, Missouri was also in economic transition. Slavery was a "real but marginal social and economic institution" because Missouri's "markets were being redirected toward the emerging manufacturing and trading colossus of the Northeast." This is not to say that there was not internal resistance to what seemed a "would-be aristocracy of slaveholders," on one side, and to the market economy spreading westward with wagon companies departing St. Joseph, followed by the railroad, on the other.[3]

In 1860, there were 1,063,489 whites in Missouri, 3,572 free blacks, and 114,931 enslaved blacks. The last group comprised 9.8% of the total population. The highest percentage of enslaved blacks of the total population had been 17.8% in 1830. This percentage had subsequently declined by two to three percent each decade. While the actual number of slaves grew steadily decade to decade, the white population almost doubled every ten years.[4] The average number of slaves per slaveholder in 1860 was a little over 4.66.

In extreme northeastern Clark County, where Athens stood overlooking Iowa, 129 whites enslaved approximately 402 blacks. The value of this "property" for tax purposes was $135,300.00.[5] The percentage of enslaved blacks in the total population of Clark County was under 5%. In Lewis County, immediately south of Clark, the percentage rose to between 10 and 14%. In the next county south, Marion, it rose to between 15 and 24%, and was as high as 37% in the most intensively slave-holding counties.[6] While Clark County whites held relatively few slaves compared to their counterparts a county or two south, they had to contend with the lure of free soil on both their northern and eastern borders.[7]

Missouri was born out of compromise. The Compromise of 1820 that gave it statehood bears its name. Southern settlers populating the Missouri territory applied for statehood as a slave state in 1817. Three acrimonious years preceded the final agreement and resulting statehood in 1821. Representatives of the northern and southern regions of the existing United States in the U.S. Congress compromised by admitting Maine in the northeast as the free counterbalance to slave Missouri. Northerners also secured legislation of the southern border of Missouri—36 degrees, 30 minutes latitude—as the line extending through the original Louisiana Purchase above which slavery would be prohibited. The principle survived the Compromise of 1850, but was effectively nullified by the Kansas-Nebraska Act. Forty years after their state entered the Union, most Missourians still preferred compromise to secession and certainly to the specter of civil war in which Missouri would literally be caught between contending states.

The Hickory leader of the 1860 campaign no doubt endorsed his candidate's Freeport doctrine. Badgered by Lincoln in that 1858 debate, Douglas navigated around the Dred Scott snag for Popular Sovereignty by arguing that antislavery territorial legislatures could simply refrain from enacting "local police regulations" conducive to slavery. In this way, the "little giant" retorted to his lanky Republican antagonist, the choice for or against slavery was retained by settlers in the territories, even after Dred Scott.[8] Resuming his senate seat in early 1859 by beating Lincoln in the Illinois legislature, Douglas now had to face the wrath of deep south spokesmen like Jefferson Davis, William Yancey, Robert Toombs, and Albert Brown for having repudiated the Dred Scott decision. The radical, cotton state view was that slavery should be protected by federal law wherever it went, even, one day, into Cuba and Central America.

This latest round of congressional vitriol followed one begun in the year preceding Douglas's campaign against Lincoln, when the former broke ranks with fellow Democrats over the pro-slavery Lecompton, Kansas, constitution. Douglas agreed with Republicans that the framers of this constitution had not correctly submitted it to Kansas voters for ratification. When the constitution was eventually submitted to the voters—who rejected it, losing Kansas to the north—enraged southerners never forgave Douglas.[9]

The regional wrangling among senate Democrats and bitterness toward Douglas spilled into the party's 1860 national convention in April in Charleston, South Carolina. When their plank demanding a federal slave code to insure that the Freeport doctrine could not be put into practice in the territories was voted out of the platform, eight cotton state delegations bolted the convention. The Democrats reconvened in June in Baltimore, but the cotton state delegates again walked out to hold their own rump convention in the same city. Douglas was nominated on the second ballot and the southerners nominated Kentuckian and former Vice-President, John C. Breckinridge. The party was now formally split along sectional lines.[10]

Douglas man David Moore consequently found himself a Northern Democrat, bound to reject the pro-slavery Southern Democratic platform. Presuming he remained a Hickory on election day and cast his vote for Douglas—with 36% of his fellow voters, making Missouri the only state carried by Douglas—Moore must certainly have continued to hope that voters in other states would chart a similar course between the Republican and Southern Democratic extremes.

Missourians statewide evidenced political moderation that election day by choosing the "compromising upper South candidate," National Constitutional Unionist Tennessean John Bell, who ran a very close second to Stephen Douglas. Bell garnered 35% of the Missouri vote running on the general principles of Constitution, Union, and law enforcement, and by urging resolution of the sectional crisis through reasoned compromise. His party hardly mentioned slavery. Breckinridge captured 19% of the Missouri vote. The remaining 10% went to Lincoln.[11]

Even Missouri voters in "Little Dixie"—counties with the densest slave populations—proved moderate in this election. Bell ran first in these counties, Douglas second, and Breckinridge third. Not surprisingly, here the Republican option was hardly entertained.[12]

In casting 71% of their ballots for Douglas and Bell, the Missouri majority navigated between what it clearly considered the extremist snags of Republican commitment to exclude slavery from the western territories, and Southern Democratic determination to force a legislative guarantee of its protection in the same territories. When their candidate lost to Lincoln, few Hickories like Moore probably felt compelled to rush into either the Republican or Southern Democratic camps.[13] If these Douglas men stuck fast to their principle of compromise, then they would have resisted non-electoral pressure both from the southern Democratic slave states— which, with South Carolina in December 1860, had begun to secede—and from the northern free states which had gone Republican. No doubt they sat tight, hoping against hope for one more national compromise to avert civil war. The attempt at one was not long in coming.

In mid-December 1860, Senator John Crittenden of Kentucky proposed a series of constitutional amendments guaranteeing that the old Missouri Compromise line of 36°30' would be reestablished and extended to the Pacific Ocean, that future states would be admitted to the Union slave or free as the people might decide, that Congress would make no law interfering with slavery where it existed or with the interstate transportation of slaves, that slave-owners would be compensated for unreturned fugitives, and that these amendments could not be revoked by future constitutional amendments.[14] Then at the end of December, Representative Charles Francis Adams of Massachusetts co-sponsored a proposal with Henry Winter Davis of Maryland to admit New Mexico as a slave state. This seeming concession to the slave states would allot to the north another free state, because in fact slavery, though it existed there, would most likely not succeed in New Mexico. Furthermore, the solidarity of the upper and lower south would be undermined. This was borne out in the committee vote, but the proposal failed on the floor in February. [15]

Likely heartened by such overtures, Douglas Democrats doubtless hoped that Unionists in the upper south could apply the brakes to Secessionist extremists, whom many northerners, including Lincoln, believed to be only a vociferous minority. At the very least, doctrinaire Hickories would have done all in their power to ensure that the moderate, compromising Missouri electorate stayed the course and kept their state neutral as secession fever spread. This would prove challenging.

On January 3, 1861, newly-elected Missouri Governor Claiborne Jackson proclaimed in his inaugural speech that his state would stand by her seceding sister states if the federal government intervened militarily to stop them.[16] Jackson had championed the extension of slavery into the territories in the 1850s but was elected now as a Hickory, having aligned himself in time with moderate Missouri opinion to win. However, like Douglas with Bell in the presidential race in Missouri, Jackson barely squeaked by Sample Orr, the National Constitutional Unionist candidate for governor.[17]

For those in the compromising Missouri mainstream, Jackson's inaugural speech had to be troubling. Putting a new twist on Popular Sovereignty, Jackson made it clear that under his administration Missouri would guarantee the right of voters in

Claiborne F. Jackson,
Governor of Missouri. (From John
McElroy, *The Struggle For Missouri*)

the state to choose their political path—even if that meant secession from United States. True Douglas men would have hardly countenanced Jackson's sleight of hand use of their principle in applying it to referenda on secession, since Douglas had constructed it to forestall just such a national debacle.

As Jackson moved into the governor's office in Jefferson City, the Secessionist tide across the deep south continued to rise. Seven states voted for disunion between December 1860 and February 1861. On February 8, 1861, delegates from South Carolina, Georgia, Alabama, Florida, Mississippi, Louisiana, and Texas formed the Confederate States of America at Montgomery, Alabama. The next day they elected Jefferson Davis and Alexander Stephens president and vice-president.

In his January 5 address, Jackson had called for "a state convention in order that the will of the people may be ascertained," that is, whether or not to secede from the Union. Election for convention delegates was held on February 18.[18] While Jackson probably intended this as an opportunity to usher Missouri into the new Confederate nation, the majority of Missourians who elected delegates to the convention thwarted him. While 30,000 did vote for avowed Secessionists, 110,000 sent different stripes of Unionists to the convention. Most of these were "conservative farmers of southern origin," on the whole conditional Unionists. They believed that the Union should be maintained through further compromise, but not by federal coercion of states that had seceded.[19]

At the opposite end of the spectrum from the Secessionists in Missouri was another minority—the Unconditional Unionists, Black Republicans, or Lincolnites, composed primarily of German immigrants concentrated in St. Louis, where Unconditional Unionist delegates were overwhelmingly chosen.[20]

The ninety-nine delegates elected to Jackson's convention met first in the Cole County court house in the heart of Little Dixie, central Missouri's hemp and tobacco region. Finding these accommodations too cramped, they reconvened in the Mercantile Library in St. Louis. Passionately debating slavery, the delegates voted finally both to remain in the Union and to remain neutral in any future showdown between the United States and the new Confederate States of America.[21]

Mainstream Missourians, having rejected secession for their state, no doubt looked to the nation's capital to come up with a solution to the looming crisis. Many continued to hope that Crittenden's, or another like compromise, might yet mollify the alienated seceded states. There seemed to be reason to hope. Statesmen, newspaper editors, and common citizens endorsed the Crittenden Compromise. Petitions supporting the plan from all over the United States were sent to Congress. From St.

Louis came "nearly a hundred foolscap pages of names, wrapped in the American flag."[22]

In January, Ohio Republican Congressman Thomas Corwin had proposed a constitutional amendment that would prohibit any future amendment that would interfere with or abolish "the domestic institutions" of any state, including that of persons held to labor or service by the laws of that state. Interestingly, the word slavery did not appear in the document. While the Crittenden Compromise was condemned by President-elect Lincoln and ultimately rejected by Congress, the Corwin Amendment, which seemed to be more specifically directed at reassuring the status quo in the border states, was supported by Lincoln and passed by both houses. Some states, such as David Moore's birth state of Ohio, went so far as to ratify it. A further olive branch offered by Corwin was a proposition to repeal personal liberty laws and faithfully enforce the Fugitive Slave Act.[23]

One last grand effort at compromise was attempted in Washington. For three weeks in February, delegates from twenty-one states met for a Peace Convention initiated by the Virginia legislature and strongly backed by Secretary of State William H. Seward. Its purpose was to craft constitutional amendments which would entice seceded states to return to the fold and to persuade border states like Missouri not to stray from it. The resulting protocol was a seven-point amendment, which basically reiterated the Crittenden Compromise. This proposal went down to defeat in the Republican dominated Congress.[24]

Problematically, from the perspective of southern radicals, none of the various attempts at compromise included what they had been demanding all along: congressional protection of slavery in the new western territories where it did not yet exist.

Despite whatever grounds for hope of an eleventh hour reconciliation these overtures offered, Claiborne Jackson's inauguration in January had set in motion a series of events in and around St. Louis that made it increasingly difficult for many Missourians to persevere on the palliative path of neutralist Unionism.

Congressman Frank Blair,[25] an Unconditional Unionist suspicious of Jackson's loyalties, tapped the politics and prior military experience of many of the St. Louis German immigrants by converting their Republican "Wide-Awake" political organizations into Unionist Home Guard units. Swiftly responding to what they called this "Black Dutch" militarization, St. Louis's southern sympathizers organized their own "minuteman" units, evoking the comparison of the German militia and U.S. troops to those of the occupying British in the Massachusetts of 1775.[26] In February, fiercely anti-secession Captain Nathaniel Lyon of the U.S. Army was transferred to St. Louis from Kansas and immediately

Frank Blair
(Library of Congress
LC-DIG-cwpb-05566)

Nathaniel Lyon
(From *Battles and Leaders of the Civil War*)

formed a close relationship with Blair. Together they worked to train and encourage the loyal Home Guards units.[27]

March saw President-elect Abraham Lincoln sworn in amidst threats of assassination. At about the same time, anti-Secessionist men in Clark County formed their own protection society. Increasingly insecure in the midst of Secessionist neighbors, they met clandestinely in the little Highland Schoolhouse between Chambersburg and Athens. Among them were John McKee, soon to be a private in Daniel Hull's company; Dan Hull himself; John's father, William McKee, who would be ordered out on picket duty the morning of August 4, 1861; some of the men he would take with him (Wash Collins, Bill Ferguson, and Henry McKee); Bart Hackney and John Cox, who would lead the defense of the Home Guard right flank at Athens; T. H. Roseberry, destined to raise and captain a home guard company; other Roseberrys, who would provide musical inspiration to what would be the First Northeast Missouri Home Guard; David McKee, who would be elected a major under Moore; and William Bishop, whose protégés would campaign vigorously for his colonelcy of the regiment against Moore.

In the little schoolhouse they drew up and signed an oath which began:

> In the presence of all now surrounding us we solemnly pledge our honor as American citizens that we will use all honorable means in aid of each other and our brethren elsewhere in the protection of each others lives, property and character from the enemies of our present United States government and any grade of secession oppression or aggression that we will at all times uphold and defend the constitution of these United States and use it in the enforcement of the laws thereof.[28]

The line in Clark County was clearly drawn by the time these men met in March. On one side, they place "American citizens" loyal to the "present United States government," ready and willing to "uphold and defend the constitution," and to employ it in the "enforcement of the laws" of "these United States." On the other, they place the "enemies of our present United States government," the agents of "secession oppression or aggression" threatening the very "lives, property and character" of these men gathered in the little Highland School.

The central motifs of this opening—United States, constitution, laws—evoke the National Constitutional Union party's platform which avowed "no political principle other than the Constitution, the Union, and law enforcement" during the campaigns of the previous year. This party's candidates ran neck and neck with those of the northern Democrats in both the gubernatorial and presidential races in Missouri, and it seems likely from the wording of this oath that many of the signers were Constitutional Unionists, or at least influenced by them. Like the platform of that party, the oath is silent on the issue of slavery. The United States or Union, the U.S. Constitution, and federal law were sufficient grounds in March 1861 on which to unite with neighbors of like mind in Clark County in opposition to the "aggression" and "oppression" of Secessionist neighbors. The signers, who undoubtedly saw themselves as guardians of the result of Missouri's referendum on secession, go on to pledge to "resist any attempt made by the authorities of this state or any other power or force to put Missouri out of the Union, unless done fairly by a majority of all the legal voters through the ballot box."

The oath to "uphold and defend the constitution" is reiterated inversely by the signers, swearing that they "will never be coerced or driven into any oath, affirmation, obligation, pledge or conspiracy, the design of which is to subvert or place us in hostile array against the government and constitution."

Concluding, the Highland School men swear each other to secrecy concerning the "object, aims, means used…signs and…bywords" of their new "organization." They swear secrecy "binding" even if one "voluntarily leave or be expelled from this order." Uncertain of who was friend or foe in Clark County this March of 1861, no longer could just any neighbor be trusted.

As March gave way to April, "talk of war" increased in Clark County, in Missouri, and across the fragmenting nation. Attention focused on South Carolina where Confederate forces demanded the evacuation of the small U.S. garrison still occupying Fort Sumter in Charleston harbor. The news that the South Carolinians had actually fired on Sumter before dawn on April 12 flashed across the wires on April 13. Two days later, Lincoln called for 75,000 volunteers to suppress the rebellion. On April 17, the ante for border states like Missouri was raised when Virginia's secession convention voted to secede from the Union.

Instead of working to fill Missouri's quota of four regiments—4,000 men—in response to Lincoln's call, Claiborne Jackson lobbied the general assembly to improve the militia's organization and upgrade its equipment, "to place the state in the proper attitude for defense." Ostensibly, this was to ensure Missouri's neutrality in the coming conflict. However, the cautious assemblymen refused to pass any legislation they suspected would be used to violate the neutralist mandate of the March convention. Secretly, Jackson, who had pointedly refused the President's call for volunteers, requested intervention from the new Confederate States of America and, on April 17, petitioned its president, Jefferson Davis, for cannon recently captured from the Baton Rouge, Louisiana, Arsenal.[29]

To avoid the appearance of hostility toward the U.S. government, Jackson exercised his power under law to invoke the 1858 Militia Act, summoning the Missouri Militia to assemble locally on May 3, thereafter to go into camp in St. Louis at a place designated by General Daniel M. Frost.[30] Jackson had intended that this camp be situated so as to threaten the St. Louis Arsenal. Lyon, who had been given full command of the arsenal on April 6, reacted swiftly to this threat. Without authority to do so, he occupied the area surrounding the arsenal. Lyon's influential political allies were able to obtain permission for him to arm the loyal militia groups of St. Louis without the approval of his immediate superior General William S. Harney, commander of the Department of the West. Beginning on April 22, Lyon swore in four regiments of volunteers, arming them with weapons from the arsenal. He kept a number in reserve for arming new regiments and sent the remainder of the weapons to safety in Illinois.[31]

When Jackson's Missouri Militia actually went into camp on May 6, the area surrounding the arsenal was already occupied by Lyon. General Frost therefore established Camp Jackson (named in honor of the Governor) in Lindell Grove, in the western part of the city. On May 8, the artillery taken by the Confederates at Baton Rouge was delivered to Camp Jackson. When Blair and Lyon were apprised of this fact, Lyon decided to reconnoiter the camp incognito. Dressed in Blair's mother-in-law's clothing and riding in her carriage, Lyon noted the camp's street signs displaying prominent Confederate names such as Davis and Beauregard. Not surprisingly, he concluded that the militia encampment was a den of Secessionists. He also saw the stolen Baton Rouge weapons.[32]

Back in uniform, Lyon and Blair ordered their new Federal troops to surround Camp Jackson on May 10 and demanded its unconditional surrender. The militiamen stacked their arms and submitted. Lyon could not resist flaunting his authority by parading these captives through the streets of St. Louis under guard of his new "Dutch" Federal troops. The crowds through which Lyon's Germans attempted to navigate swelled as they progressed, pressing in and jostling the nervous volunteers. The mob first hurled epithets and threats, then a variety of missiles. A clod of dirt, perhaps a bullet (which it was seems to depend on the politics of the reporter), struck Captain Blandowski of the Third Regiment, U.S. Reserve Corps, who exclaimed loudly at the impact. Whether this exclamation was an explicit command or not, his agitated troops took this as a command to fire and poured a volley into the crowd.

Fifteen people, including women and children, fell dead and at least twelve more were seriously wounded. Several died in the days following. [33]

Responding to the news of the "Camp Jackson Affair" and to reports that Lyon was marching his troops on the capital at Jefferson City, Governor Jackson succeeded, on May 10, in pushing through the state legislature a military bill authorizing "the Governor to take such measures as he might deem necessary or proper to repel invasion or put down rebellion."[34] The legislature gave Jackson dictatorial powers as well as the treasury. Congressional districts became military regions. And on May 18 former governor Sterling Price was given the rank of major general and made commander of the Missouri State Guard.

At about the same time, Nathaniel Lyon was promoted to brigadier general of Volunteers. Blair was secretly authorized to sack Harney

Sterling Price,
General Missouri State Guard. (Library
of Congress LC-DIG-cwpb-07527)

and elevate Lyon to the position of Commander of the Department of the West on May 20. Ten days later, with an order from the War Department in hand, he did so.[35] Whether Lyon knew or just took for granted that authorization was coming to do so, it is likely he began recruiting for Federal service and swearing in Home Guard units immediately upon learning of Jackson's and the legislature's actions of the 10th.

Assuming David Moore held the same neutralist stance as the signers of the Highland School oath, his position must have been sorely tested by the news of the attack on Fort Sumter. This one event wiped away a lot of the vacillation in the north over whether the southern states should be allowed to secede in peace. "From Ohio and the West came 'one great Eagle-scream' for the flag."[36] The compromising Stephen Douglas, in one of his last speeches before his death, said: "There are only two sides to the question. Every man must be for the United States or against it. There can be no neutrals in this war, only patriots—or traitors." A northern Democratic editor wrote: "All squeamish sentimentality should be discarded, and bloody vengeance wreaked upon the heads of the contemptible traitors who have provoked it by their dastardly impertinence and rebellious acts."[37]

In northeast Missouri, "after the fall of Fort Sumter there was nothing talked about but the war."[38] In May, the citizens of Alexandria were "getting up a company of what they called 'home guard,' to protect themselves from both parties…" Thinking that he stood a good chance of leading this apparently neutralist group as he had the Hickories in the same town, and given his military experience as a captain in the Mexican War, Moore made the trip to Alexandria from his home in Wrightsville, fifteen miles slightly southeast, to stand for the captaincy. To his chagrin, one "Tuter" Johnson polled more votes, and Moore returned home "bitterly disappointed," to form his own company of Home Guard, with a more decidedly partisan bent. When many men from the Alexandria company later enlisted in the Confederate army, specious aspersions arising from this incident were cast on Moore's sincerity in embracing the Unionist Home Guard cause and ultimately that of the Union army.[39]

It was probably soon after the watershed Camp Jackson riot that David Moore directly aligned himself with Federal authorities in St. Louis. Moore requested aid for northeast Missouri from Lyon, whom he supposedly had met during the Mexican War. About May 20, "General Lyon sent him a commission as Captain, with authority to organize and hold the country" in the northeast part of the state.[40]

Moore wasted no time in drafting a pugilistic recruitment poster and getting the Alexandria newspaper, *Delta*, to print a batch for him:

> The undersigned is authorized to raise a company of volunteers in the county, for the Union service. All who are willing to fight for their homes, their country and the flag of the glorious Union, are invited to join him, bringing with them their arms and ammunition. Until the Government can aid us we must take care of ourselves. Secessionists and rebel traitors desiring a fight can be accommodated on demand.
> D. MOORE.[41]

Moore reputedly attached one poster to the door of a neighbor he believed to be the author of an earlier ultimatum to him to leave town.[42] At about this time, to show there should be no question of where his sympathies lay, Moore is said to

Rufus Ash,
one of the original soldiers recruited by
David Moore. (Courtesy of Battle of
Athens State Historic Site)

have climbed a ladder to the gable of his general store where the words "D. Moore, Wrightsville" appeared, painted out the word "Wrightsville," and painted in "Union," allegedly commenting to onlookers: "And if I had more room I'd put 'Now and Forever' there, too."[43]

News of the Camp Jackson Affair seems to have inspired Clark County Secessionists to levels of aggression beyond those alluded to in March by the men signing the Highland School oath. Even before Camp Jackson, on April 29, U.S. Senator James S. Green stated emphatically in a speech at Monticello that "Every man willing to live under Black Republican rule ought to be kicked out of the State like a dog!"[44] Many Unionists packed whatever belongings they could carry and abandoned their homes to their Secessionist neighbors.

Such rhetoric and the actions it motivated, along with his shaken faith in the allegiances of those who rejected him for captain in Alexandria, were probably the final straws breaking the back of any hope David Moore entertained of keeping Missouri in the Union through a neutralist posture. By mid-May, the Unionist-neutralist stance of the March convention must have seemed hopelessly naive and impracticable. Moore rejected the option of flight in the classical choice and elected to stay and fight.[45]

The last shred of hope of reconciling the opposing factions in Missouri completely vanished on June 11. That day Jackson and Price met with Lyon at the Planter's House in St. Louis, attempting to persuade him not to intervene further in the affairs of what they argued was a sovereign state. After a four or five hour meeting that had accomplished nothing, the impetuous Lyon shouted them down with the words that "'rather than concede to the State of Missouri for one single instant the right to dictate to my government in any matter however unimportant, I would…see…every man, woman, and child in the state dead and buried.' Then turning to the Governor he said: 'This means war. In an hour one of my officers will call for you and conduct you out of my lines.'"[46] Not waiting for Lyon's escort out of St. Louis, Jackson and Price returned to Jefferson City, burning a bridge on the way and ordering telegraph lines cut between St. Louis and the capital.

Lyon pursued, marching his Federal troops on Jefferson City. The capital was his on June 15. Jackson fled to Boonville, where a few hundred of his State Guardsmen were encamped. Following with 2,000 troops, Lyon struck Boonville two days later, easily dispersing Jackson's protectors. With some Secessionist assemblymen in tow, the governor retreated all the way southwest to Missouri's border with Confederate Arkansas. Lyon followed.

On June 10, the day before his stormy meeting with Jackson and Price, Lyon had sent a letter to William Bishop of Alexandria authorizing him to swear into United

States service "such parties as do desire to obey such orders as I may give, or you in your judgment deem best to serve the cause of the General Government." Bishop took the "oath of service to the United States" the next day at the St. Louis Arsenal.[47] Three days later, on June 14, Bishop swore in David Moore, who by now had raised a company of fifty-five Unionist Home Guards. Moore's men were sworn in on June 15, the same day Lyon's troops occupied Jefferson City.[48]

As he watched them take the oath, one can imagine Captain Moore ardently hoping that his men realized as clearly as he that those willing to fight "for the flag of the glorious Union" had now thrown down the gauntlet to "rebel traitors."

William Bishop
(Courtesy of Clayton Bishop)

Chapter 3

June and July of 1861 were busy months for recruitment of the Union Home Guard in northeast Missouri. In Clark County, "William McKee, T. H. Roseberry, Jackson…Hackney, Spellman, Motley and Washburn raised companies and squads." Just west, in Scotland County, "William Harle, Simon Pearce, and Ellsberry Small formed companies," and in Knox County "Joseph Story, George W. Fulton, N. W. Murrow and Pierce rallied the Unionists."[1]

William Bishop had sworn in O. B. Payne at St. Francisville on June 10, Thomas Roseberry, William Jackson, David Moore, Aaron Mattley, Peter Washburn, Barton Hackney, Henry Spellman, and James Best between June 14 and 18 in Alexandria. He swore in D. F. Hull at Sweet Home on June 18, and Joseph T. Farris at Croton on June 20. Elsberry T. Small took the oath on July 19 in Alexandria.[2]

The Secessionist intimidation that brought the Highland School men together in March continued unabated into the summer. According to a *Chicago Tribune* correspondent:

> For the past three or four weeks the northeast corner of Missouri has been in a state of anarchy…This state of things originated from the attempts of secessionists to drive Union men out of the country. To effect this, they…collected in squads, visited the houses of the Unionists—mostly in the absence of the men—insulted and abused the women, and threatened that unless the family left the men would be shot or hung…the consequence has been that many Union men have abandoned everything and left the State.[3]

The mere forming of individual Home Guard companies under the Federal aegis was insufficient for defense against these outrages, because "the members, being scattered…were useless in a sudden emergency," and were "powerless to protect from assassination." Hence, the Home Guard captains and their recruits rendezvoused at "Cahokia" with the intent of consolidating under the command of one of their number.[4]

July 4, 1861, was no ordinary Independence Day in Kahoka, Missouri, for Captain David Moore and other Home Guard organizers who had been busily gathering men for the Union cause. In mid-morning the various Home Guard companies drilled in the Kahoka square under the eye of Captain Bart Hackney. This entertainment was followed by a picnic lunch. In the early afternoon a drum and bugle corps performed, composed mostly of members of the musical Roseberry family. Moore then introduced a young speaker and former neighbor of his from Sugar Creek, 17-year-old William H. Resor. Descended from slave-owners in Virginia, young Resor gave an impassioned Unionist speech, punctuated by questions, which he answered, and applause from the audience. Having captivated his listeners for two hours, Resor joined his mother watching from a hotel window. As the band played in front of the hotel, Moore and a delegation pressed the young orator to appear again in the hotel window for the crowd. Bart Hackney and Moore then spoke, as did Hiram Hiller and the Reverend Charles S. Callihan, a Methodist preacher from lower Clark County, disciple of Frederick Douglass, and one-time West Point cadet.

The Home Guard captains then gathered to elect field officers. David McKee, 2nd lieutenant in D. F. Hull's company, was elected major, edging out Hull, who in turn called the whole process into legal question.[5] Charles S. Callihan became lieutenant colonel. When lobbying began for colonel, David McKee, Henry Spellman, and others supported William Bishop, then in St. Louis on grand jury duty.[6] The Bishop faction lost and David Moore won the post. As commander, Moore made various appointments to lesser regimental posts, including Dr. Wilfred M. Wiley of Edina as surgeon and Dr. Andrew Clark of Kahoka as assistant surgeon.[7] The Chicago Tribune correspondent backhandedly endorsed the new colonel as "rough, not over bright, but withal a well-meaning and brave old soldier, who has seen service in Mexico."[8] The festivities concluded only when "darkness constrained the people to depart."[9]

While his regiment remained camped in Kahoka, the new colonel wasted no time in dealing with those who disputed his election. Within the week he sent off the disgruntled Major McKee and Captain Spellman as members of a delegation to St. Louis in search of arms. This strategy bought Moore a week of peace. Only Spellman returned, carrying a promise from William Bishop of 250 rifle-muskets to be sent

by rail to Croton, Iowa. David McKee remained with Bishop in as a recruiter for Bishop's own "Black Hawk Cavalry." Bishop would not serve under David Moore.[10]

Kahoka was of no strategic importance to Moore in securing Clark County for the United States. To remain there only made him vulnerable to State Guard attack from almost any direction. The strategic linchpin of the region was Athens, fifteen miles northeast. There Moore's regiment could secure the Des Moines River and the Keokuk & Des Moines Valley Railroad across it at Croton, both crucial lines for supply and reinforcement. And it was to Croton that Bishop was sending his coveted rife-muskets.

Just a little more than a week after Moore's election, his pro-secession counterpart, Martin Green, had been elected colonel of a regiment of State Guard volunteers.[11] His second in command was Joseph C. Porter of Lewis County. Green's mounted troops were camped only

Dr. Andrew Clark, Assistant Surgeon, First Northeast Missouri Home Guard. (Courtesy of Battle of Athens State Historic Site)

twenty-five miles south of Kahoka at Monticello, the county seat of Lewis County on Horseshoe Bend of the Fabius River. Fifteen miles west of Moore, just over the border of Clark in Scotland County at Etna, lay the camp of Green's newly elected major, Benjamin W. Shacklett. At Keller's Tavern Shacklett's men erected a liberty pole and hoisted the flag of the new Confederate nation. Secessionists were also gathering at Memphis, just northwest of Etna.[12]

Rumors abounded of an impending attack on the Kahoka Home Guard camp. Moore sent requests to Keokuk and Quincy, Illinois, for reinforcements and appealed to the governor of Iowa to "pleas scend 500 men armed and Equipt with two Days rasions to cooporate with my Reg home gards…"[sic][13] The Warsaw Greys, commanded by Captain George W. Coster, came over from Illinois. Keosauqua, Iowa, sent men. The Croton Guards came down.

These Iowa and Illinois troops apparently came to Moore's aid assuming they were to function only defensively, but the new Home Guard commander had other ideas. Moore had no intention of waiting in Kahoka to be attacked from the south and, if Shacklett consolidated his force with troops from Memphis, from the west. If Shacklett simply stole a march on him, beating him to Athens and the shipment of weapons, his Home Guard would be looking down the wrong ends of those rifle barrels. And he would still have to contend with Green. The prospect of being caught in State Guard pincers in either scenario must have figured prominently in Moore's calculations. Strengthened by the Iowa and Illinois men, the colonel-elect prepared his First Northeast Missouri Home Guard to march.[14]

At this point D. F. Hull revived his earlier challenge to Moore's election and mutinied. "When we left Kahoka," Pvt. John McKee noted, "our captain Daniel Hull refused to go, saying we were not legally organized." McKee's father, William, "having been a Black Hawk soldier took command of our company."[15]

Moore's destination of Athens lay fifteen miles almost directly north of the Kahoka encampment. But on Sunday, July 21, William McKee's company, including Pvt. John McKee, and the rest of the regiment, five hundred strong, broke camp and marched directly west. In this daring detour, Moore set out to surprise and destroy Shacklett at Etna, while he was still separated from Green.

Along the way, according to a pro-State Guard reporter who characterized the southerners as "States Rights men," Moore's Home Guardsmen "went to private houses, searched them for arms, and arrested all citizens they could lay hands upon that had ever expressed themselves against the administration."[16] If so, this was a practice Moore would repeat in his program to pacify northeast Missouri.

Late that afternoon, William McKee's company of Home Guard cavalry reached Etna, sweeping down on the State Guard encampment. "'After delivering one volley [the State Guardsmen] fled.'"[17] They fired high and no Home Guardsmen were hit. Home Guard fire did strike one of Shacklett's men who died later that evening in Keller's Tavern. Several of his comrades were taken prisoner. Moore's men made short work of the "liberty pole, eighty feet high, from the top of which a rebel flag was flying, and secured the flag."[18] Peter S. Washburn, Captain Company H, noted laconically: "July 21ˢᵗ Marched from Cahoka to Aetna, Mo., there had a skirmish."[19]

Camped on ground occupied only the night before by Shacklett, Moore must have smiled over his day's work. Rejecting the cautious option of marching directly to Athens and establishing a defensive position, he had taken the offensive, executed a police action against the seditious populace, brought the fight directly to the gathering State Guard host, put them to flight, and incurred no Home Guard casualties. No doubt he hoped that handing his men this victory would silence those who muttered about his legitimacy, and perhaps ability, to command.

The Home Guard broke camp at Etna the next day, Monday, July 22, and marched toward Athens, slightly less than 20 miles northeast. North of Luray, Washburn recorded that Moore's force skirmished with some State Guardsmen at Nick Conkle's farm in the bottoms of the Little Fox River, killing four or five. Moore's intelligence had it that Martin Green and his troops were also on the move from Monticello. Therefore, on July 23, Moore detached 300 men under Callihan and Washburn as a rear guard, leading the remainder on to Athens, where he began barricading the streets and adopting "other measures of defense." By the following Monday, July 29, the rearguard had rejoined Moore in Athens and the relocation of the First Northeast Missouri Home Guards from Kahoka to Athens was completed.[20]

Moore wasted no time in implementing his pacification program inaugurated a week and a half earlier between Kahoka and Etna. All those suspected of being disloyal were arrested. The Home Guardsmen "confiscated everything" they needed "in the way of food, clothing, forage for horses, and shelter." While impounding supplies from the loyal populace as well, "as far as possible" they "discommoded the Southern sympathizers first." Moore appropriated W. H. Spurgeon's Drygoods Store as the Home Guard hospital. He was preparing for battle and, as a veteran, knew that battle meant casualties. Home Guard troops were quartered in buildings throughout the community. Private residences were not spared, including those of Jane Gray and former County Judge William Baker.[21]

Incidents of wanton destruction against "disloyal" Athenians also took place. Moore's soldiers dumped the contents of George Gray's Water Street general store into the Des Moines, including a shipment of parasols, which they opened before throwing in the river. "The next morning, they could still be seen floating down stream."[22] The correspondent "Justicia" spares no vitriol in charging Home Guard depredations in Athens, including appropriating meat from George Gray's pork house and supplies from W. H. Spurgeon, W. Stafford, and B. Rebo. "I do not think they even gave their worthless script in exchange." According to Justicia, Moore's men did not restrict their "all manner of outrages" to Athens. They began "scouring the country for miles around" as well, "searching houses, arresting peaceful citizens, insulting women," and "appropriating private property."[23]

While fiercely partisan, Justicia may also have reported these events accurately, for Moore quickly realized that he needed to establish rules governing foraging. One Home Guardsman confiscated the suit of Barney, described as an "elderly house servant," possibly a slave, of young widow Jane Gray. She complained to Moore, who adjudicated the affair and returned Barney's suit.[24]

The Home Guard colonel knew that well-supplied troops would be less inclined to raid civilian property. Acting as his own quartermaster, Moore had written to the Committee of Public Safety in Keokuk as early as July 23 stating, "my men are

The widow Jane Gray and her son Lon, ca. 1910. (Courtesy of the Battle of Athens State Historic Site)

destitute. Can you send me 200 blankets and some bread or crackers?" Moore also requested "one piece of artillery," informing the committee that the State Guard had assembled 1,000 men as near as Memphis. The Keokuk committee appealed in turn to Iowa Governor Kirkwood. No supplies or arms were sent. However, Kirkwood's aid, Colonel Cyrus Bussey, set off to St. Louis to petition General John C. Frémont, since July commander of the Department of the West, for weapons for the Guardsmen. In the meantime, Moore purchased seven tons of ham and pork shoulders from the firm of Shreve & Scott in Farmington, Iowa.[25]

On July 25, just a day after the first of the Home Guard arrived in Athens, a delegation of "peace men" from Clark County sought a meeting with Colonel Moore at Joseph Benning's residence.[26] The delegation recounted to Moore its visit to Green's camp and described the State Guard's formidable strength. They informed the Home Guard colonel that it was not too late to compromise and avert bloodshed. If he would disband, so would Green.

Moore responded emphatically that the time for compromise was past and that a state of war already existed between his troops and those rebelling against the United States government. He cautioned these mediators that he did not "wish to hear any more propositions of this sort," and warned that if Green wished to "avoid the shedding of blood," then he should "keep his men beyond the range of my muskets!"[27] Given his attack on Shacklett only four days earlier, no one doubted Moore's resolve or capacity to fight.

However, having assumed the defensive in Athens and anticipating imminent attack, Moore suddenly found his capacity to make good on his threat seriously compromised. One account claims that he himself "furloughed a number of his men, until he had about 400 left." He immediately "began drilling" these four hundred, who became "quite proficient in the 'school of the soldier' and in company and battalion drill."[28]

It is curious that Moore would furlough a large part of his force, given continuing reports of State Guard movement in the general direction of Athens. The peculiarity of this action is only increased by the claim that Moore immediately began to drill his remaining troops, presumably preparing them for battle. Why would he, at the same time, furlough numerous others, especially given what was probably his uncertainty about the size of Green's force?

A clue is provided by the *Chicago Tribune* correspondent's account of the "peace" meeting held at Benning's. He writes that

Soon after retiring to Athens, the secessionists proposed a peace conference, and

> many Unionists went into council with them to bring about a restoration of order; but the more wary said the object of the rebels was only to get them to disperse and then they would disarm them. The effect, however, of this proposition, was to very much weaken the Union camp, and Col. Moore soon found his force reduced to less than 300 men.[29]

If the correspondent was right, it seems that Moore continued to face more and greater dissidence than that from disgruntled officers like David McKee, Henry Spellman, and Daniel Hull. The "Unionists" of which this correspondent writes appear to be the rank and file of Moore's Home Guard camp, who were intimidated by the rumor of the approaching State Guard horde. Indeed, it was the object and proposal of the peace delegation that "Col. Moore and his men immediately lay down their arms and return at once to their homes" to avoid bloodletting. While Moore reportedly scoffed at this proposal, throwing down his own gauntlet to Green, the *Chicago Tribune* correspondent matter-of-factly records that many of his men took it seriously and decamped. This turn of events would explain Moore immediately throwing himself into drilling his remaining force.[30]

Pro-State Guard Athenians, chafing under Moore's occupation, no doubt took some heart at what may have been a mutiny and mass desertion. Yet they no doubt yearned for complete liberation of their town from the coarse and hostile Home Guard.[31]

About a week after the disarmament delegation made its proposal to Moore, Martin Green issued a proclamation to the citizens of Knox County on Friday, August 2. It was a masterful attempt to bestow the mantle of "lawfulness" on his State Guard and to construe their mission as the protection of "constitutional rights" of all the citizenry, regardless of politics. Most of the proclamation attempts to mollify the citizens of Knox County concerning the "foraging" of the State Guard, which Green claims to be "the lawful militia of Missouri." Green's troops incurred the same resentment as Moore's of their supplying themselves at the local populations' expense.

Green explicitly states his aim as being "to restore quiet," and he pledges to "protect all citizens, regardless of their opinion, in the enjoyment of their constitutional rights." He concludes with virtually the same message the "peace" delegation bore to Athens:

> ...to those who have taken up arms against us I would say, whenever you lay down your arms and return to your business, as citizens, you, too, shall be protected in your rights, both you and your property...and whenever the causes that placed us in the field cease to exist, we shall most gladly accept the opportunity to disband our forces and return to our homes.[32]

This proclamation may have found its way to Athens and conjoined with the peace delegation's message "to very much weaken the Union camp" by some of the Home Guard "furloughing" themselves. It may well have been that Green's proclamation and the overture of the peace delegation to Moore, were twin prongs of a political strategy of the State Guard organization.[33]

Green's proclamation was attended by even more disconcerting news for Home

Guard morale: Major E. V. Wilson's Knox County Home Guard company had been routed by the State Guard at Edina, forty miles southwest of Athens. Decamping from near Monticello, the State Guard had marched west toward Edina. Near sundown on July 30, Knox County Unionists under Wilson met them at Troublesome Creek, three miles east of town. However, Wilson apparently lost his nerve and ordered a retreat thirty-five miles south, all the way to Macon. Green then occupied Edina, from which place he had issued his proclamation.[34]

It was no doubt clear to Moore, and probably to most of his troops, that Green would march unimpeded north toward a rendezvous with the State Guard at Memphis, only twenty-five miles southwest of Athens. Once he concentrated his forces at Memphis, there could be little doubt of his destination.

So it was that forty or so cavalrymen of Captain Sample's company went up to Athens from Keokuk on Saturday, August 3, based on reports "of dissensions among the Union men" at Athens. Sample understood that a "large part of the regiment had abandoned their arms" at the same time "that an attack was feared from the rebels." As far as the Iowans could understand, the wrangling in Kahoka on July 4 over "whether Bishop or Moore should be Colonel," which had persisted with Daniel Hull's mutiny on July 21, still bedeviled the Home Guard ranks in the very face of the enemy. And it was said "Moore's loyalty was doubted because he has two sons in the ranks of the rebel forces."[35]

The Home Guard decamping at Athens may have been due to continuing dissension over whether Moore was their legitimate commander, to distrust of his motives, to belief that bloodshed could still be avoided through compromise, to panic at the news of Wilson's folding at Troublesome Creek, to the general anxiety of raw recruits anticipating battle, to the need to attend to "usual vocations," or likely to a chemistry of some or all of these reasons. Whatever the explanation, the Iowans wanted to know if Moore's depleted ranks could prevent a State Guard incursion into their state, or whether the Des Moines River at Athens would become a second, and for them much more troublesome, Troublesome Creek.

If battle was joined, it would not be "just the unadorned, long-drawn-out line of ragged, dirty blue against the long-drawn-out line of dirty, ragged butternut" for these Missourians, as one soldier described the opposing lines of battle less than two years later.[36] If these men were to fire on an opposing battle line, then they would most likely be firing on neighbors, acquaintances, and, in some cases, family. It is not difficult to understand why some may have held out the hope of resolution into the last week of July or the first week of August, or beyond, or why some may have been willing to lay down their arms as a good-faith response to Green's offer.

But at last the outnumbered Home Guard force at Athens received their long sought supplies. A shipment from St. Louis of some 30 tons of rations, clothing, and perhaps more muskets, ammunition, and accoutrements arrived in Croton on August 1.[37] Now the odds of making a successful stand against the State Guard, while certainly not stacked in their favor, were improved.

Colonel Cyrus Bussey, an aide to Iowa Governor Kirkwood, had also been keeping an eye on northeast Missouri. On June 15, the day Moore's original company was sworn in, he had advised Kirkwood that "trouble in the northern counties of Missouri" may well "extend to Iowa." On July 30 Bussey was in St. Louis petitioning General Frémont for muskets and ammunition for the Missouri and Iowa border militias. The Pathfinder could spare no arms for home guard militias, but gave Bussey fifty thousand rounds of rifle ammunition and permission to move the 5th and 6th Iowa Infantries, some 2,000 men, from Burlington to Keokuk if he thought circumstances called for it.[38]

Bussey was a man with a will who found a way. Back in Keokuk on August 2, he learned that a shipment of 1,000 U.S. Springfield rifle-muskets were sitting on a freight train bound for the 4th Iowa Infantry, then mustering under Grenville Dodge at Council Bluffs in far northwest Iowa. Bussey seized the muskets. He dis-

Cyrus Bussey
(From A. A. Stuart,
Iowa Colonels and Regiments)

pensed two hundred to Sample's mounted Keokuk Rangers and Belknap's Keokuk City Rifles. The remaining eight hundred were loaded on a Keokuk & Des Moines Valley Railroad train which departed northeast toward Croton. Bussey deposited two hundred more muskets at Croton for the First Northeast Missouri Home Guard and proceeded to dispense the remaining six hundred to militias upriver.[39]

Bussey's determination to upgrade the militia's arms and equipage, combined with his willingness to incur the wrath of Kirkwood, Dodge, and others, played no small role in the outcome of the fight brewing at Athens. Bussey may not have known on August 2 how timely his delivery of the 1000 muskets was. John McKee, the 19-year-old cavalryman in the Home Guard reported that he replaced his double-barreled shotgun (with only one barrel fireable) with a new government-issue rifle-musket on Sunday night, August 4.[40]

Dave Moore's recruiting handbill of earlier in the summer had enjoined those volunteering to bring "with them their arms and ammunition," because "until the government can aid us, we must take care of ourselves."[41] However, it was easier to request than to accomplish that the volunteers "take care of ourselves" in this manner.

Surprising as it may be to twenty-first century readers accustomed to thinking of their forebears as armed to the teeth, arms both of sufficient number and quality were significantly lacking at the establishment of many of the Home Guard companies. Sometime after his mustering-in by Bishop on June 18, Dan Hull found that among his forty-two horsemen there were only twenty odd revolvers, rifles, and shotguns. Similarly Bart Hackney, mustered the same day, also by Bishop, found his situation even more perilous. He could find only twenty-eight guns among his one hundred and five recruits! Petitioning for arms, Hull wrote that "if wee had armes I think it would hav an attendency to do the cose a gradeel of (good)... they hav armes and wee hav not.[sic]"[42]

By Sunday night this situation had been substantially rectified thanks to Bishop

and Bussey. No doubt Pvt. John McKee, Colonel David Moore, and many other
Home Guardsmen, slept better the night of Sunday, August 4, 1861, knowing that
most, if not all of their ranks, as well as the Iowa men just across the river, were
armed with U.S. issue muskets. Nevertheless, the Colonel made certain that "during
the night the line of sentinels was often visited by grand rounds and instructed of
their duty."[43]

Athens, Missouri: Then

Croton, Iowa, taken from an upper floor of a building on Water Street in Athens,
ca. 1857. (Courtesy of Battle of Athens State Historic Site)

Hanson's Blacksmith Shop, southeast corner of Spring and Polk Streets, ca. 1908.
Camera is facing north. Pictured are sister and brother Bertha and Kenneth Doud.
(Courtesy of Battle of Athens State Historic Site)

Spurgeon's Drygoods Store, northeast corner of Spring and Thome Streets, ca. 1910. Camera is facing northwest. Beyond are Kern's Furniture and Undertaking Parlor and the McKee House. The building was torn down in 1915. (Courtesy of Battle of Athens State Historic Site)

Athens School, northeast corner of Elm and Virginia Streets, ca. 1890. Camera is facing southwest. John McKee's cavalry bivouac would have been behind and to the left of the camera. The school was built around 1850 and torn down in 1902. (Courtesy of Battle of Athens State Historic Site)

General Store, southeast corner of Spring and Thome Streets (with men standing under porch roof),
ca. 1890. Camera is in Spring Street, approximately in front of the Susan Anthony House, facing east.
(Courtesy of Battle of Athens State Historic Site)

General Store (same as previous), camera is facing northeast, ca. 1916. The last general store in Athens,
it burned down in about 1917. (Courtesy of Battle of Athens State Historic Site)

Athens Ferry, ca. 1916. Camera is facing north. Established in the 1830s by Isaac Gray, the ferry operated until the 1920s. (Courtesy of Battle of Athens State Historic Site)

Athens Mill (foundation), ca. 1907. Camera is facing west. Athens's principle business, the mill was built
in the 1840s by Arthur Thome and continued to operate under various owners until the mid-1880s.
Pictured are Doris and Neva Bedill. (Courtesy of Battle of Athens State Historic Site)

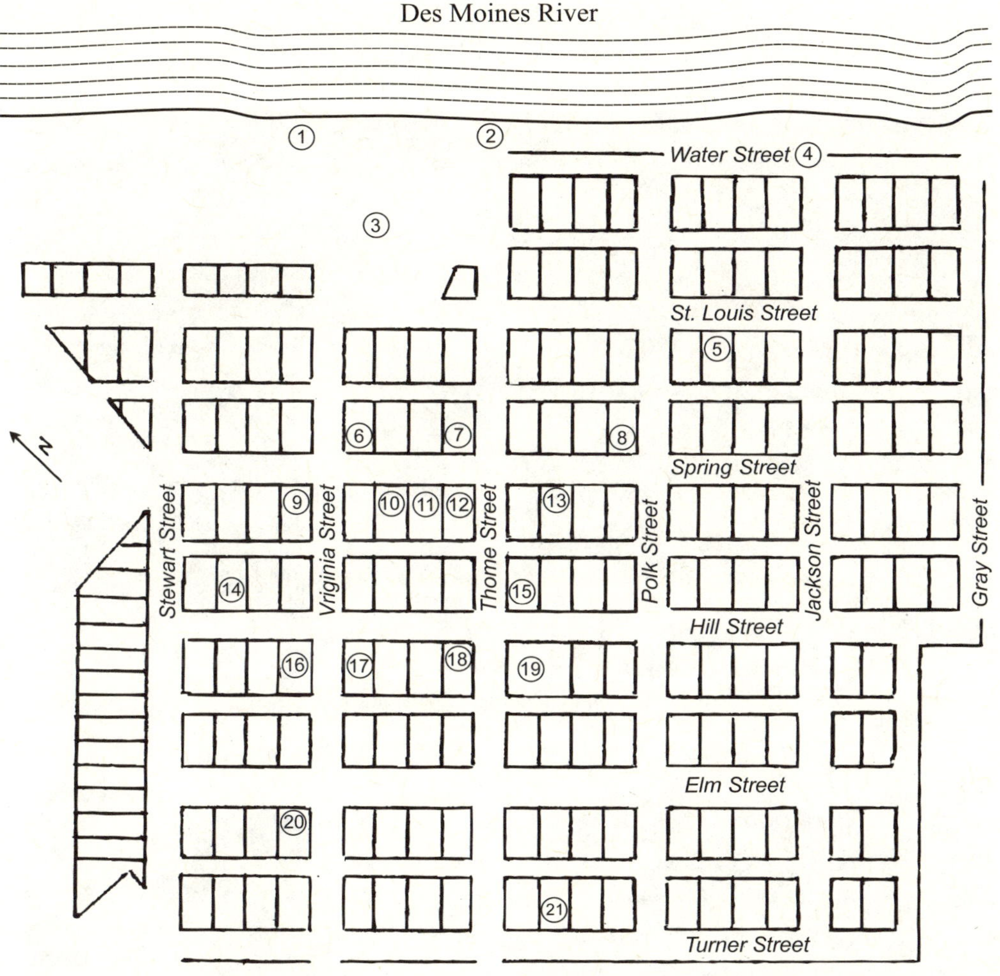

1. Athens Mill
2. Athens Ferry
3. Benning House
4. Water Street Businesses
   Jackson Hotel
   George Gray's Store
   George Gray's Woodyard
   George Gray's Meatpacking
   Town Meeting Hall
5. Masonic Hall
6. Susan Anthony House
7. General Store
8. Hanson Blacksmith Shop
9. McKee House
10. Kern's Furniture and Undertaking
11. Oldenhague's Harness Shop
12. Spurgeon's Drygoods
13. Post Office
14. Townsend-Stafford Feed Lot
15. Townsend-Stafford Warehouse
16. Townsend-Stafford Feed Warehouse
17. Townsend-Stafford General Store
18. Townsend-Gray House
19. Faxon Wagon Works
20. Athens School
21. Methodist Church (1868)

Athens businesses and home sites
(Map drawn by Matt Kantola)

Athens, Missouri: Today
(Except where noted all pictures were take in the mid 1990s by the author)

Susan Anthony House, looking north.

Spring Street, looking northwest, McKee House in the distance.
Camera is in approximately the same position as in the photo of Spurgeon's Drygoods Store.

McKee House, looking north.

Spring Street, looking southeast, McKee House is on the right, Anthony House is partially visible on the left. House in the distance on the left was not present in 1861. Moore's line of battle formed up along this street facing right. Virginia Street intersects in the middle distance.

Mill ruins, from Croton, Thome-Benning House is visible at the top of the bluff.

Stallion Branch, looking toward the Des Moines River.

Des Moines River, looking toward Croton, at about the point where Callihan and Spellman retreated.

Thome Street, looking southwest from the middle of Moore's line. State Guard artillery was posted on the ridge in the distance, and further to the right. Townsend-Gray House is in the middle distance on the right (to the left of the "CC" sign).

Townsend-Gray House, corner of Hill and Thome Streets, looking southwest toward State Guard line. William Sullivan and Jabez Harrison were killed here.

Virginia Street, looking northeast, McKee House in the distance, from Elm Street. Athens School would have been on the left in the middle distance, McKee's cavalry camp to the right. This is the approximate position of the State Guard's barricade.

Cemetery Hill, looking southeast. Shacklett's State Guard approached Moore's left flank from right to left under cover of this hill.

Cemetery Hill, as seen from the corner of the Jane Gray House. Shacklett's State Guard moved from right to left around the hill, then attacked toward the house through the cornfield.

Jane Gray House, looking northeast, Des Moines River is in the distance. Only the front of the house is original. The addition on the back (and the tank) were not present in 1861.
(Picture taken in 1988, courtesy Battle of Athens State Historic Site)

Jane Gray House, looking southwest toward Athens, river is behind the camera. The addition on the back of the house and the structure to the right were not present in 1861.
(Picture taken in 1988, courtesy Battle of Athens State Historic Site)

Chapter 4

Our boys stood fire!

Private John McKee was up frying "pancakes and other things on the fire" for his father's cavalry company as Monday, August 5, 1861, dawned.[1] The Home Guard cavalry were bivouacked on a block on the west side of Athens bounded by Virginia, Elm, Turner, and Thome Streets, across from the Athens school on the corner of Virginia and Elm.[2]

Athens, Missouri, now occupied by the First Northeast Missouri Home Guard and soon to be a battlefield, was laid out in 1844 atop and down two sides of a hill overlooking the Des Moines River. Its grid of streets and blocks turned expectantly northeast toward the river, which its founders hoped would make it a prosperous port.

From St. Louis Street atop the bluff above the Des Moines, the town descended precipitously some sixty or seventy feet to aptly-named Water Street at the river's edge. Transplanted Kentuckian, Arthur Thome, built his house on the edge of the bluff, west of the street named for him, beyond this northwestern line of the original town. Below his house on the river he erected a dam and built a saw, grist, and wool carding mill (all in the same building).

Other enterprises sprang up below on the river bank near Thome's mill. When his financial fortunes fell, Thome sold his house and businesses to Joseph Benning. In addition to the mill acquired from Thome, Benning ran a slaughterhouse. Nearby his uncle, George Gray, who had opened one of the first general stores under the bluff on Water Street, operated a packing plant and no doubt packed carcasses dressed at his nephew's slaughterhouse. Gray's brother Isaac was the first to operate a ferry at Athens.[3]

Southwest, away from the river, a block or so from Thome's house and across a small hollow, the ground leveled approaching Spring Street, which ran parallel to St. Louis Street. Here David Moore would place the center of his battle line, running two blocks or more, early in the morning of August 5, 1861.

The original town extended another block southwest to Hill Street, then southeast to Polk Street, then descended some forty or fifty feet through two more blocks and Jackson Street to Gray Street. There, in the fertile river bottom where corn grew tall, just up from the river, sat a small house occupied by Jane Gray, who had at least one "servant" named Barney, who owned at least one suit.

Additions more than doubling the size of the original town to the northwest and southwest, and to the southeast by half a block, were laid out between 1857 and early 1861, primarily by Isaac Gray and Joseph Benning. On the corner of Spring and Virginia Streets, part of the first additions on the northwest, sat a two story

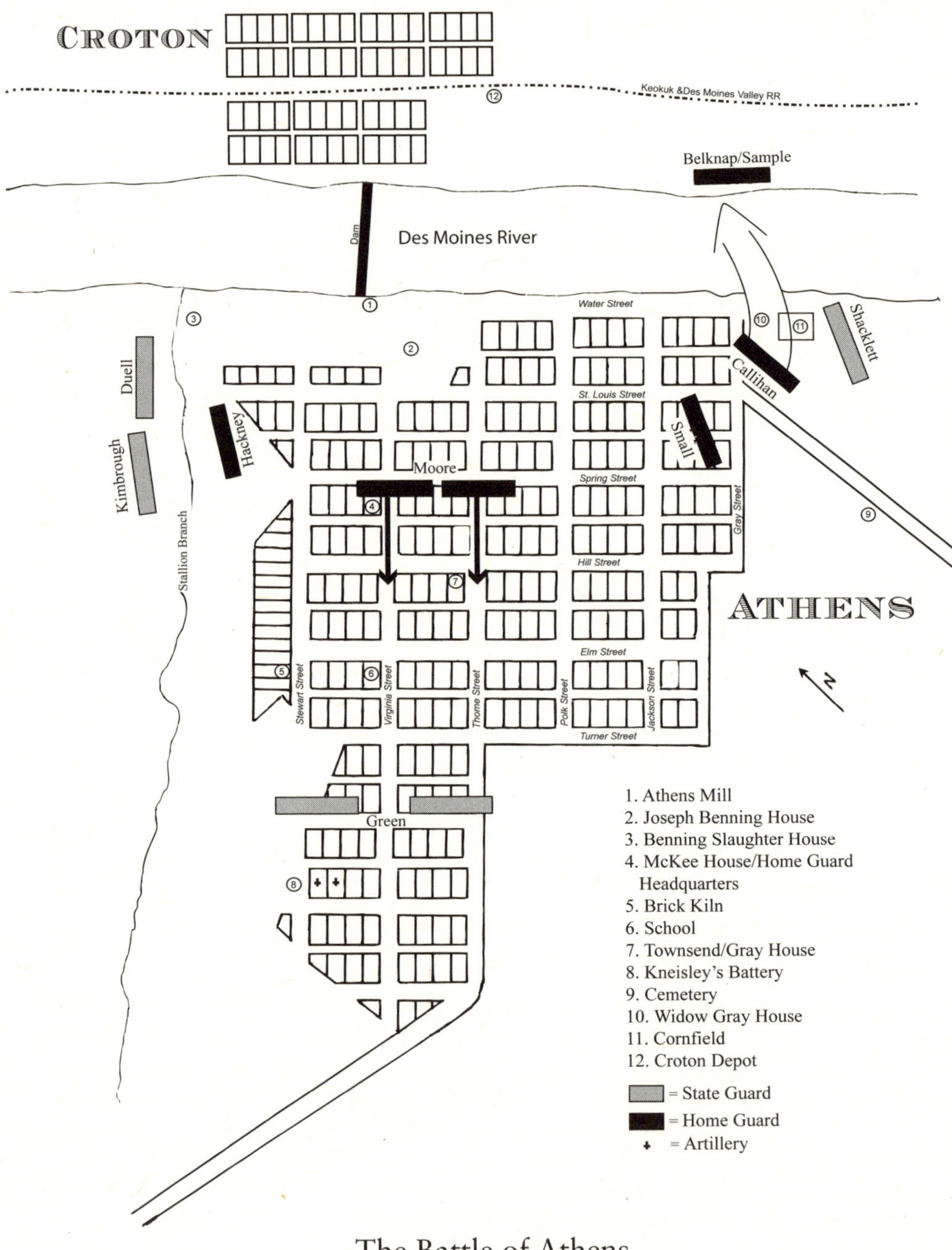

1. Athens Mill
2. Joseph Benning House
3. Benning Slaughter House
4. McKee House/Home Guard
   Headquarters
5. Brick Kiln
6. School
7. Townsend/Gray House
8. Kneisley's Battery
9. Cemetery
10. Widow Gray House
11. Cornfield
12. Croton Depot

= State Guard
= Home Guard
= Artillery

The Battle of Athens
(Map drawn by Matt Kantola)

frame house owned by William McKee and provided to David Moore as a headquarters. Not far to the north of the McKee house, the hill descended seventy or eighty feet, almost vertically for stretches, to Stallion Branch, a creek emptying into the Des Moines. Depending on rainfall, it could be a swelled torrent or bone dry.

Diagonally across the street from the McKee house lived Susan Clark Anthony and her several children, destined to become some of the first refugees of the war. Across Spring Street from Mrs. Anthony was Kern's Furniture and Undertaking. One door to the southeast, John Henry Oldenhage, a German and staunch Unionist, plied his trade as a harness maker. Next door, on the corner of Spring and Thome, W. H. Spurgeon ran a Drygoods Store in a long brick building, competing with another run by Charles Stafford not far away. Spurgeon's loyalties were suspect, at least to the Colonel of the encamped Home Guard, who appropriated his store to be used as a hospital in the event of a fight. Across the street from Spurgeons was a general store, one of six in Athens at this time, and the only one that would persist into the 20th century. Just down the street, near the intersection of Spring and Polk, was Armstrong's storeroom, recently destroyed in a storm. It would soon function as the anchor of the left end of Moore's center.

By August 1861, Thome Street, the main street into town running northeasterly straight down to the river and the ferry landing, more or less bisected Athens—at least as laid out, if not as yet built. From Gray Street at the extreme southwestern tip of a recent addition, to Water Street on the river, Athens ran some eight blocks, or a little more than half a mile. From Stewart Street on the northwest, to Gray Street down below the main town on the southeast, it ran five blocks, or slightly more than a third of a mile.

Rising above St. Louis Street, winding its way down past the Gray farm on the southeast edge of town, stood Cemetery Hill. With shafts of sunlight glancing off them this August Monday, the gravestones of Isaac Gray and other departed settlers stood like sentinels surveying the Des Moines just beyond the cornfield below, Croton on the plain across the river to the north, and finally the hills rising up in the distance to the horizon. A stone's throw to the northwest stood the neighboring hill of Athens, where smoke rose from breakfast fires and young John McKee tended his sizzling skillets.

Had they been able, these denizens of the cemetery would have spied State Guard troops moving under cover of their hill, and some Unionists among them might have shouted to John that they were heading toward the cornfield and Moore's pickets down by Isaac Gray's. Unstopped, they would swarm up the hill of Athens and overrun the breakfasting Home Guard camp.

Wood smoke curled from other cooking fires across the camp, mingling with the smell of coffee, pancakes, and horse manure. Drawn by the smell of breakfast, some Iowa militiamen forded the Des Moines from the Croton side and clambered up the bluff in search of Missouri hospitality.[4] Obliging Home Guardsmen filled their plates. Over the rooftops of Athens toward Cemetery Hill the sky was brightening with the promise of another hot day.

John McKee was about to dish up breakfast for the Home Guard cavalry when pickets led by Lt. William Harle came pounding into camp, shouting that State Guard troops were on their heels. John protested that breakfast was ready. "Never mind about breakfast, the enemy is coming and we are going to have a fight!" his father William McKee shouted, ordering his cavalry to mount and fall into line. Abandoning his spatula for his new musket, John jumped to his saddle. With Wash Collins and a few other men commanded by Captain Oliver B. Payne, he galloped southwest through town and up the hill rising some seventy feet above their camp.[5]

In less than a quarter of a mile, they reined in their mounts "where Harland and old Captain Baker lived." From this vantage point they could see the advancing lead column of State Guardsmen. Payne ordered his detachment of "just eighteen" into line of battle "to meet the enemy."[6] Gripping their muskets, John McKee and his comrades studied the approaching State Guardsmen. "Their cannon came first" followed by "many men." The artillerists halted and began "uncovering the gun," preparing it for action.[7]

McKee fastened his eyes on "a man riding the lead horse, a big don [*sic*]," and raised his musket. But Captain Payne was having second thoughts about engaging these State Guardsmen and their cannon with eighteen men. He ordered his little detachment to withdraw. Undeterred, Private McKee "drew" his musket on the man on the "don" horse, "but before I could fire, my horse whirled and started to follow our boys. Wash Collins fired his old holester [*sic*] at them and we fled, pell mell down the hill."[8]

Driven in by the sight of the State Guard artillery, Payne's mounted patrol returned to where the Home Guard was hastily assembling. One of the Roseberrys slung on his drum and began beating "the long roll," calling his comrades to arms. Hearts pounding, lounging men sprang up, grabbed their gleaming muskets, and ran in the direction of the drumming. "In one minute," Moore recalled, "a line of battle was formed and told off in groups of forty men."[9]

About three hundred and thirty Home Guardsmen[10] hastily fell in line along Spring Street "between the Armstrong storeroom (the one blown down)," near the intersection of Spring and Polk, and "the frame house owned by Wm. McKee" at the intersection of Spring and Virginia.[11] The men in the center of this line faced Oldenhage's harness shop and Spurgeon's Drygoods Store next door on the corner of Thome and Spring. A block and a half behind their backs were the steep bluffs descending to the Des Moines River.

Moore may have immediately refused his right and left flanks—wheeling them back perpendicular to the Des Moines forming a three-sided rectangle with the river as the fourth side—when the State Guard opened fire, or only when they actually attacked him on both flanks. However, in ordering his flanks to press forward toward the east and west, he may have left them "in the air"—with gaps between them and his main line of battle through which the enemy could penetrate. In either case, geography was on the Home Guard side because Moore had chosen his position well. He held the high ground on his right and left and had the "interior line." Green was forced to spread his larger force, double or more that of Moore's, in a semi-circular exterior line around the town. State Guardsmen attacking Moore's right and left would be forced to navigate steep inclines—from Stallion branch on the right and from the plain with Gray Street on the left—into daunting fire from the top of

James Kneisley, Captain Missouri State Guard. (Courtesy of Battle of Athens State Historic Site)

each.

The minute it took for the Home Guardsmen to form a line of battle was not one too soon. They were not yet "fully rally d" when State Guard artillery opened with solid shot and ersatz canister. "Scraps of iron broken castings pot legs etc.," sprayed over the Home Guard's heads.[12] Along with geography, luck was also on the Home Guard side. The green State Guard artillerists, wrestling not only with the terrain but with hitting an enemy at least partially shielded by buildings, "had a fine chance at us," noted Hiller, "but owing to the unskillfullness of their gunner or some other cause their cannon fail d to kill or crippl a sengle man [*sic*]."[13]

State Guard artillery Captain James W. Kneisley had set up his six and nine-pound guns on the hill along Baker Street, near where his approach had been earlier observed by Payne's Home Guards.[14] Along with his two iron cannon, Kneisley had brought an improvised gun made from a hollowed out log reinforced with steel bands. It was not reinforced enough, however. For the gun exploded the first time it was fired, wounding some of its crew.[15]

Kneisley's men sent one solid shot careening into the Croton Railroad Depot across the river. Depressing their barrel, the gunners sent another ball crashing through Benning's house atop the bluff on the Athens side. Entering beside the front door, the shot clipped the corner of a kitchen cupboard, narrowly missed Mrs. Benning emerging from the cellar with coffee for her husband and friends in the kitchen, and exited the back wall of the house. An ardent Southern sympathizer, Mrs. Benning was in the midst of cooking her contribution to a victory feast she and other pro-Southern Athenian women were preparing for their State Guard liberators.[16]

Taking no more chances, Mrs. Benning herded her eight children into the cellar as cannon and musket fire exploded across the hollow. Other Athenians took similar refuge or fled town altogether.[17] "Royal took Harriet and Billy & Alexander into Iowa in a buggy just as the fight commence d," wrote John Hiller later that day.[18] Just feet behind Moore's battle line, Susan Anthony abandoned her property to shot whizzing over her roof, reputedly ferrying her

Detail of Thome-Benning House showing cannon ball hole. (Author's collection)

children across the Des Moines in a large molasses pan![19]

Athenians seeking refuge in Croton found its citizens abandoning their town with equal frenzy. The "barrage produced a general panic," sending "women and children, crying and half-clad" running "into the ravines and forests back of town, for safety."[20] Moore did not order his artillery to answer Kneisley because he had none. The piece he had requested from the Committee of Public Safety in Keokuk on July 23 had not been sent.[21]

Amidst the flying iron, the river at his back, Moore knew that the better part of valor was to avoid casualties which might set off a panic. If his line broke, the State Guard would drive his men to the bluffs and shoot them like fish in a barrel as they splashed across the Des Moines. If he could not rally them on the Iowa shore the supplies, arms, and munitions at Croton, to say nothing of the railroad, would fall into Green's open hands. Moore "ordered his men to lie down and withhold their fire until the opportune moment,"[22] while Moore himself paced bravely up and down his line to encourage his raw troops, receiving in the process a wound in his knee from a piece of rebel canister. His men did not disappoint their Colonel. "Remarkably for raw soldiers" they "stood fire." At Moore's command they reciprocated with "a volley of musket balls."[23]

As the State Guard artillerists worked their guns and the Home Guardsmen heated up their new muskets from the centers some four hundred yards apart, gunfire suddenly erupted down below the Home Guard right and left. The State Guard "attacked us on both flanks," wrote John Hiller.[24] According to John McKee, "the rebels were now all around us, some on the west down the hollow" at Stallion Branch attempting to flank the Home Guard right, "some on the hill with the cannon, some down by the cemetery" on the east, and "some at Jane Gray's near the sugar camp" below cemetery hill, striking toward the Home Guard left through a stand of corn.[25] At this point McKee matter-of-factly observed that "it became too hot for us." He and the rest of Payne's cavalry turned and spurred their mounts across "the river above the mill."[26]

It was not lost on Colonel Moore that "when the artillery opened, my mounted horsemen filed across the river."[27] According to one of Captain James S. Best's men in Moore's center, Payne's cavalry hardly even stopped to position themselves once they rode in, as McKee claimed. Instead, they "quietly rode past our line, down the hill and across the river, many of them never to come back."[28]

Payne's cavalry breaking in their rear did little to nerve the men enduring cannon fire for the first time on their bellies in Moore's center. "Say," Moore is supposed to have bellowed amidst the roar, "whoever heard of anybody being killed by a cannon!"[29] With their Colonel's "extraordinary volume of voice" steadying them, and the State Guard cannon fire dying out, his Home Guardsmen poured volley after volley into the opposing ranks.[30]

Captain Joe Farris, guarding southern sympathizers along with arms and equipage in Croton, had posted pickets on the Iowa side of the river the night before. One of them, Elijah Starr, passed the night at a ford of the Des Moines downriver. Reporting in at daylight, he heard gunfire up the hill in Athens across the river and saw

State Guardsmen advancing over the flat, thick with corn between Cemetery Hill and the Des Moines. Commanded by Ben W. Shacklett, these troops swung around in a northeasterly direction under cover of Cemetery Hill, descended, then crossed St. Louis Street, coming on toward Moore's left.[31]

Moore recalled that "Major Shacklett, with his battalion was on Green's right with their flank opposite the Iowa boys on the other side of the river." Shacklett's "strong force" faced northwestward, advanced through "the cornfield immediately below Wm. Gray's house," and "opened a brisk fire" on Moore's pickets and a contingent of Farmington militia on his left. Once Moore up on Spring Street heard this

Benjamin Shacklett, Major Missouri State Guard. (Courtesy of Battle of Athens State Historic Site)

firing, he ordered Captains Henry Spellman and Ellsberry Small under the command of Lt.-Col. Callihan into position on his left.[32]

The Iowa militiamen on the Missouri side had come intending to eat, not to fight. Discharging a few rounds, they "began to retreat across the river" under "a perfect shower of bullets." A number were hit. Their comrades on the Iowa side did their best to cover the retreat by returning the State Guard fire.[33] Tramping through the corn in pursuit of the fleeing Farmington men, Shacklett's men were no doubt momentarily stunned and stymied by the sound of gunfire from their right. They faced their tormentors across the river and returned fire.

As the Battle of Athens began, the 70 militiamen of the Keokuk Rifles and Rangers who had arrived at Croton late the previous night were relaxing around the depot. According to Station Agent Beaman, Belknap and Sample were not able to get their men organized and marched to the river in good order or soon enough to make a crossing to assist Moore. Reaching the Iowa bank of the river, across from a grove of maple trees on the Missouri side, the Keokuk men could hear and see plainly that shooting had begun in the area of the cornfield. The Rifles and Rangers, joining their Farmington brethren, took cover behind maple trees on the Iowa side and opened fire.[34] Their first rounds fell short, striking "the water near the opposite shore." However, they were able "to get the range readily" and from then on kept "the rebels dodging behind the trees in Ike Gray's grove."[35] Some of Shacklett's men took cover in the Gray house and returned fire from its windows.[36]

Undeterred by the Iowans' enfilading fire on their right, Shacklett's men managed to direct fire from the cornfield at both the Iowans and the Missourians advancing on their front. Bullets ripping through the high corn from unseen muskets and fleeing militiamen falling in the river were more than Spellman's horsemen approaching from Athens hill could bear. "Taken with a panic," they "made a stampede for Croton." From the cornfield, the maple grove, and Jane Gray's house, Shacklett's men poured merciless fire into the Home Guard's rear "but with little effect, shooting over." Nevertheless, "the flag that was carried over was pierced with nine balls."[37]

Sprouse House in Croton (1964). (Author's collection)

Spellman himself brought off the rent colors.[38] "Captain Spellman, with his company" retreated across the Des Moines "with his colors flying," Moore recalled.[39]

It may have been during this retreat that Pvt. William Sprouse was shot. He was severely wounded and taken to a house in Croton, which was set up as hospital, where he died later in the day.[40]

This rout "occasioned a panic" in Croton beyond that already instigated by Kneisley's cannon fire. "Some soldiers, citizens, women and children, with wagons, fled back into the country, spreading alarm and terror all around."[41] One can imagine southeast Iowan farm wives anxiously scanning the horizon to the south, expecting hordes of Missouri Secessionists to sweep down on them at any moment.

Advancing southeast down the hill atop which Athens sat, not long behind Spellman's cavalry, came Moore's refused left flank of infantry commanded by the "elephantine" Captain Ellsberry T. Small.[42] Amidst the panic, as the State Guard tide rolled out of the cornfield toward the hill to Athens and Moore's center, Captain Small proved himself the man for the hour. Armed with a "huge rifle," Small "cheered his men," encouraging "them to fight the harder, and successfully resisted every effort to drive him back."[43] This Home Guard company "stood just where they were posted," according to their colonel.[44]

John Hiller also "crossed the river and rallyd a small force probably 30 or 40 men behind the fence…"[45] He and his comrades were aided by the Iowa militiamen men who, having found the range, were "pouring a galling fire into the flank of the enemy's right wing across the river, with their Minie rifles."[46] Still enfiladed on their right, Shacklett's drive was halted at the edge of the corn by the steady fire from Small in their front. As D. C. Beaman saw it from the Iowa side, the "union reinforcement from Colonel Moore" on the Missouri side "put the rebels in the grove under a cross fire."[47] For the time being at least, no State Guard wave would crest the hill from the southeast, crashing into the left of Moore's center along Spring Street.

Fighting behind his fence on the Iowa side, Hiller claimed that "we soon drove the force from the cornfield and the old log house where they fought from the doors and windows."[48] The Keokuk newspaper, ascribing the retreat from the Gray house to the Keokuk men firing from the Iowa side, probably more accurately states that their fire drove "the rebels from the Gray house," but not from the cornfield, only "into" it.[49]

Small's infantry standing their ground and firing into Shacklett's front played a major psychological role, for "seeing their companions standing firm, many" who had skedaddled "returned and took part in the fight."[50] At some point, Shacklett received a serious wound and had to relinquish command.[51] This casualty and a half hour or so of simultaneous fire on their front and right flank was more than the State Guardsmen could bear. They began to fall back through the cornfield, leaving some of their dead.[52]

As musket fire crackled and powder smoke rolled between the State and Home Guard centers and down in the cornfield, State Guardsmen led by Captains John Duell and John K. Kimbrough advanced along Stallion Branch on the northwest side of town, moving to flank Moore on his right, precipitating a firefight similar to that in the cornfield. The summer had been hot with little rainfall. Running at the bottom of the precipitous bluff, with a plain on the west bank, Stallion Branch was probably low or dry.[53] To meet this threat, Moore sent Captain Bart Hackney and Sergeant John Cox with about sixty men.[54]

Occupying the top of the bluff descending from the west side of Athens to Stallion Branch, Hackney and his men could have repelled virtually any force attempting to cross the creek and advance up the bluff to threaten Moore's line on Spring Street. At least some of them probably descended the bluff to get a better shot at the State Guardsmen across the creek.[55]

Having skedaddled under fire from Kneisley's battery at the outset, and once safely across on the Iowa side, some of Payne's men turned to harass Duell and Kimbrough. John McKee and his comrades "fired a number of shots at them from the Iowa side as the enemy came down the hollow" of Stallion Branch, reminiscent of the fields of fire in the cornfield fight. Neglecting to mention the presence across the river of Hackney, Cox, and their sixty Home Guard comrades, McKee writes that the State Guardsmen "thought we had been joined by reinforcements

John H. Cox, 2nd Sergeant, Co F, Methodist preacher in Clark County, known for abolitionist sermons. (Courtesy of Battle of Athens State Historic Site)

and they started to retreat."[56] "We" may imply Hackney's presence or refer to the Home Guard generally. Duell and Kimbrough, no doubt unaware of Payne's flight, and suddenly finding their left enfiladed from across the river, may have mistakenly assumed fresh Home Guard reinforcements were counterattacking from the Iowa side.

Hiller and his rallied troops had moved upriver from their position opposite the Gray house once they saw the latter evacuated. Whether they waited until the general retreat of Shacklett's men back through the cornfield was in progress or not is unclear. Like McKee, Hiller saw that the State Guard "attacking from the point at Benning's Slaughter House attempted to take possession of the point below the run."[57] But unlike McKee, Hiller maintains that it was Hackney and his men who discouraged this attempt by Duell and Kimbrough to take the ground on the Athens side of Stallion Branch. If Hiller witnessed this "dislodging" first-hand from the Iowa side, then it seems likely that McKee, on the same side and apparently in about the same position, would also have been aware of it.

"For two hours the battle raged on flanks and center," recalled State Guardsman, J. T. Norris.[58] He and his comrades in Green's center fought most of the time behind a breastwork of fence rails they had built shortly after their arrival on the outskirts of Athens around 4:00 a.m.[59]

Like their Keokuk compatriots sniping from the Croton bank of the Des Moines, the Missouri Home Guardsmen in the center soon "got the range" on the State Guardsmen behind their fence rails, firing their "shotguns and...old-fashioned squirrel rifles." Ten year old Oliver Morrison, who had come to the battle with his uncle observed that

> The men with Moore had regular army muskets. A good marksman could kill a man a mile away with one of them. These musket balls would go right through a fence rail or an oak board, and through two or three men on the other side, if they happened to be in line.[60]

Young Morrison claimed to have witnessed at least twenty-five State Guardsmen killed by the Home Guard's long range fire. It didn't take the men in Green's center long to realize that "the trouble was" the Home Guards' "regular army muskets."[61]

At least one Home Guard soldier took it upon himself to work his way closer to the rebel barricade. William Sullivan, 76-year-old veteran of the War of 1812 and a private in Company K, advancing alone or with others on the left of Moore's line, was shot a block forward in the vicinity of the Townsend-Gray House on Thome Street between Hill and Elm, obviously within sight of the rest of Moore's line. Reverend Jabez Harrison mounted his horse and rode out between the lines to rescue Sullivan. As Harrison dismounted, a State Guardsman took aim. His ball struck the chaplain square in the mouth, killing him. Sullivan's wound also proved fatal. Harrison's mount, "Old Frank," cantered over to the State Guard line and was caught.[62]

At some point, "pleasing intelligence," albeit false, of Shacklett's victory in the cornfield spread swiftly down the demoralized State Guard center. The "squirrel rifles" of Shacklett's men, the report ran, "had slaughtered over 500 of the enemy."

The Des Moines, "almost choked with dead bodies of the Federals," had "become a rich carmine hue."[63] If Shacklett's makeshift weaponry had so destroyed Moore's left, then there was no reason why such could not prevail against his center. Perhaps seeing at least two shots connecting with the enemy (Sullivan and Harrison) emboldened the rebels. Maybe one decisive blow would send these "Yankees" skedaddling over the bluff and into the river. State Guardsmen up and down the line gripped their antiquated weapons with renewed determination, "cheered and started forward," to charge the Home Guard center.[64]

It may have been now that one panicked man in Moore's line yelled, "Colonel, I can't stand it. I've got to go!" No doubt enraged by Payne's defection and probably aware of Spellman's, but likely informed that his flanks were now holding and even driving the enemy, Moore responded in his inimitable tone, striking every faint heart in the line, "Damn it, you've got to stand it!"[65]

With Moore's voice booming, the Home Guard line erupted in a sheet of flame as Green's men rushed toward it shouting. But with minie balls whizzing by their heads, the State Guardsmen faltered, falling suddenly silent. The fact that "the enemy's muskets would shoot nearly twice as far as our hunting guns" struck them anew with a vengeance. It probably dawned quickly on not a few of them as well that the inspiring "story of the dead Federals" down on their right "was all a piece of fiction."[66]

Moore saw the crisis in the fight was at hand and seized the initiative. Ordering "those posted on the right and left" at the cornfield and Stallion Branch "to stand fast," he commanded the men of his "center to fix bayonets and move forward in common time." Through the smoke, the faltering State Guards were now the ones to see enemy ranks advancing, bayonets fixed. [67]

Shoulder to shoulder, Moore's men quickened their pace. Seeing State Guardsmen beginning to throw down their weapons, suddenly they "broke into a charge," coming at the State Guard line on a dead run, screaming at the tops of their lungs. Ordering this fait accompli so loud some said as to be heard on the Croton side of the Des Moines, Moore ran along bellowing, "Give the rebels hell, Boys! Charge!"[68] Moore's sons William and Eugene were fighting on the State Guard side. Supposedly, when they heard their father's voice above the battle, they told their comrades: "Boys, do you hear the old man? He means what he says and will be here in about a minute…" They turned tail and ran, adding to their fellows' panic.[69]

Howling, Moore's Home Guards stormed toward Green's wavering center. Green's Chaplain Reverend John Rowe rode among the fleeing Guardsmen, swinging his hat, shouting "Give them hell, boys! God's on our side!" to no avail.[70] The stunned State Guardsmen, facing onrushing bayonets, ignored "experienced warriors" admonishing them to rally and fight. Instead they "took a notion that they wanted to go somewhere" and quickly "lit out." "Every fellow made a break for his horse. Did I run too? Sure I did!" admitted J. T. Norris.[71]

This "stampede" for the rear, this reverse Bull Run "out here in old Missouri," as Norris termed it, reached the timber where the State Guard had tethered their horses earlier that morning. With Moore's men rushing down on them:

You never saw such a mix-up as there was when the fugitives tried to unhitch their horses. Some slashed the bridles with a knife; others tried to jerk them loose by main force. The horses contracted the terror of their masters and jumped around frantically, aiding in the confusion. Many broke loose and rushed wildly about the field. Some of the excited soldiers struck out across the country without taking time to get their horses. The cannon—those fearful engines of destruction—were dragged off the field and hidden in some hazel brush, a most undignified ending of their career.[72]

So thorough was the rout that some of Green's men retreated all the way home to "Macon, Lewis, Shelby, Scotland and other counties. One man went as far as Lancaster in Schuyler County. There were no prisoners taken on the retreat and but very few lives lost. While Col. Moore's men could outshoot us they couldn't outrun us—not that day, and it was a hot one too," remembered Norris.[73]

Green's right and left were probably in retreat virtually at the same time as Moore's center charged.[74] Down in the cornfield, Ben Shacklett, himself with "a grisly wound in his neck, sought to draw off his command, but lost control of his men, who fled incentively [*sic*], some running down the river straight to the east."[75] On Moore's right, Hiller recalled: "As soon as the flanks were driven back our small force waded the river below the dam[,] filed up the hollow between Mrs. Marshbank's and Jo Benning's to reinforce our main body but found the enemy retreating."[76]

Hiller, McKee, and others of Payne's errant cavalry probably joined forces on the Iowa side of the Des Moines across from the action at Stallion Branch. McKee narrates:

> We again crossed the river and by this time Colonel Moore had them on the run. We were ordered to follow. Up the hill we went, but could see nothing of them until we got to John Bedells'. There we fired a few shots and followed through the prairie. Then we formed a line just east of John Bedman's. There was about 150 of the enemy across the hollow in the hazelbrush, about one-fourth mile away. I fired a few shots at them in there and they soon left that shelter. We followed them, came to Ranson's house, here halted awhile, then pushed on to the Stafford house. Here a number of shots were fired while they were in front of Robert Gray's. These were the last shots exchanged.[77]

Hiller, finding the rout in progress, "mounted a contraband horse," one rushing "wildly about the field," having broken loose in the State Guard panic, and

> got a case of holster pistols and a musket and with about 25 others followed in pursuit. Their forces of probably 80 or 100 covering the retreat of their cannon made a halt on the rise beyond Beidman's. We charged on them. When they retreated rapidly we all got shots at them as they rose [up] the hill at Bob Grays we being at Staffords. We then fell back as if retreating and formd an ambush but they were too cowardly to pursue[78]

It was the retreat of Kneisley's battery which Hiller claims was being covered by the "80 or 100" State Guard whom he and his party were pursuing. These guns were mounted on carriages "not of the regulation pattern, and were rather light." The drivers "tried to keep up" in this "rapid retreat from the field at Athens" but, when the carriage of the six-pounder straddled a stump about six miles south of Athens, the elevating screw caught and was bent so that it was impossible to depress or elevate the piece until the injury should be repaired. Pressed for time and a little panicky anyhow, the cannoneers drove the gun off the road and into the thick brush as far as possible, and, unhitching the horses, abandoned it.[79]

Moore's Home Guard collected spoils from the battle,[80] but Kneisley's 6-pounder was not among them. Having determined that the Home Guard had not discovered it, some of Green's men slipped back to its hiding place one night several days later and pulled it to their camp.[81]

The Home Guardsmen who returned from their brief pursuit of Green's forces "had the pleasure of visiting the cellars and hiding places of the 'Secesh,' in Athens, and of feasting on the meats, chickens, pies, and cakes which they," like Susan Benning, had prematurely "prepared and hidden for their friends, the rebel army."[82]

In addition to Jabez Harrison's horse, Old Frank, the State Guard took some Home Guard prisoners. Two of these "escaped" a short distance below Luray, having been "left in the rear" by their guards who apparently wanted no impedimenta. Returning to the Athens camp the following morning, they reported that "Green ordered the rebels to keep behind, and threatened to shoot them, but they pressed on, regardless of orders, swearing and cursing Green for leading them into a slaughter pen, and declaring they would go home. They were utterly demoralized."[83]

Chapter 5

Rejoiced over victory.

By 7:00 or 8:00 a.m. on August 5, 1861, small arms fire ceased, hazy black powder smoke dissipated, and the August sun climbed higher. For John Hiller, Athens was now even less a friendly community than during the preceding tumultuous days. Across their own streets and yards, neighbors had fired upon him, and he upon them. That same day he wrote to his brother that "Hiram & I both hold positions in this Regement he is Adjutant and I was appointed Judge Advocate and I shall be kept busy for some time trying the prisoners we took. Hon Wm Moreland prisoner Capt Baker Rev Walker Sam Kite Jessie Mullins Jonathan Bedell A O Bedell William Spurgin John Stewart and many of our neighbors were engaged against us [*sic*]."[1] It is likely that the property of these neighbors aligned against the Home Guardsmen came in for further indiscriminate use by them, as had already been the case during their occupation of Athens.[2]

Scenes and events to be repeated innumerable times and in as many places over the next four years followed the battle. Spurgeon's Drygoods Store at the corner of Spring and Thome Streets, facing Moore's battle line short hours before, became the hospital where Dr. William Aylward of Memphis treated the wounded of both sides.[3]

Readers consumed lists of the dead and wounded accompanying newspaper battle reports. These specified the location of wounds (arm, shoulder, leg, foot, hip, back, groin, forearm), their degree of seriousness, (not dangerous, severely, seriously, slightly, dangerously), and their prognoses (probably lose arm, probably mortal).[4] Home Guard Captain Aaron Mattley, listed as having a probably mortal shoulder wound, was found by the doctor to have had his lungs punctured as well. He survived. Foster Fuller, listed as "wounded in the leg, dangerously," had his leg amputated.[5] Similar lists by name of wounded State Guardsmen who had been captured were published. The battle was a local affair and many of the named casualties were known throughout the area.

Compared to battles yet to come, this was carnage on a small scale. Yet it was no doubt curious to many of those observing it, accustomed though they were, as mid-19th century people, to the frequency and proximity of death. John McKee noted that "one of the rebels" he and his party discovered "had been shot in the jaw, the bullet going through and showing under the skin on the other side." John Moore saw "young Thompson…shot in the mouth, so that a half circle was cut out of his upper lip."[6]

John Hiller summed up the battle's casualties as he understood them:

> I think the battle lasted about an hour or more. Our loss in killd so far as known is
> three. Two or three are mortally wounded and probabably 8 or 10 less severely.
> The loss of the enemy is not known as they had wagons and carried many away.
> We found three dead on the ground and several mortally wounded. Jim McArtor
> was wounded in the hip not mortal (Secession) I am not acquainted with any of the
> killd[sic][7]

On the Home Guard side, in addition to Jabez Harrison, William Sullivan, and William Sprouse, Pvt. Joseph Knox of Captain Hackney's company was killed.[8]

The State Guard dead not carried away in the initial retreat lay on the field where they had fallen. Monday afternoon State Guardsmen came into the Athens camp under a flag of truce. No doubt part of their mission was to remove their remaining dead comrades.[9] As so many future battlefields would do, Athens disgorged those it claimed for some time after the rattle of musketry and thunder of cannon ceased. Three more State Guard dead were discovered lying in the cornfield the day after the battle.[10]

G. W. Shacklett, the Major's son and a soldier in Green's force, is said to have stated that "upwards of forty dead Confederates, killed in the Athens fight, were buried that night in the pasture of the Harr place."[11] Young Oliver Morrison reported the same: "I saw a number of dead Confederates buried at the Harr farm exactly as Mr. Shacklett has related the incident."[12]

Spurgeon's Drygoods Store in Athens and the house where William Sprouse died in Croton were not the only field hospitals set up after the battle. Murphy's farm, two miles south of Ashton, was located on the retreat route of the State Guard.[13] According to J. W. Murphy:

> A large party of Confederate fugitives from the battle…camped on the evening after
> the engagement at my father's farm… I remember also that there were a great many
> wounded men in this party. They took all of our sheets, pillow cases and cotton
> clothes to make bandages for the wounded. They also pumped the well dry early in
> the evening. The weather was intensely hot and our family soon were in desperate
> straits for water. My father hitched up the team, placed some barrels in the wagon
> and was in the act of starting to the Wyaconda for a load of water, when a rebel
> officer stopped him. Finally he was allowed to proceed. When he got back with the
> water the soldiers took it all. The upshot of the matter was that they kept him busy
> hauling water all night, and finally we little folks of the family were permitted to
> indulge in the luxury of a drink.[14]

Given that at least some of the retreating State Guard could bivouac no more than 12 miles from the battlefield, Moore's initial pursuit of Green must have broken off after only few miles. As noted in Chapter 4, elements of the 5th and 6th Iowa regiments had arrived in Croton mid-morning on the day of the battle. Colonel John A. McDowell, commander of the 6th Iowa, quickly formed up three companies of the 6th and sent them across the Des Moines with their shoes in their hands and their pant legs rolled up. However, finding that the battle was over, they did not pursue the State Guard. That night the Iowa volunteers furnished pickets and camp guards for Athens.[15]

Thinking the rebels were no more than eight or nine miles west of Athens, on Monday night Colonel William H. Worthington of the 5th Iowa Infantry, commander of all Iowa volunteers in Keokuk, sent five companies of the 5th under Lt.-Col. Charles L. Matthies across the Des Moines at Sweet Home, two miles below Athens. Matthies was to swing around and attack Green's rear, while Worthington with the balance of the 5th would attack Green from the east. Before going half the distance, Matthies learned from his scouts that Green was more like 25 miles away and still retreating, so the operation was called off. Matthies and Worthington returned to Croton, thence back to Keokuk, and on to St. Louis.[16]

Elements of the State Guard remained scattered throughout northeast Missouri, while Green attempted to consolidate his forces in the area of Edina in the days following the battle. Moore was drawn out of Athens to join with Colonel Humphrey M. Woodyard of the Second Northeast Missouri State Guard and other Federal volunteers under General Stephen Hurlburt and John Pope to attempt to finally bag Martin Green. The State Guard commander was able to elude his pursuers (and even to give battle on a few occasions, such as Bee Branch near Kirksville on August 19 and Shelbina September 4), until receiving a summons from Sterling Price to join in the advance on Lexington, Missouri. After tying up Union forces in northeast Missouri for a month (which no doubt contributed to Price's success at Wilson's Creek in southwest Missouri on August 10), Martin Green's army crossed the Missouri River on September 12, 1861.[17]

Rumors of renewed attacks on Athens continued in the pages of the *Keokuk Daily Gate City,* followed by still more train loads of Keokuk militiamen mustered to ride to the rescue.[18] But in fact, though the residents of the area might not have realized it at the time, the border between northeast Missouri and southeast Iowa was now secure for the duration of the war.

"We are much rejoiced over the victory," wrote the exuberant John Hiller to his brother later on the day of the battle. In his rejoicing was no small amount of pride for having bested the vaunted rebels: "as they claim they can whip 5 to 1 and as some of their party said they did not know about these skim milk yankees fighting, they may find out, to their sorrow."[19]

Appendix.

The Hawkins Taylor Roster

In the chaotic early months of the Civil War, at least two citizens of northeast Missouri sought authority from the Federal military commander in St. Louis, Nathaniel Lyon, to raise troops for the protection of their persons and property and the property of the federal government from "combinations too powerful to be suppressed by the ordinary course of judicial proceedings," as Abraham Lincoln had put it in his first call for volunteers on April 15, 1861.[1] These two were David Moore, a merchant in Wrightsville, Clark County, and William Bishop, a prominent businessman and Republican activist in Alexandria, Missouri. In his communication with Bishop, in which he conveyed general authority to swear in troops, Lyon pointed out that "all those who thus enlist and render service to the General Government will have a claim against it…"[2]

On December 17, 1861, Representative Frank Blair of Missouri introduced in Congress "A bill to secure to the officers and men actually employed in the western department, or department of Missouri, their pay, bounty, and pension."[3] This act was approved on March 25, 1862, but not signed into law until February 16, 1863. On March 6, 1863, President Lincoln put forth the names of Hawkins Taylor of Iowa and Augustus A. Fleming and Francis T. Russell of Missouri to serve as commissioners.[4] Their job was to find every Missouri Home Guard unit commander and collect reconstructed rosters of all the men who had served in the Home Guard.[5]

Hawkins Taylor was born in Kentucky November 11, 1811, and came to the "Black Hawk Purchase" in 1836, settling in what would become Lee County, Iowa. He was elected to the House of the First Legislative Assembly when Iowa became a territory in 1838. In 1857 he was mayor of Keokuk, and in 1860 he was a delegate to the Republican National Convention. When Abraham Lincoln was elected president, Taylor moved to Washington, working as a lawyer and often serving in minor government offices. He died November 15, 1893.[6]

The following roster contains 1097 names. Not all who are listed served at Athens or in the follow-up campaign against Martin Green in northeast Missouri. Many who fought at Athens are missing from the roster. Each entry is arranged thus: last name, first name, company, rank, muster-in date (MI_date), place of muster (MI_place), date of discharge (D_date), and remarks.

Last Name	First Name	Company	Rank	MI_date	MI_place	D_date	Remarks
Abrams	Benjamin	B	Pvt	6/18	Memphis	10/24/1861	
Ackland	George	K	2Corp	6/17	Luray	10/1/1861	
Ackland	James	K	Pvt	6/17	Luray	10/1/1861	
Adams	Isaac	D	Pvt	6/20	Scotland Co.	10/24/1861	
Adams	Philip	D	Pvt	6/20	Scotland Co.	10/24/1861	
Adams	Alexander	B	Pvt	6/18	Memphis	10/24/1861	
Adams	Allen	B	Pvt	6/18	Memphis	10/24/1861	
Adams	John Q.	B	Pvt	6/18	Memphis	10/24/1861	
Alexander	Sidon	G	Pvt	7/19	Alexandria	7/20/1861	Deserted, to receive no pay or allowance
Alexander	James H.	G	Pvt	7/19	Alexandria	10/24/1861	
Allen	John W.	H	Pvt	6/15	Kahoka	10/26/1861	Never served, to receive no pay or allowance
Allen	Samuel A.	H	Pvt	6/15	Kahoka	10/26/1861	Never served, to receive no pay or allowance
Amand	Anthony	L	Pvt	6/22	Sweet Home	8/15/1861	
Amend	John	F	Pvt	6/18	Alexandria	8/27/1861	
Anderson	George	I	Pvt	6/16	Fairmount	2/14/1862	Rendered no service, to receive no pay
Anderson	Alfred F. C.	M	Pvt	7/12	Edina	8/1/1861	
Anderson	John P.	C	2Lieut	6/17	Alexandria	8/17/1861	
Anderson	John	I	Pvt	6/16	Fairmount	10/25/1861	
Anderson	Anros	F	Pvt	6/18	Alexandria	8/27/1861	
Anderson	Albert	O	Pvt	6/15	St. Francisville	8/5/1861	
Anderson	Jacob	F	Pvt	6/18	Alexandria	8/27/1861	
Anderson	John J.	I	5Corp	6/16	Fairmount	8/7/1861	
Andrews	William	E	Pvt	7/15	Croton	8/20/1861	
Anthony	Robert (Sr)	D	Pvt	6/20	Scotland Co.	10/10/1861	
Anthony	Robert (Jr)	D	Pvt	6/20	Scotland Co.	7/1861	Discharged for disability
Anthony	Isaac	D	Pvt	6/20	Scotland Co.	11/6/1861	
Anthony	William	D	Pvt	6/20	Scotland Co.	9/1861	
Anthony	John	C	Pvt	6/17	Alexandria	8/17/1861	
Anthony	Merrit	D	Pvt	6/20	Scotland Co.	11/6/1861	
Anthony	George H.	F	Pvt	6/18	Alexandria	8/27/1861	
Anthony	Charles	C	Pvt	6/17	Alexandria	8/17/1861	
Antony	Herrick	A	Pvt	11/6	Memphis	12/4/1861	
Armstrong	Albert	Moore's	Pvt	6/15	Wrightsville	10/24/1861	
Armstrong	William	Murray's	Pvt	7/1	Edina	10/24/1861	
Armstrong	Thomas	Murray's	Pvt	7/1	Edina	7/20/1861	
Armstrong	John	B	Pvt	6/18	Memphis	10/24/1861	
Armstrong	James R.	B	Pvt	6/18	Memphis	10/24/1861	
Arnold	Sidney	B	Pvt	6/18	Memphis	10/24/1861	
Ash	Rufus	I	6Corp	6/16	Fairmount	10/25/1861	

Ash	Rufus	Moore's	Pvt	6/15	Wrightsville	10/24/1861	
Ashberry	Jackson	F	Pvt	6/18	Alexandria	8/27/1861	
Aylward	William	B	Pvt	6/18	Memphis	10/24/1861	
Bach	Amos	A	Pvt	11/6	Memphis	12/4/1861	
Baggs	Collupe	L	Pvt	6/22	Sweet Home	8/15/1861	
Baggs	John	L	Pvt	6/22	Sweet Home	8/15/1861	
Baley	Adam	O	Pvt	6/15	St. Francisville	10/25/1861	Rendered no service, to receive no pay
Ball	Jacob	F	Pvt	6/18	Alexandria	8/27/1861	
Ball	Edward	H	Pvt	6/15	Kahoka	10/26/1861	
Bamard	John	Murray's	Pvt	7/1	Edina	10/24/1861	
Barden	Stephen T.	K	Pvt	6/17	Luray	10/1/1861	Rendered no service, to receive no pay
Barnes	Daniel H.	K	Pvt	6/17	Luray	8/1/1861	
Barnes	David B.	H	Pvt	6/28	Kahoka	8/30/1861	To receive no pay or allowance
Barrett	Joseph	H	Pvt	6/15	Kahoka	10/26/1861	
Barrow	Laund	L	Pvt	6/22	Sweet Home	8/15/1861	
Barrows	William P.	O	Pvt	6/15	St. Francisville	8/15/1861	
Bartlett	Scott	Moore's	Pvt	6/15	Wrightsville	10/24/1861	Rendered no service, to receive no pay
Batton	John	E	3Corp	7/15	Croton	8/20/1861	
Battzel	A. M.	N	1Lieut	6/15	St. Francisville	8/15/1861	
Baxley	Columbus C.	I	Pvt	6/16	Fairmount	2/14/1862	Rendered no service, to receive no pay
Beach	Nathan	D	3Corp	6/20	Scotland Co.	11/6/1861	
Beach	Amos	D	Pvt	8/10	Memphis	11/6/1861	
Beaman	David C.	E	1Ser	7/15	Croton	8/20/1861	
Bear	Simon	A	Pvt	11/6	Memphis	12/4/1861	
Bear	Simon	D	5Corp	6/20	Scotland Co.	11/6/1861	
Beboret	G. N.	H	Pvt	6/15	Kahoka	10/26/1861	To receive no pay or allowance
Beckwith	Wright	N	Pvt	6/15	St. Francisville	8/15/1861	
Beel	William	Murray's	Pvt	7/1	Edina	7/10/1861	
Beel	Daniel	Murray's	Pvt	7/1	Edina	7/10/1861	
Beeman	David	H	2Lieut	6/15	Kahoka	10/24/1861	
Benedict	Jason	D	Pvt	6/20	Scotland Co.	11/6/1861	
Bertram	Frederick	I	7Corp	7/21	Etna	2/14/1862	
Best	James S.	B	Capt	6/15	Alexandria	9/4/1861	Resigned Sept. 4, 1861
Best	James	A	Pvt	9/28	Memphis	12/4/1861	
Bills	George	H	Pvt	6/15	Kahoka	8/30/1861	
Bills	John	H	Pvt	6/15	Kahoka	10/26/1861	To receive no pay or allowance
Bills	Presley D.	H	Pvt	6/15	Kahoka	10/26/1861	
Bills	Isaac	H	Pvt	6/15	Kahoka	8/20/1861	
Billups	James H.	B	Pvt	6/18	Memphis	10/24/1861	
Birge	John	L	Pvt	6/22	Sweet Home	8/15/1861	
Bise	George W.	I	Pvt	7/21	Fairmount	10/25/1861	
Bise	William R.	I	Pvt	7/21	Fairmount	10/25/1861	

Bise	John A.	I	8Corp	6/16	Fairmount	10/25/1861	
Bishop	John H.	H	Pvt	6/15	Kahoka	8/15/1861	
Bishop	Nelson	I	Pvt	6/15	Fairmount	10/25/1861	
Bishop	Nelson	Moore's	Pvt	6/15	Wrightsville	10/24/1861	
Black	John W.	K	Pvt	6/17	Luray	10/1/1861	
Blair	A. M.	M	Pvt	7/12	Edina	9/8/1861	Disallowed, no proof of service
Blair	Wilson C.	M	1Corp	7/12	Edina	9/5/1861	
Bloom	Jacob	H	Pvt	6/15	Kahoka	7/21/1861	To receive no pay or allowance
Bloom	John	H	Pvt	6/15	Kahoka	7/21/1861	To receive no pay or allowance
Bloom	Abraham	H	Pvt	6/15	Kahoka	10/26/1861	To receive no pay or allowance
Bloomfield	Harry	E	Pvt	7/15	Croton	8/20/1861	
Blop	A. C.	C	Pvt	6/17	Alexandria	8/17/1861	
Blurcha	Benjamin	O	Pvt	6/15	St. Francisville	8/15/1861	
Bodkins	Harmon	F	Pvt	6/18	Alexandria	7/17/1861	
Booth	Joseph	K	Pvt	6/17	Luray	10/1/1861	
Borden	Thomas L.	K	Pvt	6/17	Luray	10/1/1861	
Borden	James A.	K	Pvt	6/17	Luray	10/1/1861	
Boswell	William	O	Pvt	6/15	St. Francisville	8/5/1861	
Botts	Thompson	M	Pvt	7/12	Edina	8/1/1861	
Botts	William F.	M	Pvt	7/12	Edina	8/1/1861	Disallowed, no proof of service
Bowen	John	O	Pvt	6/15	St. Francisville	8/5/1861	
Bowen	Glenn	N	Pvt	6/15	St. Francisville	8/15/1861	
Bower	Isaac	C	Pvt	6/17	Alexandria	8/17/1861	
Bowers	George	Murray's	Pvt	7/1	Edina	10/24/1861	
Bradfield	George W.	K	Pvt	6/17	Luray	7/24/1861	
Bradley	Samuel G.	C	Pvt	6/17	Alexandria	8/17/1861	
Bradley	William B.	G	Pvt	7/19	Alexandria	10/24/1861	
Bramble	William	B	4Ser	6/18	Memphis	10/24/1861	
Brand	Thomas	N	Pvt	6/15	St. Francisville	8/15/1861	
Brandis	Henry	C	Pvt	6/17	Alexandria	8/17/1861	
Brax	Adam	I	1Lieut	6/16	Fairmount	8/27/1861	
Bremei	William	G	Pvt	7/19	Alexandria	10/24/1861	
Bresee	John A.	D	Pvt	6/20	Scotland Co.	11/6/1861	
Bresel	John J.	A	Pvt	9/28	Memphis	12/4/1861	
Brester	John	F	Pvt	6/18	Alexandria	8/22/1861	
Brewer	William	D	Pvt	8/12	Scotland Co.	11/6/1861	
Brewer	William	A	Pvt	11/6	Memphis	12/4/1861	
Briggs	Andy	H	3Corp	6/15	Kahoka	10/26/1861	
Briggs	Robert L.	H	Pvt	6/15	Kahoka	10/26/1861	
Brightenbaker	George	K	Pvt	6/17	Luray	8/12/1861	
Brockaw	Aaron	K	Pvt	6/17	Luray	10/1/1861	
Brown	Albert	L	1Corp	6/22	Sweet Home	8/15/1861	

Brown	William	E	Pvt	7/15	Croton	8/20/1861	
Brown	Samuel	K	Pvt	6/17	Luray	10/1/1861	
Brown	Henry	K	Pvt	6/17	Luray	8/1/1861	
Brown	Albert	K	Pvt	6/17	Luray	8/3/1861	
Brown	Stewart	I	2Corp	6/16	Fairmount	9/14/1861	
Bruce	John	E	Pvt	7/15	Croton	8/20/1861	
Brumbaugh	John	E	Pvt	7/15	Croton	8/20/1861	
Bruster	George	F	Pvt	6/18	Alexandria	8/22/1861	
Bryan	William M.	B	Pvt	6/18	Memphis	10/24/1861	
Bryan	Nicholas	B	Pvt	6/18	Memphis	10/24/1861	
Bucher	Geroge	N	Pvt	6/15	St. Francisville	8/15/1861	
Buehler	Henry C.	I	Pvt	9/18	Kahoka	10/25/1861	
Bumer	James	H	Pvt	6/15	Kahoka	10/26/1861	
Bundy	Samuel	E	Pvt	7/15	Croton	8/20/1861	
Burfield	Collins	K	Pvt	6/17	Luray	10/1/1861	
Burner	Gustav	I	4Corp	7/21	Kahoka	2/14/1862	
Burnett	Matthew	K	Pvt	6/17	Luray	8/1/1861	
Burns	Jacob	D	Pvt	6/20	Scotland Co.	8/20/1861	
Burtram	Conrad	I	Pvt	7/2	Etna	10/25/1861	
Burtram	Henry	I	Pvt	6/16	Fairmount	2/14/1862	
Butcher	James H.	O	Pvt	6/15	St. Francisville	8/15/1861	
Butler	Joseph	D	Pvt	6/20	Scotland Co.	9/1861	
Butler	Isaac	D	Pvt	6/20	Scotland Co.	9/1861	
Butler	George	D	Pvt	6/20	Scotland Co.	11/6/1861	
Butlin	William	E	2Corp	7/15	Croton	8/20/1861	
Byrne	Harrison	B	Pvt	6/18	Memphis	10/24/1861	
Byron	Hanson H.	A	2Ser	9/28	Memphis	12/4/1861	
Calvert	Isaac H.	C	Pvt	6/17	Alexandria	8/17/1861	
Campbell	H. C.	N	Pvt	6/15	St. Francisville	8/15/1861	
Campbell	J. R.	N	Pvt	6/15	St. Francisville	8/15/1861	
Canady	John	E	Pvt	7/15	Croton	7/22/1861	Disloyal, to receive no pay or allowance
Canfield	Edward	K	Pvt	6/17	Luray	8/6/1861	
Cants	Samuel	H	Pvt	6/15	Kahoka	10/26/1861	
Carder	James M.	O	Pvt	6/15	St. Francisville	10/25/1861	
Cardwell	Aurelius	K	Pvt	6/17	Luray	8/1/1861	
Caroter	James M.	O	Pvt	6/15	St. Francisville	10/25/1861	
Carothers	Charles H.	I	Pvt	ukn	Fairmount	ukn	
Carothers	John R.	I	Pvt	ukn	Fairmount	ukn	
Carter	Charles E.	K	Pvt	6/17	Luray	10/1/1861	
Cary	Jerry	B	Pvt	6/18	Memphis	10/24/1861	
Case	Holmes	L	Pvt	6/22	Sweet Home	8/15/1861	
Case	O. P.	L	Pvt	6/22	Sweet Home	8/15/1861	

Casey	William	H	Pvt	6/15	Kahoka	10/26/1861	
Cashman	Michael	G	Pvt	7/19	Alexandria	10/24/1861	
Casse	William	Murray's	Pvt	7/1	Edina	8/1/1861	
Caywood	Thomas	O	Pvt	6/15	St. Francisville	10/25/1861	
Cecil	Miles	H	1Corp	6/15	Kahoka	10/26/1861	
Cecil	Joseph	H	5Ser	6/15	Kahoka	10/26/1861	
Chamberlain	Israel B.	H	8Corp	6/15	Kahoka	10/26/1861	Not allowed
Chamrel	John W.	I	Pvt	ukn	Fairmount	ukn	
Chapman	James	I	Pvt	6/16	Fairmount	10/25/1861	
Chidester	William N.	E	1Corp	7/15	Croton	8/20/1861	
Chidester	Samuel	E	Pvt	7/15	Croton	8/20/1861	
Childers	Benjamin	C	Pvt	6/17	Alexandria	8/17/1861	
Christian	William	G	Pvt	7/19	Alexandria	10/24/1861	
Christian	Clinton	G	Pvt	7/19	Alexandria	10/24/1861	
Christian	Lewis	G	Pvt	7/19	Alexandria	10/24/1861	
Christian	Loudin	L	Pvt	6/22	Sweet Home	8/15/1861	
Christie	John S.	F	Pvt	6/18	Alexandria	7/17/1861	
Church	George	Moore's	6Corp	6/15	Wrightsville	10/24/1861	
Church	George	I	Pvt	6/15	Fairmount	10/25/1861	
Church	George	I	Pvt	ukn	Fairmount	ukn	
Church	George	N	Pvt	6/15	St. Francisville	8/15/1861	
Cinduff	William	C	Pvt	6/17	Alexandria	8/17/1861	Disloyal and to receive no pay or allowance
Clark	W. W.	C	2Ser	6/17	Alexandria	8/17/1861	Did no service and to receive no pay
Clark	Abraham J.	F	Pvt	6/18	Alexandria	8/27/1861	
Clarke	Julius	Moore's	Pvt	6/15	Wrightsville	10/24/1861	Rendered no service, to receive no pay
Clawson	Henry C.	M	Pvt	7/12	Edina	9/8/1861	
Clawson	John	Moore's	7Corp	6/15	Wrightsville	10/24/1861	
Clements	Ebenezer N.	K	Pvt	6/17	Luray	10/1/1861	
Clemments	James H.	A	Pvt	9/28	Memphis	12/4/1861	
Clemons	James H.	G	Pvt	7/19	Alexandria	10/24/1861	
Clemons	Owen	B	Pvt	6/18	Memphis	10/24/1861	
Clifton	Thomas	Moore's	Pvt	6/15	Wrightsville	10/24/1861	
Cline	J. L.	N	Pvt	6/15	St. Francisville	8/15/1861	
Cline	Henry	N	Pvt	6/15	St. Francisville	8/15/1861	
Clyne	William	F	Musician	6/18	Alexandria	8/27/1861	
Cobber	David	L	Pvt	6/22	Sweet Home	8/15/1861	
Colgan	William	F	3Ser	6/18	Alexandria	8/27/1861	
Collands	Washington S.	L	1Ser	6/22	Sweet Home	8/15/1861	Wounded at Battle of Athens
Collins	William L.	Murray's	3Ser	7/1	Edina	10/24/1861	
Collins	Amos S.	B	Pvt	6/18	Memphis	10/24/1861	
Collonywee	Edward	B	Pvt	6/18	Memphis	10/24/1861	

Collonywee	Claron	B	Pvt	6/18	Memphis	10/24/1861	
Colmstock	Daniel	L	Pvt	6/22	Sweet Home	8/15/1861	
Combs	Charles R.	C	1Lieut	6/17	Alexandria	8/17/1861	
Congdon	Dorr	I	Pvt	ukn	Fairmount	ukn	
Congdon	Elijah	I	Pvt	ukn	Fairmount	ukn	
Conkle	George	K	Pvt	6/17	Luray	10/1/1861	
Conner	Benjamin	K	Pvt	6/17	Luray	8/6/1861	
Cook	Claudius	Moore's	Pvt	6/15	Wrightsville	10/24/1861	Rendered no service, to receive no pay
Cooke	Robert	L	Pvt	6/22	Sweet Home	8/15/1861	
Cooper	David B.	G	Pvt	7/19	Alexandria	7/21/1861	Deserted, to receive no pay
Cope	Samuel B.	Moore's	4Corp	6/15	Wrightsville	8/5/1861	Deserted Aug. 5, 1861, to receive no pay
Cope	George	B	Pvt	6/18	Memphis	10/24/1861	
Cope	John Q. A.	Moore's	1Ser	6/15	Wrightsville	8/5/1861	Deserted Aug. 5, to receive no pay
Coumins	Grantson	Moore's	Pvt	6/15	Wrightsville	10/24/1861	
Covy	Edward	Moore's	2Lieut	6/15	Wrightsville	10/24/1861	
Covy	William	Moore's	Pvt	6/15	Wrightsville	10/24/1861	Rendered no service, to receive no pay
Cox	John Henry	F	2Ser	6/18	Alexandria	8/27/1861	
Coy	William	Murray's	Pvt	7/1	Edina	8/1/1861	
Crandall	Jeremiah	D	4Corp	6/20	Scotland Co.	11/6/1861	
Crane	James E.	C	Pvt	6/17	Alexandria	8/17/1861	
Crane	James	H	Pvt	6/15	Kahoka	8/16/1861	
Craren	William	I	Pvt	ukn	Fairmount	ukn	
Craren	Archabald F.	I	Pvt	ukn	Fairmount	ukn	
Crassman	Minor	H	Pvt	6/15	Kahoka	7/16/1861	To receive no pay or allowance
Craven	William A.	I	Pvt	ukn	Fairmount	ukn	
Creger	Andrew	H	Pvt	6/15	Kahoka	10/26/1861	To receive no pay or allowance
Creger	William	H	Pvt	6/15	Kahoka	8/13/1861	
Cronen	Cephas	F	Pvt	6/18	Alexandria	8/27/1861	
Cronen	James	F	Pvt	6/18	Alexandria	8/27/1861	
Cronen	Joseph	F	Pvt	6/18	Alexandria	8/27/1861	
Crook	Henry	D	Pvt	6/20	Scotland Co.	8/20/1861	
Cross	Orris	K	4Ser	6/17	Luray	10/1/1861	
Crosswhite	Perry	Murray's	1Corp	7/1	Edina	10/24/1861	
Crowel	Thomas	H	Pvt	6/15	Kahoka	8/17/1861	
Culler	Michael	H	Pvt	6/15	Kahoka	8/6/1861	To receive no pay or allowance
Culler	John	H	Pvt	6/15	Kahoka	8/17/1861	
Cummings	Granson	I	Pvt	ukn	Fairmount	ukn	
Cuoy	Matheny	N	Pvt	6/15	St. Francisville	8/15/1861	
Cuoy	William	N	Pvt	6/15	St. Francisville	8/15/1861	
Cutshaw	John	I	Pvt	9/18	Fairmount	10/25/1861	
Cutshaw	John	I	Pvt	ukn	Fairmount	ukn	
Dalling	William W.	E	Pvt	7/15	Croton	8/20/1861	

Danson	William	A	Pvt	9/28	Memphis	12/4/1861	
Danson	Andrew J.	A	Pvt	9/28	Memphis	12/4/1861	
Dare	William C.	C	Pvt	6/17	Alexandria	8/17/1861	
Dart	H. J.	O	Pvt	6/15	St. Francisville	8/15/1861	
Dart	F. L.	O	Pvt	6/15	St. Francisville	10/25/1861	
Daugherty	R. C.	B	2Lieut	6/15	Memphis	9/14/1861	Resigned Sept. 14, 1861, became Capt. Co A
Daugherty	Francis	E	Pvt	7/15	Croton	8/20/1861	
Daugherty	R. C.	A	Capt	9/28	Memphis	12/4/1861	
Daugherty	Newton	B	Pvt	6/18	Memphis	10/24/1861	
Daughters	Henry	O	Pvt	6/15	St. Francisville	8/15/1861	
Davis	Wilbur F.	I	5Ser	6/16	Fairmount	2/14/1862	
Davis	Ebenezer	I	Pvt	ukn	Fairmount	ukn	
Davis	Wilber F.	I	Pvt	ukn	Fairmount	ukn	
Davis	Ezekiel	H	Pvt	6/15	Kahoka	10/26/1861	To receive no pay or allowance
Davis	Milton	B	Pvt	6/18	Memphis	10/24/1861	
Davis	Seth	K	Pvt	6/17	Luray	10/1/1861	
Davison	William	B	Pvt	6/18	Memphis	10/24/1861	
Day	William	H	Pvt	6/15	Kahoka	8/17/1861	
Day	James	F	Pvt	6/18	Alexandria	8/27/1861	
Day	Joseph	F	Pvt	6/18	Alexandria	8/27/1861	
Dean	Perry	B	Pvt	6/18	Memphis	10/24/1861	
Dean	Silas	B	Pvt	6/18	Memphis	10/24/1861	
Delap	Joseph	E	Pvt	7/15	Croton	8/20/1861	
Dell	John (Sr)	I	Pvt	ukn	Fairmount	ukn	
Dell	John (Jr)	I	Pvt	ukn	Fairmount	ukn	
Dempsey	Joseph	L	Pvt	6/22	Sweet Home	8/15/1861	
Dennis	Isaac	I	Pvt	ukn	Fairmount	ukn	
Denny	Thomas	F	Pvt	6/18	Alexandria	8/27/1861	
Devance	Charles	H	Pvt	6/15	Kahoka	10/26/1861	
Devance	John	H	Pvt	6/15	Kahoka	10/26/1861	
Devance	James	H	Pvt	6/15	Kahoka	10/26/1861	
Dewall	Isaac	O	Pvt	6/15	St. Francisville	10/15/1861	
Dewalt	Samuel	O	7Corp	6/15	St. Francisville	8/5/1861	
Dickinson	Thomas	D	Pvt	6/20	Scotland Co.	11/6/1861	
Dickson	Thomas M.	A	Pvt	9/28	Memphis	12/4/1861	
Dillon	Price C.	Moore's	Pvt	6/15	Wrightsville	10/24/1861	
Ditmus	Henry	O	Pvt	6/15	St. Francisville	8/15/1861	
Dobbins	George	K	1Corp	6/17	Luray	10/1/1861	
Dobbins	Louis B.	K	Pvt	6/17	Luray	6/20/1861	No pay allowed
Dockum	Henry	I	Pvt	ukn	Fairmount	ukn	
Dolton	Frank	G	4Ser	7/19	Alexandria	10/24/1861	
Door	James T.	O	4Corp	6/15	St. Francisville	10/25/1861	

Dorsly	Andrew J.	H	Pvt	6/15	Kahoka	10/26/1861	
Driskell	William	G	Pvt	7/19	Alexandria	10/24/1861	
Duke	James	D	Pvt	6/20	Scotland Co.	9/5/1861	
Dunn	Aaron	D	Pvt	6/20	Scotland Co.	11/6/1861	
Dunn	Jackson	Moore's	Pvt	6/15	Wrightsville	10/24/1861	Rendered no service, to receive no pay
Dunn	James D,	D	Pvt	6/20	Scotland Co.	11/6/1861	
Dunn	John	H	Pvt	6/15	Kahoka	10/26/1861	
Dunn	Jeremiah	D	Pvt	6/20	Scotland Co.	11/6/1861	
Dust	Michael	F	Pvt	6/18	Alexandria	8/27/1861	
Duty	John	F	Pvt	6/18	Alexandria	8/27/1861	
Dyer	William G.	D	Pvt	6/20	Scotland Co.	11/6/1861	
Early	James	O	Pvt	6/15	St. Francisville	10/25/1861	
Early	Samuel C.	O	Pvt	6/15	St. Francisville	8/15/1861	
East	John	Moore's	Pvt	6/15	Wrightsville	10/24/1861	Rendered no service, to receive no pay
East	Samuel	Moore's	Pvt	6/15	Wrightsville	10/24/1861	
Eaton	James	G	Pvt	7/19	Alexandria	10/24/1861	
Eberling	Frederick	D	Pvt	6/20	Scotland Co.	8/20/1861	
Eberling	William	D	Pvt	6/20	Scotland Co.	11/6/1861	
Edwards	William D.	B	Pvt	6/18	Memphis	10/24/1861	
Edwrds	Joseph	B	Pvt	6/18	Memphis	10/24/1861	
Eggleton	Daniel	M	2Lieut	7/12	Edina	9/8/1861	
Elder	William (Jr)	F	Pvt	6/18	Alexandria	8/27/1861	
Elder	William (Sr)	F	Pvt	6/18	Alexandria	8/27/1861	
Eliott	Samuel	M	Pvt	7/12	Edina	7/26/1861	
Emery	Daniel	C	Pvt	6/17	Alexandria	8/17/1861	
Emory	Thomas	O	8Corp	6/15	St. Francisville	8/5/1861	
Englehart	Philip	G	Pvt	7/19	Alexandria	10/24/1861	
Ensighn	John	H	Pvt	6/15	Kahoka	10/26/1861	
Epperhart	Julius C.	C	Pvt	6/17	Alexandria	8/17/1861	
Epperhart	Henry	C	Pvt	6/17	Alexandria	8/17/1861	
Etheridge	William	K	Pvt	6/17	Luray	8/4/1861	
Evans	Geroge M.	M	Pvt	7/12	Edina	9/8/1861	
Fairboother	John F.	Moore's	1Corp	6/15	Wrightsville	10/15/1861	Joined Black Hawk Cavalry, Oct. 15, 1861
Fairgo	Marton	Moore's	Pvt	6/15	Wrightsville	10/24/1861	
Fanler	James J.	Murray's	3Corp	7/1	Edina	10/24/1861	
Farris	Joseph T.	E	Capt	6/20	Croton	8/20/1861	
Farris	Joseph T.	M	4Corp	7/12	Edina	9/1/1861	
Faunichol	Charles	E	Pvt	7/15	Croton	8/20/1861	
Fauven	Henry	B	Pvt	6/18	Memphis	10/24/1861	
Fell	John G.	H	Pvt	6/15	Kahoka	10/26/1861	
Fellows	Hart	K	Pvt	6/17	Luray	8/7/1861	
Ferguson	William	L	3Corp	6/22	Sweet Home	8/15/1861	

Ferguson	Allen	H	Pvt	6/15	Kahoka	7/31/1861	
Ferril	George	D	Pvt	6/20	Scotland Co.	9/27/1861	
Fetters	James	Murray's	6Corp	7/1	Edina	10/24/1861	
Fight	Andrew J.	M	2Corp	7/12	Edina	9/5/1861	Disallowed, no proof of service
Finch	John P.	Murray's	Pvt	7/1	Edina	10/24/1861	
Fine	Joseph	L	Pvt	6/22	Sweet Home	8/15/1861	
Fine	Alfred	L	Pvt	6/22	Sweet Home	8/15/1861	Disloyal, to receive no pay or allowance
Fine	Sullivan	F	Pvt	6/18	Alexandria	7/17/1861	Discharged for disability
Fine	Jacob	L	2Corp	6/22	Sweet Home	8/15/1861	
Finley	James	G	Pvt	7/19	Alexandria	10/24/1861	
Fisher	Alexander	E	Pvt	7/15	Croton	8/20/1861	
Fitzsimmons	John	H	Pvt	6/15	Kahoka	8/6/1861	To receive no pay or allowance
Fleetwood	James	D	Pvt	6/20	Scotland Co.	11/6/1861	
Flemming	John W.	K	Pvt	6/17	Luray	10/1/1861	
Fleshman	Benjamin	I	Musician	6/16	Fairmount	10/25/1861	
Fletcher	Jefferson	F	Pvt	6/18	Alexandria	8/27/1861	
Flour	W. H. T.	N	3Corp	6/15	St. Francisville	8/15/1861	
Fordman	Jackson	D	Pvt	6/20	Scotland Co.	11/6/1861	
Forester	Acklin G.	Murray's	Pvt	7/1	Edina	7/12/1861	
Fortune	John	K	Pvt	6/17	Luray	10/1/1861	
Foster	William	D	Pvt	6/20	Scotland Co.	11/6/1861	
Foster	Silas	M	Pvt	7/12	Edina	9/8/1861	
Fowler	Reson K.	Murray's	Pvt	7/1	Edina	10/24/1861	
Fowler	Fendrick T.	Murray's	Pvt	7/1	Edina	7/15/1861	
Fowler	Milford	Murray's	Pvt	7/1	Edina	7/20/1861	
Fowler	Emanuel	D	Pvt	6/20	Scotland Co.	11/6/1861	
Fray	George	B	Pvt	6/18	Memphis	10/24/1861	
Frazier	Lewis	F	Pvt	6/18	Alexandria	8/27/1861	
Frazier	John W.	M	Pvt	7/12	Edina	7/26/1861	
Free	George	H	Pvt	6/15	Kahoka	10/26/1861	
French	Humphrey	M	Pvt	7/12	Edina	7/26/1861	Deserted, to receive no pay
French	William	H	Pvt	6/15	Kahoka	10/26/1861	
French	Charles	L	Pvt	6/22	Sweet Home	8/15/1861	
Fulk	Daniel N.	B	Pvt	6/18	Memphis	10/24/1861	
Fuller	Gilbert	O	Pvt	6/15	St. Francisville	8/15/1861	
Fuller	Albert	O	Pvt	6/15	St. Francisville	8/15/1861	
Fuller	Porter	O	4Ser	6/15	St. Francisville	10/25/1861	Wounded at Battle of Athens (lost a leg)
Gainoro	Jacob	K	Pvt	6/17	Luray	8/1/1861	
Gallahore	Hanson	B	Pvt	6/18	Memphis	10/24/1861	
Gallahore	Thomas	B	Pvt	6/18	Memphis	10/24/1861	
Gallian	John	C	Pvt	6/17	Alexandria	8/17/1861	Discharged for disability

Galloope	John	L	4Corp	6/22	Sweet Home	8/15/1861	
Gallope	Lewis	Moore's	2Ser	6/15	Wrightsville	10/24/1861	
Gallope	David	C	Pvt	6/17	Alexandria	8/17/1861	Discharged for disability
Galloway	William	D	Pvt	6/20	Scotland Co.	9/18/1861	
Gammon	Samuel	L	Pvt	6/22	Sweet Home	8/15/1861	
Gammon	William	L	Pvt	6/22	Sweet Home	8/15/1861	
Gammon	Robert	F	Pvt	6/18	Alexandria	8/27/1861	
Gammon	Josiah	F	Pvt	6/18	Alexandria	8/27/1861	
Garlock	John	Murray's	Pvt	7/1	Edina	7/8/1861	
Garrett	David	O	Pvt	6/15	St. Francisville	10/25/1861	Rendered no service, to receive no pay
Garrison	John	G	Pvt	7/19	Alexandria	10/24/1861	
Gates	Jacob	Moore's	Pvt	6/15	Wrightsville	10/24/1861	
Gilmore	Christopher	K	4Corp	6/17	Luray	10/1/1861	
Ginn	Joseph	B	Pvt	6/18	Memphis	10/24/1861	
Goddard	James W.	E	Pvt	7/15	Croton	8/20/1861	
Goodwin	Wallace	H	Pvt	6/15	Kahoka	10/26/1861	
Goodwin	George S.	C	Pvt	6/17	Alexandria	8/17/1861	
Goodwin	James	Moore's	Pvt	6/15	Wrightsville	10/24/1861	
Gough	Francis M.	B	Pvt	6/18	Memphis	10/24/1861	
Grade	Joseph	L	Pvt	6/22	Sweet Home	8/15/1861	
Graham	Joseph	D	Pvt	6/20	Scotland Co.	9/2/1861	
Graham	Harrison	D	Pvt	6/20	Scotland Co.	9/2/1861	
Graves	James B.	K	3Corp	6/17	Luray	10/1/1861	
Gray	Thomas	Moore's	Pvt	6/15	Wrightsville	10/24/1861	
Greegg	Thomas	B	Pvt	6/18	Memphis	10/24/1861	
Griggs	R. N.	M	Pvt	7/12	Edina	9/1/1861	
Grinell	Ovid	N	Pvt	6/15	St. Francisville	8/15/1861	
Grover	Alanason	H	5Corp	6/15	Kahoka	10/26/1861	Never served, to receive no pay or allowance
Guthrie	Dempsey	B	Pvt	6/18	Memphis	10/24/1861	
Hackney	John F.	B	Pvt	6/18	Memphis	10/24/1861	
Hackney	Barton P.	F	Capt	6/18	Alexandria	8/27/1861	
Haggerty	Morris	B	Pvt	6/18	Memphis	10/24/1861	
Hales	William	F	Pvt	6/18	Alexandria	8/27/1861	
Ham	William F.	A	Pvt	9/28	Memphis	11/20/1861	Transferred 50th Regiment Illinois Volunteers
Hamersly	William H.	I	Pvt	6/21	Fairmount	8/1/1861	
Hamersly	George B.	I	Pvt	6/21	Fairmount	8/5/1861	Deserted, to receive no pay or allowances
Hamersly	Andrew Z.	I	Pvt	6/21	Fairmount	8/1/1861	
Hamiliton	William S.	G	Pvt	7/19	Alexandria	10/24/1861	
Hamilton	Robert	B	Pvt	6/18	Memphis	10/24/1861	
Hamilton	Charles	B	Pvt	6/18	Memphis	10/24/1861	
Hamilton	William W.	G	Pvt	7/19	Alexandria	10/24/1861	

Hamilton	Jeremiah	B	Pvt	6/18	Memphis	10/24/1861	
Hamilton	Lemuel	G	Pvt	7/19	Alexandria	10/24/1861	
Hamilton	Ezra	G	Pvt	7/19	Alexandria	10/24/1861	
Hammersly	James O.	I	Pvt	6/21	Fairmount	8/1/1861	
Han	William	G	Pvt	7/19	Alexandria	10/24/1861	
Hannon	John L.	A	Pvt	11/6	Memphis	12/4/1861	
Hannon	Bradford B.	K	Pvt	6/17	Luray	10/1/1861	Was hospital steward from Aug. 5, 1861
Hanson	Rueben	F	Pvt	6/18	Alexandria	8/27/1861	Did no service, to receive no pay or allowance
Hanson	Hamilton	F	Pvt	6/18	Alexandria	8/27/1861	
Hanson	Robert	F	Pvt	6/18	Alexandria	8/27/1861	Did no service, to receive no pay or allowance
Happee	August	C	1Ser	6/17	Alexandria	8/17/1861	
Hardee	William	F	Pvt	6/18	Alexandria	8/27/1861	
Harld (Harle)	William	B	1Lieut	6/18	Memphis	10/24/1861	
Harle	Thomas B.	B	Pvt	6/18	Memphis	10/24/1861	
Harlen	Aaron W.	E	Pvt	7/15	Croton	8/20/1861	
Harmon	J. L.	D	Pvt	6/20	Scotland Co.	9/2/1861	
Harmon	Jacob	K	Pvt	6/17	Luray	10/1/1861	
Harr	John	L	Pvt	6/22	Sweet Home	8/15/1861	
Harr	Charles	L	Pvt	6/22	Sweet Home	8/15/1861	
Harris	William H.	M	Pvt	7/12	Edina	9/8/1861	No proof of service, disallowed
Harris	Moses	O	Pvt	6/15	St. Francisville	10/25/1861	
Harrison	Daniel	G	Pvt	7/19	Alexandria	10/24/1861	
Harryman	Hugh	D	Pvt	6/20	Scotland Co.	9/2/1861	
Harvey	Geroge W.	B	Pvt	6/18	Memphis	10/24/1861	
Harwell	John	O	Pvt	6/15	St. Francisville	8/15/1861	
Havens	John H.	K	Pvt	6/17	Luray	9/5/1861	
Hawhee	William W.	Murray's	Pvt	7/1	Edina	10/24/1861	
Hawkins	William	H	3Lieut	6/15	Kahoka	8/6/1861	Deserted, to receive no pay or allowance
Hayes	Thomas	Murray's	Pvt	7/1	Edina	10/24/1861	
Hays	Theodore	M	Pvt	7/12	Edina	7/26/1861	
Hays	Joshua	E	Pvt	7/15	Croton	8/20/1861	
Hays	Henry F.	M	3Corp	7/12	Edina	9/5/1861	Disallowed, no proof of service
Haywood	R. M.	N	Pvt	6/15	St. Francisville	8/15/1861	
Heely	M. U.	N	1Ser	6/15	St. Francisville	8/15/1861	
Heler	A.	O	Pvt	6/15	St. Francisville	8/15/1861	
Hendricks	John S.	Murray's	Pvt	7/1	Edina	10/24/1861	
Hendricks	David	Murray's	Pvt	7/1	Edina	10/24/1861	
Hendricks	Milton	M	Capt	7/12	Edina	9/8/1861	
Henslow	George	Moore's	Pvt	6/15	Wrightsville	10/24/1861	
Henson	Martin	E	Pvt	7/15	Croton	8/20/1861	

Last	First	Co.	Rank	Enlisted	Place	Date	Notes
Henson	John	E	Pvt	7/15	Croton	8/20/1861	
Herdman	Robert	F	Pvt	6/18	Alexandria	8/27/1861	
Herdman	John	L	Pvt	6/22	Sweet Home	8/15/1861	
Hessum	Harvey	F	Pvt	6/18	Alexandria	8/27/1861	
Hicks	Sylvanus E.	Moore's	1Lieut	6/15	Wrightsville	7/4/1861	Promoted to Adjutant of Regiment, July 4, 1861
Higbee	Joseph	Moore's	4Ser	6/15	Wrightsville	9/1/1861	Joined Missouri State Militia
High	Henry	O	Pvt	6/15	St. Francisville	10/25/1861	
Hill	John G.	A	1Ser	9/28	Memphis	12/4/1861	
Hiller	Hiram	F	1Ser	6/18	Alexandria	8/1/1861	Joined Missouri State Guard
Hilliard	Zeno	I	Pvt	6/16	Fairmount	10/25/1861	
Hindman	James	G	Pvt	7/19	Alexandria	10/24/1861	
Hinds	Joseph G. E.	K	Pvt	6/17	Luray	8/12/1861	
Hobbs	James C.	Murray's	Pvt	7/1	Edina	10/24/1861	
Hobbs	James	K	Pvt	6/17	Luray	10/1/1861	
Hogan	Benjamin F.	Murray's	Pvt	7/1	Edina	7/13/1861	
Hogan	George W.	Murray's	Pvt	7/1	Edina	7/16/1861	
Holeman	Timothy	Murray's	Pvt	7/1	Edina	10/24/1861	
Holeman	Timothy	G	Pvt	7/19	Alexandria	10/24/1861	
Holmes	James L.	H	7Corp	6/15	Kahoka	10/26/1861	
Holmes	James C.	K	Pvt	6/17	Luray	8/1/1861	
Holmes	Edward	Murray's	7Corp	7/1	Edina	10/24/1861	
Homer	Jasper N.	I	Pvt	6/16	Fairmount	10/25/1861	
Hopkins	Richard	O	Pvt	6/15	St. Francisville	9/15/1861	
Horle	Wilson F.	B	Pvt	6/18	Memphis	10/24/1861	
Horle	James H.	B	Pvt	6/18	Memphis	10/24/1861	
Horner	Frederick A.	I	Pvt	6/16	Fairmount	10/25/1861	
Hostadt	Lewis	B	Pvt	6/18	Memphis	10/24/1861	
Hostadt	Hiram	B	Pvt	6/18	Memphis	10/24/1861	
Hostadt	Luther A.	K	Pvt	6/17	Luray	9/5/1861	
Hostadt	John W.	B	Pvt	6/18	Memphis	10/24/1861	
Hotchkiss	Thomas	M	2Ser	7/12	Edina	9/5/1861	Disallowed, no proof of service
Houston	H. P.	O	6Corp	6/15	St. Francisville	10/25/1861	
Howel	Abner	N	Pvt	6/15	St. Francisville	8/15/1861	
Howell	Thomas	O	Pvt	6/15	St. Francisville	8/15/1861	
Howell	John	O	Pvt	6/15	St. Francisville	8/15/1861	
Huff	Stephen	C	Pvt	6/17	Alexandria	8/17/1861	
Hugenberg	Anthony	C	Pvt	6/17	Alexandria	8/17/1861	
Huggins	William	D	Pvt	6/20	Scotland Co.	9/2/1861	
Hull	D. F.	L	Capt	6/18	Sweet Home	8/15/1861	
Hull	Samuel	F	3Corp	6/18	Alexandria	8/27/1861	
Hume	Zandy	M	Pvt	7/12	Edina	8/20/1861	
Humphrey	D. A.	C	Pvt	6/17	Alexandria	8/17/1861	

Hunsaker	B. W.	C	Pvt	6/17	Alexandria	8/17/1861	
Hunssucor	Henry	Moore's	Pvt	6/15	Wrightsville	10/24/1861	
Hyde	Silas	B	Pvt	6/18	Memphis	10/24/1861	
Hyde	David E.	B	Pvt	6/18	Memphis	10/24/1861	
Hyde	William	B	Pvt	6/18	Memphis	10/24/1861	
Imbler	John (Sr)	M	Pvt	7/12	Edina	9/8/1861	No proof of service, disallowed
Imbler	Ephraim	M	Pvt	7/12	Edina	8/12/1861	
Imbler	William B.	M	Pvt	7/12	Edina	8/12/1861	
Imbler	John A.	M	Pvt	7/12	Edina	9/1/1861	
Imbler	Daniel	M	Pvt	7/12	Edina	9/8/1861	
Imbler	Samuel S.	M	Pvt	7/12	Edina	9/1/1861	
Imbler	Willaim	M	Pvt	7/12	Edina	9/1/1861	
Ireland	Joseph	C	Pvt	6/17	Alexandria	8/17/1861	
Jackson	Riley	F	Pvt	6/18	Alexandria	7/17/1861	
Jackson	William	H	Capt	6/15	Alexandria	10/26/1861	
Jarvis	Edward	Murray's	1Ser	7/1	Edina	10/24/1861	
Jarvis	Patrick	Murray's	Pvt	7/1	Edina	10/24/1861	
Jeffreis	Henry C.	M	3Ser	7/12	Edina	8/1/1861	
Jewit	Alvin	N	Pvt	6/15	St. Francisville	8/15/1861	
Johnson	Daniel	D	Pvt	6/20	Scotland Co.	9/2/1861	
Johnson	James N.	O	Pvt	6/15	St. Francisville	9/15/1861	
Johnson	James E.	O	Pvt	6/15	St. Francisville	10/15/1861	
Johnson	David	O	Pvt	6/15	St. Francisville	10/25/1861	Rendered no service, to receive no pay
Johnson	Dan	A	Pvt	11/6	Memphis	12/4/1861	
Jones	Ephraim P.	K	Pvt	6/17	Luray	10/1/1861	
Jones	Charles	O	1Lieut	6/14	Alexandria	10/25/1861	
Jones	Orlando	I	Pvt	8/9	Memphis	10/25/1861	
Jones	Orlando	D	Pvt	6/20	Scotland Co.	9/8/1861	
Jones	Greenberry R.	K	2Ser	6/17	Luray	10/1/1861	
Jones	William	B	Pvt	6/18	Memphis	10/24/1861	
Jones	Thomas	B	Pvt	6/18	Memphis	10/24/1861	
Jones	Isaac R.	K	Pvt	6/17	Luray	8/8/1861	
Jones	Robert C.	K	Pvt	6/17	Luray	10/1/1861	
Jones	Robert H.	M	Pvt	7/12	Edina	8/26/1861	
Joslin	Adolphus	F	1Corp	6/18	Alexandria	8/27/1861	
Juert	Robert	Moore's	Pvt	8/6	Athens	10/24/1861	
Just	Charles H.	I	Pvt	8/9	Memphis	10/25/1861	
Justice	David	G	Pvt	7/19	Alexandria	10/24/1861	
Kay	William	F	Pvt	6/18	Alexandria	8/27/1861	
Keever	Edward	Murray's	2Corp	7/1	Edina	10/24/1861	
Keever	Edward	G	Pvt	7/19	Alexandria	10/24/1861	
Kehoe	Jeremiah	M	Pvt	7/12	Edina	8/12/1861	

Kehoe	Patrick	M	Pvt	7/12	Edina	9/8/1861	No proof of service, disallowed
Keith	Anderson G.	M	Pvt	7/12	Edina	9/8/1861	
Keith	James M.	M	Pvt	7/12	Edina	9/8/1861	
Keith	George P.	M	Pvt	7/12	Edina	9/8/1861	
Kell	Benjamin	Moore's	Pvt	6/15	Wrightsville	10/24/1861	
Kell	William	Moore's	Pvt	6/15	Wrightsville	10/24/1861	
Kelly	James	Murray's	Pvt	7/1	Edina	10/24/1861	
Kelsey	John S.	F	Pvt	6/18	Alexandria	8/27/1861	
Kemnaw	Anderson	M	1Lieut	7/12	Edina	9/8/1861	
Kenayer	Samuel	Murray's	Pvt	7/1	Edina	10/24/1861	
Kenayer	Eli	Murray's	Pvt	7/1	Edina	10/24/1861	
Kendall	Joshua	Murray's	4Corp	7/1	Edina	10/24/1861	
Kendall	Adam	Murray's	Pvt	7/1	Edina	10/24/1861	
Kendall	Elijah	Murray's	Pvt	7/1	Edina	9/1/1861	
Kennelt	John G.	G	Pvt	7/19	Alexandria	10/24/1861	
Kennett	Joseph	D	Pvt	6/20	Scotland Co.	7/20/1861	
Kerns	William	E	Pvt	7/15	Croton	8/20/1861	
Kertz	John	Murray's	Pvt	7/1	Edina	10/24/1861	
Kincaid	John	O	5Corp	6/15	St. Francisville	10/25/1861	
Kincaid	William	O	3Ser	6/15	St. Francisville	8/5/1861	
Kincaid	George W.	O	2Lieut	6/14	Alexandria	10/25/1861	
Kincaid	David	F	Pvt	6/18	Alexandria	8/27/1861	
Kine	Henry	E	Pvt	7/15	Croton	8/20/1861	
King	H. G.	L	Pvt	6/22	Sweet Home	8/15/1861	
Kinman	William A.	M	Pvt	7/12	Edina	9/8/1861	No proof of service, disallowed
Kirk	John	G	Pvt	7/19	Alexandria	10/24/1861	
Kisling	Daniel	B	Pvt	6/18	Memphis	10/24/1861	
Kisling	James M.	B	Pvt	6/18	Memphis	10/24/1861	
Kniser	James	F	Pvt	6/18	Alexandria	8/27/1861	
Knox	Joseph	F	Pvt	6/18	Alexandria		Killed at Athens
Kreiger	John C.	M	Pvt	7/12	Edina	9/8/1861	
Lacket	James H.	M	1Ser	7/12	Edina	9/5/1861	
Ladden	Thomas	Murray's	5Corp	7/1	Edina	10/24/1861	
Lafeever	Jephta	G	Pvt	7/19	Alexandria	10/24/1861	
Lafferty	Nicholas	F	Pvt	6/18	Alexandria	8/27/1861	
Lafranz	John	I	Wag-oner	6/16	Fairmount	10/25/1861	
Lamasters	Geroge	O	Pvt	6/15	St. Francisville	9/15/1861	
Lancaster	Robert H.	B	Pvt	6/18	Memphis	10/24/1861	
Langley	John	O	Pvt	6/15	St. Francisville	10/25/1861	
Laporte	William	C	3Corp	6/17	Alexandria	8/16/1861	Killed at Lone Jack, MO, Aug. 16, 1861
Laughlin	Robert	I	Musi-cian	6/16	Fairmount	2/14/1862	

Lecumber	Edward Sen.	A	Pvt	11/6	Memphis	12/4/1861	
Lecumber	Edward (Sr)	D	Pvt	6/20	Scotland Co.	11/6/1861	
Lecumber	Edward (Jr)	D	Pvt	6/20	Scotland Co.	11/6/1861	
Lecumber	Edward Jr.	A	Pvt	11/6	Memphis	12/4/1861	
Lee	John	F	Pvt	6/18	Alexandria	8/27/1861	
Lee	Benjamin	F	2Corp	6/18	Alexandria	8/27/1861	
Lee	Martin	O	Pvt	6/15	St. Francisville	7/15/1861	
Lemming	David	C	4Corp	6/17	Alexandria	8/17/1861	
Lemon	Peter	B	Pvt	6/18	Memphis	10/24/1861	
Lewis	James	G	Pvt	7/19	Alexandria	10/24/1861	
Lewis	James J.	G	Pvt	7/19	Alexandria	10/24/1861	
Lewis	Sprague	D	6Corp	6/20	Scotland Co.	11/6/1861	
Lewis	Marsena	I	Pvt	6/16	Fairmount	10/25/1861	
Lewis	William L.	O	Pvt	6/15	St. Francisville	9/15/1861	
Lewis	David B.	O	Pvt	6/15	St. Francisville	10/25/1861	
Lewis	William H.	Murray's	Pvt	7/1	Edina	10/24/1861	
Liburger	Lewis	B	Pvt	6/18	Memphis	10/24/1861	
Lightner	Frederick	C	Pvt	6/17	Alexandria	8/17/1861	
Linkenfetter	James	Murray's	Pvt	7/1	Edina	10/24/1861	
Lips	John	I	Pvt	6/16	Fairmount	10/25/1861	
Little	Robert J.	A	Pvt	9/28	Memphis	12/4/1861	
Little	William R.	A	Pvt	9/28	Memphis	12/4/1861	
Little	John	A	Pvt	9/28	Memphis	12/4/1861	
Long	Samuel	I	Pvt	6/16	Fairmount	2/14/1862	
Lonigan	Henry W.	I	Pvt	6/16	Fairmount	10/25/1861	
Loomis	Caleb	K	Pvt	6/17	Luray	10/1/1861	
Lord	Little W.	H	6Corp	6/15	Kahoka	10/26/1861	
Lory	Franklin	Murray's	Pvt	7/1	Edina	10/24/1861	
Lory	Joseph	Murray's	Pvt	7/1	Edina	10/24/1861	
Louis	William	I	Pvt	7/1	Kahoka	9/5/1861	
Lowery	Charles	B	Pvt	6/18	Memphis	10/24/1861	
Loy	Nicholas	I	Pvt	6/16	Fairmount	10/25/1861	
Luther	Alfred	G	4Corp	7/19	Alexandria	10/24/1861	
Lyon	John W.	E	Pvt	7/15	Croton	8/20/1861	
Mack	George	F	Pvt	6/18	Alexandria	8/27/1861	
Maggard	John	Murray's	Pvt	7/1	Edina	8/11/1861	
Mangles	Henry	I	Pvt	6/16	Fairmount	10/25/1861	
Mans	Austin	N	2Lieut	6/15	St. Francisville	8/15/1861	
Mansperger	Samuel	Moore's	Pvt	6/15	Wrightsville	10/24/1861	Rendered no service, to receive no pay
Mansperger	George	Moore's	Pvt	6/15	Wrightsville	10/24/1861	Rendered no service, to receive no pay
March	Rudolphus	G	Pvt	7/19	Alexandria	10/24/1861	
Marris	James K.	G	Pvt	7/19	Alexandria	10/24/1861	

Marshall	Ralph	G	Pvt	7/19	Alexandria	10/24/1861	
Martin	Patrick	O	Pvt	6/15	St. Francisville	9/15/1861	
Martin	John A.	I	Pvt	10/3	Memphis	2/14/1862	
Mason	James M.	O	Pvt	6/15	St. Francisville	10/25/1861	
Massa	Jacob	I	Pvt	6/16	Fairmount	10/25/1861	
Massa	John	I	Pvt	6/16	Fairmount	10/25/1861	
Mathey	Newton D.	O	Pvt	6/15	St. Francisville	8/15/1861	
Matlich	Zachariah	G	Pvt	7/19	Alexandria	10/24/1861	
Matlick	Zachariah	Murray's	2Lieut	7/1	Edina	10/24/1861	
Matlick	Josiah	Murray's	2Ser	7/1	Edina	7/15/1861	
Matlick	William	Murray's	Pvt	7/1	Edina	10/24/1861	
Matlick	Edgar	Murray's	Pvt	7/1	Edina	10/24/1861	
Matlick	Elijah	Murray's	Pvt	7/1	Edina	10/24/1861	
Matt	R. B.	N	3Ser	6/15	St. Francisville	8/15/1861	
Mattley	Aaron R.	D	Capt	6/16	Alexandria	11/6/1861	Wounded at Battle of Athens, Aug. 5, 1861
Mauck	David	L	Pvt	6/22	Sweet Home	8/15/1861	
McBree	Robert	O	Pvt	6/15	St. Francisville	8/16/1861	Rendered no service, to receive no pay
McCain	John	B	Pvt	6/18	Memphis	10/24/1861	
McCaslin	John	D	Pvt	9/15	Scotland Co.	11/6/1861	
McCay	James	D	Pvt	6/20	Scotland Co.	10/22/1861	
McClamroch	John	Murray's	Pvt	7/1	Edina	7/15/1861	Deserted July 15, 1861, to receive no pay
McClellan	George W.	D	4Ser	6/20	Scotland Co.	11/6/1861	
McClellan	Evan M.	D	2Lieut	6/20	Scotland Co.	10/23/1861	Resigned Oct. 23, 1861
McClintock	John M.	N	1Corp	6/15	St. Francisville	8/15/1861	
McClintock	David	C	Pvt	6/17	Alexandria	8/17/1861	
McClure	David	O	Pvt	6/15	St. Francisville	8/15/1861	
McColister	Thomas	G	1Lieut	7/19	Alexandria	10/24/1861	
McConnell	George	O	Pvt	6/15	St. Francisville	8/15/1861	
McCoun	William	L	Pvt	6/22	Sweet Home	8/15/1861	
McCoy	Chambers	M	Pvt	7/12	Edina	9/8/1861	No proof of service, disallowed
McCue	Benjamin	Moore's	Pvt	6/15	Wrightsville	10/24/1861	Rendered no service, to receive no pay
McCully	William	M	Pvt	7/12	Edina	8/1/1861	
McCully	Samuel	M	Pvt	7/12	Edina	9/8/1861	
McDaniel	Jesse	O	Pvt	6/15	St. Francisville	9/15/1861	
McDonald	Harvey	G	Pvt	7/19	Alexandria	10/24/1861	
McDonald	Sterling	A	Pvt	11/6	Memphis	12/4/1861	
McDonald	Samuel	A	Pvt	11/6	Memphis	12/4/1861	
McDonald	Sterling	D	5Ser	6/20	Scotland Co.	11/6/1861	
McDonald	Samuel M.	D	1Corp	6/20	Scotland Co.	11/6/1861	
McDonald	Samuel	I	Pvt	6/16	Fairmount	10/25/1861	
McDougal	James	C	Pvt	6/17	Alexandria	8/17/1861	

McGovern	Joseph	B	Pvt	6/18	Memphis	10/24/1861	
McHenry	Benjaimin F.	B	Pvt	9/28	Memphis	10/24/1861	
McKee	Woodfore	O	Pvt	6/15	St. Francisville	8/16/1861	
McKee	James	L	Pvt	6/22	Sweet Home	8/15/1861	
McKee	John	L	Pvt	6/22	Sweet Home	8/15/1861	
McKee	David	L	2Lieut	6/22	Sweet Home	8/15/1861	
McKee	Henry L.	L	2Ser	6/22	Sweet Home	8/15/1861	
McKee	William	L	Pvt	6/22	Sweet Home	8/15/1861	
McKee	Preston M.	D	Pvt	6/20	Scotland Co.	11/6/1861	
McKenny	John A.	E	Pvt	7/15	Croton	8/20/1861	
McKoy	John	C	Pvt	6/17	Alexandria	8/17/1861	
McLane	John	C	3Ser	6/17	Alexandria	8/17/1861	
McLaughlin	William	N	Pvt	6/15	St. Francisville	8/15/1861	
McMee	Henry W.	Murray's	Pvt	7/1	Edina	10/24/1861	
McNamar	Isaac	F	1Lieut	6/18	Alexandria	8/27/1861	
McNeely	William	Murray's	Pvt	7/1	Edina	7/15/1861	
McNeil	James S.	E	Pvt	7/15	Croton	8/20/1861	
Means	James	N	Pvt	6/15	St. Francisville	8/15/1861	
Means	John	O	Pvt	6/15	St. Francisville	8/15/1861	
Means	Joseph	N	Pvt	6/15	St. Francisville	8/15/1861	
Merritt	Caleb H.	H	3Ser	6/15	Kahoka	10/26/1861	
Meyers	Tilford	Murray's	5Ser	7/1	Edina	10/24/1861	
Meyers	A. D.	M	Pvt	7/12	Edina	9/8/1861	
Michael	B. N.	N	4Corp	6/15	St. Francisville	8/15/1861	
Miles	Henry	F	Pvt	6/18	Alexandria	8/27/1861	
Miles	Frank	F	Pvt	6/18	Alexandria	8/27/1861	
Miller	Phillip	D	Pvt	6/20	Scotland Co.	11/6/1861	
Miller	Alexander	L	Pvt	6/22	Sweet Home	8/15/1861	
Miller	George D.	D	2Corp	6/20	Scotland Co.	11/6/1861	
Miller	William	B	Pvt	6/18	Memphis	10/24/1861	
Miller	Thomas	B	Pvt	6/18	Memphis	10/24/1861	
Miller	Warren	Murray's	Pvt	7/1	Edina	7/25/1861	
Miller	Joseph	Murray's	Pvt	7/1	Edina	8/1/1861	
Miller	Harrison	B	Pvt	6/18	Memphis	10/24/1861	
Mills	Marvin	I	Pvt	6/16	Fairmount	8/7/1861	
Mills	Vernon	K	Pvt	6/17	Luray	9/1/1861	
Mills	John	G	Pvt	7/19	Alexandria	10/24/1861	
Mingels	Henry	I	Pvt	6/16	Fairmount	8/1/1861	
Mitchell	Harvey	G	3Corp	7/19	Alexandria	10/24/1861	
Moody	Benjamin	D	Pvt	6/20	Scotland Co.	8/8/1861	
Moore	David	Moore's	Capt	6/14	Alexandria	7/4/1861	Promoted to Colonel of Regiment, July 4, 1861
Moore	John W.	F	Pvt	6/18	Alexandria	7/17/1861	

More	J. B.	O	Pvt	6/15	St. Francisville	9/15/1861	
Morris	Phinias S.	G	Pvt	7/19	Alexandria	10/24/1861	
Morris	Doddridge	B	Pvt	6/18	Memphis	10/24/1861	
Morris	William	B	Pvt	6/18	Memphis	10/24/1861	
Morris	Benjamin F.	B	Pvt	6/18	Memphis	10/24/1861	
Morris	Justice	N	Pvt	6/15	St. Francisville	8/15/1861	
Morris	David R.	B	Pvt	6/18	Memphis	10/24/1861	
Mosier	Frank	F	Pvt	6/18	Alexandria	8/27/1861	Did no service, to receive no pay or allowance
Mott	George	B	Pvt	6/18	Memphis	10/24/1861	
Mure	James	B	Pvt	6/18	Memphis	10/24/1861	
Murphy	Alexander	O	Pvt	6/15	St. Francisville	8/15/1861	
Murray	Gilbert E.	Murray's	Capt	7/1	Edina	10/20/1861	Died Oct. 20, 1861
Murry	Benjamin F.	Murray's	Pvt	7/1	Edina	7/10/1861	
Myers	Peter	Murray's	Pvt	7/1	Edina	7/15/1861	
Myers	Mathias M.	Murray's	Pvt	7/1	Edina	10/24/1861	
Myers	Andrew	Murray's	Pvt	7/1	Edina	10/24/1861	
Myers	Mack	Murray's	Pvt	7/1	Edina	8/4/1861	
Myers	Henry	Murray's	Pvt	7/1	Edina	7/11/1861	
Myers	John W.	Murray's	Pvt	7/1	Edina	7/10/1861	
Myers	Nathaniel	Murray's	Pvt	7/1	Edina	7/9/1861	
Myres	Matthew	B	Pvt	6/18	Memphis	10/24/1861	
Neal	John	Moore's	Pvt	6/15	Wrightsville	10/24/1861	
Neal	John	I	Pvt	7/12	Memphis	10/25/1861	
Neal	George	Moore's	Pvt	6/15	Wrightsville	10/24/1861	
Needham	William	G	Pvt	7/19	Alexandria	10/24/1861	
Needham	David	G	Pvt	7/19	Alexandria	10/24/1861	
Nelson	L. B.	O	Pvt	6/15	St. Francisville	8/15/1861	
NewHome	Joseph M.	F	Pvt	6/18	Alexandria	8/27/1861	
Newlitze	Lewis	C	2Corp	6/17	Alexandria	8/17/1861	
Niday	Clark C.	D	Pvt	6/20	Scotland Co.	9/20/1861	
Niday	John A.	D	Pvt	6/20	Scotland Co.	11/6/1861	
Niday	David	D	Pvt	6/20	Scotland Co.	10/10/1861	
Nigh	Oliver	O	1Corp	6/15	St. Francisville	8/5/1861	
Nigh	John	O	Pvt	6/15	St. Francisville	8/11/1861	
Nigh	William	O	Pvt	6/15	St. Francisville	10/25/1861	
Norton	George S.	Murray's	Pvt	7/1	Edina	8/10/1861	
Norton	James K.	Murray's	Pvt	7/1	Edina	8/15/1861	
Norton	John J.	Murray's	1Lieut	7/1	Edina	10/24/1861	
Norton	John H.	Murray's	4Ser	7/1	Edina	10/24/1861	
Numire	George	O	1Ser	6/15	St. Francisville	8/5/1861	Wounded at Battle of Athens
Oaks	Oberon	M	Pvt	7/12	Edina	8/1/1861	
Oaks	Ransom	M	Pvt	7/12	Edina	8/1/1861	

O'Blennis	Charles	C	Pvt	6/17	Alexandria	8/6/1861	Transferred to 1st Regt Iowa Cavalry
O'Blennis	Mathias	C	Pvt	6/17	Alexandria	8/6/1861	Transferred to 1st Regt Iowa Cavalry
Ochiltree	Thomas E.	O	Pvt	6/15	St. Francisville	8/15/1861	
Ochiltree	D. F.	O	Pvt	6/15	St. Francisville	10/25/1861	
Ochiltree	Madison	O	Pvt	6/15	St. Francisville	8/15/1861	
Ochsenbecker	John	I	Pvt	8/9	Memphis	10/25/1861	
Ocker	James	Murray's	8Corp	7/1	Edina	10/24/1861	
O'Day	Andrew	F	Pvt	6/18	Alexandria	8/27/1861	
Oliver	Joseph	B	2Ser	6/18	Memphis	10/24/1861	
O'Neil	Jasper	E	2Ser	7/15	Croton	8/20/1861	
Oroal	Grifith	O	Pvt	6/15	St. Francisville	10/25/1861	Rendered no service, to receive no pay
Overhaus	Benjamin	D	Pvt	6/20	Scotland Co.	11/6/1861	
Owens	Edward	Murray's	Pvt	7/1	Edina	8/15/1861	
Owens	W. H. T.	M	4Ser	7/12	Edina	8/1/1861	Disallowed, no proof of service
Owens	William	H	4Corp	6/15	Kahoka	10/26/1861	
Oyler	William H.	B	Pvt	6/18	Memphis	10/24/1861	
Padock	Henry	Moore's	8Corp	6/15	Wrightsville	10/24/1861	
Padock	Jonathan (Sr)	Moore's	Pvt	6/15	Wrightsville	10/24/1861	Rendered no service, to receive no pay
Padock	Jonathan (Jr)	Moore's	5Corp	6/15	Wrightsville	10/24/1861	
Page	David	B	Pvt	6/18	Memphis	10/24/1861	
Paine	P. J.	O	Pvt	6/15	St. Francisville	8/15/1861	
Palmer	Benjamin S.	G	Pvt	7/19	Alexandria	10/24/1861	
Palmerton	William	K	Pvt	6/17	Luray	10/1/1861	
Parrish	Ira	D	Pvt	6/20	Scotland Co.	11/6/1861	
Parsons	Charles	E	Pvt	7/15	Croton	8/20/1861	
Parsons	Wesley	L	Pvt	6/22	Sweet Home	8/15/1861	
Parsons	Jeffeson	D	Pvt	6/20	Scotland Co.	11/6/1861	
Past	E.	O	Pvt	6/15	St. Francisville	8/15/1861	
Patten	David N.	Murray's	Pvt	7/1	Edina	10/24/1861	
Payden	Harden	E	Pvt	7/15	Croton	8/20/1861	
Payden	Nathaniel	E	Pvt	7/15	Croton	8/20/1861	
Payden	Joseph	E	2Lieut	7/15	Croton	8/20/1861	
Payne	O. B.	N	Capt	6/10	St. Francisville	8/15/1861	
Payne	P. J.	N	Pvt	6/15	St. Francisville	8/15/1861	
Payne	Hiram	Moore's	Pvt	6/15	Wrightsville	10/24/1861	
Pearce	Ransom	G	Pvt	7/19	Alexandria	10/24/1861	
Pearce	James	G	Pvt	7/19	Alexandria	10/24/1861	
Pearce	Kinney	D	Pvt	6/20	Scotland Co.	11/6/1861	
Pearce	Simon	G	1Corp	7/19	Alexandria	10/24/1861	
Pearce	William	G	Pvt	7/19	Alexandria	10/24/1861	
Pearce	Lewis K.	G	Pvt	7/19	Alexandria	10/24/1861	
Pearson	John	F	Pvt	6/18	Alexandria	8/27/1861	Did no service, to receive no pay or allowance

Peck	Samuel	I	1Corp	6/16	Fairmount	12/14/1861	
Peck	Samuel E.	Moore's	3Corp	6/15	Wrightsville	10/15/1861	Joined Black Hawk Cavalry, Oct. 15, 1861
Peden	John P.	G	Pvt	7/19	Alexandria	10/24/1861	
Perrigo	William	F	Pvt	6/18	Alexandria	8/27/1861	
Perrigo	Justice	F	Pvt	6/18	Alexandria	8/27/1861	
Perry	Gideon M.	A	Pvt	9/28	Memphis	12/4/1861	
Perry	Benjamin M.	B	Pvt	6/18	Memphis	10/24/1861	
Perry	Benjamin A.	B	Pvt	6/18	Memphis	10/24/1861	
Perry	Oliver H.	K	Pvt	6/17	Luray	8/6/1861	
Pettit	Aaron	M	Pvt	7/12	Edina	8/1/1861	
Phelps	George	O	Pvt	6/15	St. Francisville	8/15/1861	
Pherigo	Elijah	D	Pvt	6/20	Scotland Co.	10/24/1861	
Pherigo	John M.	D	Pvt	6/20	Scotland Co.	10/24/1861	
Phillips	Andrew H.	K	Pvt	6/17	Luray	10/1/1861	
Pickering	Thomas	C	Pvt	6/17	Alexandria	8/17/1861	
Pickering	Henry C.	C	Pvt	6/17	Alexandria	8/17/1861	
Pickering	William	C	1Corp	6/17	Alexandria	8/16/1861	Killed at Lone Jack, MO, Aug. 16, 1861
Pierce	Stephen	F	Pvt	6/18	Alexandria	7/11/1861	
Pierce	George W.	B	Pvt	6/18	Memphis	10/24/1861	
Pierpont	Henry	O	Pvt	6/15	St. Francisville	8/15/1861	
Pilcher	William	K	Pvt	6/17	Luray	8/19/1861	
Pilcher	Hiram G.	K	Pvt	6/17	Luray	10/1/1861	
Plunket	T. J.	M	Pvt	7/12	Edina	7/26/1861	
Poe	Henderson G.	B	Pvt	6/18	Memphis	10/24/1861	
Postlethwait	Charles	I	Pvt	8/20	Athens	2/14/1862	
Poulson	Harrison	E	Pvt	7/15	Croton	8/20/1861	
Pugh	David	C	Pvt	6/17	Alexandria	8/2/1861	Discharged for disability
Pullins	James	K	Pvt	6/17	Luray	8/1/1861	
Purmert	Wallace W.	G	1Ser	7/19	Alexandria	10/24/1861	
Rainey	William	B	Pvt	6/18	Memphis	10/24/1861	
Rains	George	E	Pvt	7/15	Croton	8/20/1861	
Randolph	David	F	Pvt	6/18	Alexandria	8/27/1861	
Ransom	David	F	Pvt	6/18	Alexandria	8/27/1861	
Rathbun	William H. H.	D	Pvt	6/20	Scotland Co.	9/20/1861	Wounded at Battle of Athens
Rathbun	John B.	D	Pvt	6/20	Scotland Co.	11/6/1861	
Rathbun	Job O. C.	D	3Ser	6/20	Scotland Co.	11/6/1861	
Rathbun	Elon G.	D	2Ser	6/20	Scotland Co.	11/6/1861	
Read	Elias C.	K	Pvt	6/17	Luray	9/20/1861	
Ree	L. D. W.	N	4Ser	6/15	St. Francisville	8/15/1861	
Reeg	Henry	I	Pvt	8/9	Memphis	10/25/1861	
Reese	Joseph	Murray's	Pvt	7/1	Edina	10/24/1861	

Reidy	James	F	Pvt	6/18	Alexandria	8/27/1861	Did no service, to receive no pay or allowance
Reiter	L.	F	Pvt	6/18	Alexandria	8/27/1861	
Resor	Hamilton	Moore's	2Corp	6/15	Wrightsville	10/24/1861	Rendered no service, to receive no pay
Rice	Hudson	B	3Ser	6/18	Memphis	10/24/1861	
Richardson	Thomas H.	G	2Lieut	7/19	Alexandria	10/24/1861	
Richey	James	F	Pvt	6/18	Alexandria	8/27/1861	
Richey	John	F	Pvt	6/18	Alexandria	8/27/1861	
Richey	Isaac	F	Pvt	6/18	Alexandria	8/27/1861	
Ridgeley	William	D	Pvt	6/20	Scotland Co.	11/6/1861	
Riggels	Josiah	L	Pvt	6/22	Sweet Home	8/15/1861	
Riggs	Elias K.	K	Pvt	6/17	Luray	8/1/1861	
Riggs	Elias C.	K	Pvt	6/17	Luray	8/1/1861	
Right	Levi	Murray's	Pvt	7/1	Edina	8/15/1861	
Rinehart	Charles B.	K	Pvt	6/17	Luray	8/4/1861	
Robb	Lewis B.	Moore's	3Ser	6/15	Wrightsville	8/29/1861	Joined Black Hawk Cavalry, Aug. 29, 1861
Robert	Jesse	G	2Corp	7/19	Alexandria	10/24/1861	
Robert	Samuel	G	Pvt	7/19	Alexandria	10/24/1861	
Roberts	Alexander	O	Pvt	6/15	St. Francisville	8/15/1861	
Roberts	Zamastus	O	2Corp	6/15	St. Francisville	8/5/1861	
Roberts	John	O	Pvt	6/15	St. Francisville	10/25/1861	
Roberts	James	N	Pvt	6/15	St. Francisville	8/15/1861	
Roberts	Daniel	O	Pvt	6/15	St. Francisville	10/25/1861	
Robertson	R. Franklin	I	Pvt	6/16	Fairmount	10/25/1861	
Robertson	Benjamin J.	I	2Lieut	6/16	Fairmount	2/14/1862	
Robinson	Edward	Moore's	Pvt	6/15	Wrightsville	10/24/1861	
Robison	Bodberry	Moore's	Pvt	6/15	Wrightsville	10/24/1861	
Rodgers	Albert	E	Pvt	7/15	Croton	8/20/1861	
Rogers	Milton	G	Pvt	7/19	Alexandria	10/24/1861	
Rollins	John	Moore's	Pvt	8/6	Athens	10/24/1861	
Root	A. S.	M	Pvt	7/12	Edina	9/8/1861	No proof of service, disallowed
Rordbaugh	James T.	B	Pvt	6/18	Memphis	10/24/1861	
Rose	Comfort	C	Pvt	6/17	Alexandria	8/10/1861	Transferred to 1st Regt Iowa Cavalry
Rose	Thomas	D	Pvt	6/20	Scotland Co.	11/6/1861	
Roseberry	John	L	1Lieut	6/22	Sweet Home	8/15/1861	
Roseberry	Thomas H.	O	Capt	6/14	Alexandria	8/25/1861	
Roseberry	James	F	Musi-cian	6/18	Alexandria	8/27/1861	
Roseberry	Reed H.	O	Pvt	6/15	St. Francisville	8/15/1861	
Roseberry	Hughes	F	Musi-cian	6/18	Alexandria	8/27/1861	
Ross	Blair W.	M	Pvt	7/12	Edina	9/1/1861	
Ross	A. J.	M	Pvt	7/12	Edina	9/1/1861	

Rothburn	William H. H.	A	Pvt	11/6	Memphis	12/4/1861	
Rothburn	Job O. C.	A	Pvt	11/6	Memphis	12/4/1861	
Rotherburn	Elon G.	A	Pvt	11/6	Memphis	12/4/1861	
Royce	Moses	F	Pvt	6/18	Alexandria	8/27/1861	
Ruark	James	F	Pvt	6/18	Alexandria	7/29/1861	
Rudd	John	O	Pvt	6/15	St. Francisville	8/15/1861	
Rynearson	John	I	Pvt	8/9	Memphis	10/25/1861	
Sales	Edward	N	Pvt	6/15	St. Francisville	8/15/1861	
Sallyers	Isaac	F	Pvt	6/18	Alexandria	8/27/1861	
Sallyers	William	F	Pvt	6/18	Alexandria	8/27/1861	
Salse	Perry R.	Murray's	Pvt	7/1	Edina	10/24/1861	
Salse	George	Murray's	Pvt	7/1	Edina	10/24/1861	
Samens	John	D	Pvt	8/11	Scotland Co.	11/6/1861	
Sanders	William	E	Pvt	7/15	Croton	8/20/1861	
Schee	John	L	Pvt	6/22	Sweet Home	8/15/1861	
Schoam	Isaac C.	Moore's	Pvt	6/15	Wrightsville	10/24/1861	
Schofield	Matthew B.	K	Pvt	6/17	Luray	10/1/1861	
Schram	Isaac C.	I	Pvt	6/15	Union	2/14/1862	
Scott	John	F	Pvt	6/18	Alexandria	8/27/1861	
Scott	Walden	E	3Ser	7/15	Croton	8/20/1861	
Scott	Andy	H	2Corp	6/15	Kahoka	9/1/1861	Deserted, to receive no pay or allowance
Scott	John	O	Pvt	6/15	St. Francisville	8/11/1861	
Scott	Miles	C	Pvt	6/17	Alexandria	8/17/1861	
Scovern	William	C	Pvt	6/17	Alexandria	8/17/1861	
Sellers	William	D	Pvt	6/20	Scotland Co.	11/6/1861	
Setens	Benjamin J.	I	Pvt	6/16	Fairmount	10/25/1861	
Sewers	John W.	F	Pvt	6/18	Alexandria	8/27/1861	
Sewers	Oliver P.	F	Pvt	6/18	Alexandria	8/27/1861	
Shaffer	James	F	Pvt	6/18	Alexandria	8/27/1861	
Shaffer	James	F	Pvt	6/18	Alexandria	8/27/1861	
Shannon	Ebeneezer	H	4Ser	6/15	Kahoka	10/26/1861	
Sharp	John	L	Pvt	6/22	Sweet Home	8/15/1861	
Sharp	James	L	Pvt	6/22	Sweet Home	8/15/1861	
Shearer	George	I	Pvt	6/16	Fairmount	10/25/1861	
Shearer	John	I	Pvt	6/16	Fairmount	11/5/1861	
Sheets	Benjamin F.	K	Pvt	6/17	Luray	10/1/1861	
Sheets	Moses	K	Pvt	6/17	Luray	10/1/1861	Rendered no service, to receive no pay
Sheets	Andrew F.	C	Pvt	6/17	Alexandria	8/17/1861	
Shenick	Joseph	O	Pvt	6/15	St. Francisville	8/15/1861	
Sherwood	William	Moore's	Pvt	6/15	Wrightsville	10/24/1861	Rendered no service, to receive no pay
Sherwood	Charles	Moore's	Pvt	6/15	Wrightsville	10/24/1861	Rendered no service, to receive no pay
Shields	William	D	Pvt	6/20	Scotland Co.	8/12/1861	

Shirick	William	E	4Ser	7/15	Croton	8/20/1861	
Shivak	Jacob	D	Pvt	6/20	Scotland Co.	9/20/1861	
Shoemaker	John	O	3Corp	6/15	St. Francisville	10/25/1861	
Shorts	Casper	C	Pvt	6/17	Alexandria	8/17/1861	
Shuler	Matthew	C	Pvt	6/17	Alexandria	8/17/1861	
Shuler	John	D	Pvt	6/20	Scotland Co.	8/18/1861	
Shuler	D. F.	L	4Ser	6/22	Sweet Home	8/15/1861	
Shure	Mathias	L	Pvt	6/22	Sweet Home	8/15/1861	
Silver	Hartwell	K	Capt	6/17	Luray	10/1/1861	
Simpson	Andrew	Moore's	Pvt	6/15	Wrightsville	10/24/1861	Rendered no service, to receive no pay
Simpson	William	G	2Ser	7/19	Alexandria	10/24/1861	
Sinclair	William G.	G	Pvt	7/19	Alexandria	10/24/1861	
Singmaster	W. B.	N	2Ser	6/15	St. Francisville	8/15/1861	
Sittle	Edward B.	I	Pvt	6/16	Fairmount	10/25/1861	
Slichfield	John	O	Pvt	6/15	St. Francisville	8/15/1861	
Small	Ellsberry T.	G	Capt	7/19	Alexandria	10/24/1861	
Smallwood	Wilkison	N	Pvt	6/15	St. Francisville	8/15/1861	
Smallwood	Wilkinson	O	Pvt	6/15	St. Francisville	8/15/1861	
Smith	Thomas N. A	A	Pvt	9/28	Memphis	12/4/1861	
Smith	John	E	Pvt	7/15	Croton	8/20/1861	
Smith	James	B	Pvt	6/18	Memphis	10/24/1861	
Smith	Augustus	B	Pvt	6/18	Memphis	10/24/1861	
Smith	Thomas M.	G	Pvt	7/19	Alexandria	10/24/1861	
Smith	Allison	O	2Ser	6/15	St. Francisville	8/5/1861	
Smith	James P.	F	Pvt	6/18	Alexandria	8/27/1861	
Smith	Henry	C	Pvt	6/17	Alexandria	8/17/1861	
Smith	Elijah	Moore's	Pvt	6/15	Wrightsville	10/24/1861	
Smith	George	B	Pvt	6/18	Memphis	10/24/1861	
Smith	Thomas	Murray's	Pvt	7/1	Edina	10/24/1861	
Smith	William	A	Pvt	9/28	Memphis	12/4/1861	
Smulling	John D.	I	1Ser	6/16	Fairmount	10/25/1861	
Snodgrass	William	D	Pvt	8/11	Scotland Co.	11/6/1861	
Socket	Erastus	K	3Ser	6/17	Luray	10/1/1861	
Spangular	Samuel	O	Pvt	6/15	St. Francisville	8/15/1861	Rendered no service, to receive no pay
Spelman	Henry P.	C	Capt	6/17	Alexandria	8/17/1861	
Spencer	Thame S.	K	Pvt	6/17	Luray	10/1/1861	
Spencer	William	L	3Ser	6/22	Sweet Home	8/15/1861	
Sprague	Hanson H.	A	Pvt	9/28	Memphis	12/4/1861	
Sprague	William S.	A	Pvt	9/28	Memphis	12/4/1861	
Sprague	William	D	Pvt	6/20	Scotland Co.	11/6/1861	
Springer	Orrin V.	N	2Corp	6/15	St. Francisville	8/15/1861	
Sprouse	William	K	Pvt	6/17	Luray	9/5/1861	Mortally wounded at the Battle of Athens

Stapleton	Richard	D	Pvt	8/11	Scotland Co.	11/6/1861	
Star	Loring E.	E	Pvt	7/15	Croton	8/20/1861	
Starr	William	F	Pvt	6/18	Alexandria	8/27/1861	Did no service, to receive no pay or allowance
Starr	Washington	I	Pvt	6/16	Fairmount	10/25/1861	
Steele	Frederick	K	Pvt	6/17	Luray	8/6/1861	
Steele	Theodore	K	Pvt	6/17	Luray	8/6/1861	
Steeples	Harrison	D	Pvt	9/13	Scotland Co.	11/6/1861	
Steidly	John H.	M	Pvt	7/12	Edina	7/26/1861	No proof of service, disallowed
Stephens	Charles R.	I	Pvt	6/16	Fairmount	10/25/1861	
Sterret	Robert E.	B	Pvt	6/18	Memphis	10/24/1861	
Stevens	Drury	I	Pvt	6/16	Fairmount	10/25/1861	
Stevens	James	I	Pvt	6/16	Fairmount	10/25/1861	
Stevens	Daniel P.	I	2Ser	6/16	Fairmount	2/14/1862	
Stevens	Buel	B	1Ser	6/18	Memphis	10/24/1861	
Stewart	Henry H.	Moore's	Pvt	6/15	Wrightsville	10/24/1861	Rendered no service, to receive no pay
Stewart	John	G	Pvt	7/19	Alexandria	10/24/1861	
Stewart	Elmer	Moore's	Pvt	6/15	Wrightsville	10/24/1861	
Stone	Calvin	F	Pvt	6/18	Alexandria	8/27/1861	
Strowsnider	Emanuel	D	Pvt	6/20	Scotland Co.	8/21/1861	
Strowsnider	Abraham	D	1Ser	6/20	Scotland Co.	11/6/1861	Wounded at Battle of Athens, Aug. 5, 1861
Strowsnider	Remley	D	Pvt	6/20	Scotland Co.	8/21/1861	
Stump	Joseph	O	Pvt	6/15	St. Francisville	8/15/1861	
Stump	David	N	Pvt	6/15	St. Francisville	8/15/1861	
Stump	Ansel	O	Pvt	6/15	St. Francisville	8/15/1861	
Stungs	N. B.	O	Pvt	6/15	St. Francisville	8/15/1861	
Stungs	Joseph	O	Pvt	6/15	St. Francisville	8/15/1861	
Stungs	John	O	Pvt	6/15	St. Francisville	8/15/1861	
Sullivan	William E.	K	Pvt	6/17	Luray	8/5/1861	Killed at the Battle of Athens
Sumens	John	A	Pvt	9/28	Memphis	12/4/1861	
Summers	John	I	Pvt	8/9	Memphis	10/25/1861	
Summers	John	Moore's	Pvt	8/10	Athens	10/24/1861	
Sutherland	A. B.	H	2Ser	6/15	Kahoka	10/26/1861	
Swarts	Dennis	I	Pvt	8/9	Memphis	10/25/1861	
Swasey	Hiram H.	A	Pvt	9/28	Memphis	12/4/1861	
Sweet	Philander	O	Pvt	6/15	St. Francisville	10/25/1861	
Tabbatt	John P.	E	1Lieut	7/15	Croton	8/20/1861	
Tames	George	O	Pvt	6/15	St. Francisville	8/15/1861	
Tayler	James H.	C	4Ser	6/17	Alexandria	8/17/1861	
Taylor	George	N	Pvt	6/15	St. Francisville	8/15/1861	
Taylor	William	F	Pvt	8/5	Alexandria	8/27/1861	
Taylor	Darius	F	Pvt	6/18	Alexandria	8/27/1861	

Last	First	Co.	Rank		Place		Remarks
Thomas	Joseph	O	Pvt	6/15	St. Francisville	8/15/1861	
Thomas	David	D	Pvt	6/20	Scotland Co.	11/6/1861	
Thomas	David	A	Pvt	11/6	Memphis	12/4/1861	
Thomas	Paul	F	Pvt	6/18	Alexandria	8/27/1861	
Thomas	Elijah	B	Pvt	6/18	Memphis	10/24/1861	
Thomas	Charles B.	B	Pvt	6/18	Memphis	10/24/1861	
Thompson	James P.	F	Pvt	6/18	Alexandria	8/27/1861	
Thompson	Henry	F	4Corp	6/18	Alexandria	8/27/1861	
Thomson	Samuel	L	Pvt	6/22	Sweet Home	8/15/1861	
Thomson	Dennis	I	Pvt	6/16	Fairmount	10/25/1861	
Thorp	J. A.	C	Pvt	6/17	Alexandria	8/17/1861	
Thorp	William	K	1Ser	6/17	Luray	10/1/1861	
Thrush	Abraham	D	Pvt	6/20	Scotland Co.	8/20/1861	
Thurman	Elijah	Murray's	Pvt	7/1	Edina	10/24/1861	
Tillison	John	G	Pvt	7/19	Alexandria	10/24/1861	
Todd	William	K	Pvt	6/17	Luray	10/1/1861	Rendered no service, to receive no pay
Tompson	John	C	Pvt	6/17	Alexandria	8/17/1861	
Toopis	Harrison	F	2Lieut	6/18	Alexandria	8/1/1861	Resigned Aug. 1, 1861
Toops	John	F	Pvt	6/18	Alexandria	7/25/1861	
Toops	Alexandria	F	Pvt	6/18	Alexandria	7/19/1861	
Toops	Michael	F	Pvt	6/18	Alexandria	7/19/1861	
Townsen	A. C.	O	Pvt	6/15	St. Francisville	8/15/1861	Rendered no service, to receive no pay
Tracy	John	G	Pvt	7/19	Alexandria	10/24/1861	
Tracy	William	G	Pvt	7/19	Alexandria	10/24/1861	
Trarlkill	George	G	3Ser	7/19	Alexandria	10/24/1861	
Troth	Francis S.	B	Pvt	6/18	Memphis	10/24/1861	
Troth	Francis M.	B	Pvt	6/18	Memphis	10/24/1861	
Vanfossen	Thomas E.	L	Pvt	6/22	Sweet Home	8/15/1861	
Vanpatton	Cornelius J.	K	Pvt	6/17	Luray	8/7/1861	
Viles	John	C	Pvt	6/17	Alexandria	8/17/1861	
Vires	Walter	K	Pvt	6/17	Luray	10/1/1861	
Waid	Meredith	I	Pvt	6/16	Fairmount	10/25/1861	
Waid	Peter	I	3Corp	6/16	Fairmount	9/14/1861	
Wainsley	James	M	Pvt	7/12	Edina	8/1/1861	
Wakey	Jacob	D	Pvt	6/20	Scotland Co.	11/6/1861	
Wakey	Jacob	A	Pvt	11/6	Memphis	12/4/1861	
Waltman	Seder	I	Pvt	6/16	Fairmount	10/25/1861	
Walton	William	K	Pvt	6/17	Luray	10/1/1861	Correct name is William Yalton
Ward	Samuel A.	E	Pvt	7/15	Croton	8/20/1861	
Ward	James	Murray's	Pvt	7/1	Edina	10/24/1861	
Ward	James D.	K	1Lieut	6/17	Luray	8/28/1861	Transferred to 7th Missouri Cavalry
Washburn	George P.	I	Pvt	6/16	Fairmount	2/14/1862	Rendered no service, to receive no pay

Washburn	Peter S.	I		Capt	6/16	Alexandria	2/14/1862	
Washburn	Alvin M.	I		Pvt	6/16	Fairmount	2/14/1862	
Washburn	Hiram	A		Pvt	11/6	Memphis	12/4/1861	
Washburn	Hiram	D		1Lieut	6/20	Alexandria	11/6/1861	
Washburn	Lither	H		1Lieut	6/15	Alexandria	10/26/1861	
Watson	Charles	G		Pvt	7/19	Alexandria	7/25/1861	Deserted, to receive no pay or allowance
Weber	Leroy Z.	I		Pvt	6/16	Fairmount	10/25/1861	Disloyal, to receive no pay
Weber	Thomas R.	I		3Ser	6/16	Fairmount	9/29/1861	Killed by guerrillas near Memphis, MO, while on duty
Weber	Daniel	I		Pvt	6/16	Fairmount	10/25/1861	
Weber	Dudley	I		Pvt	6/16	Fairmount	10/25/1861	Disloyal, to receive no pay
Weber	Edmund	I		4Ser	6/16	Fairmount	2/14/1862	
Weisner	Philip	C		Pvt	6/17	Alexandria	8/17/1861	
Welch	John A.	F		4Ser	6/18	Alexandria	8/27/1861	
Wells	George W.	D		Pvt	8/11	Scotland Co.	11/6/1861	
Wells	William	K		Pvt	6/17	Luray	10/1/1861	
Wells	Jesse C.	C		5Ser	6/17	Alexandria	8/17/1861	
Wells	William	D		Pvt	8/11	Scotland Co.	11/6/1861	
Wells	George	N		Pvt	6/15	St. Francisville	8/15/1861	
Wesel	Ephraim	F		Pvt	6/18	Alexandria	8/27/1861	
Westfall	Thomas L.	E		Pvt	7/15	Croton	8/20/1861	
Wetherbee	F. G.	M		Pvt	7/12	Edina	9/8/1861	
Weyer	Andrew J.	E		Pvt	7/15	Croton	8/20/1861	
Weyer	James R.	A		Pvt	9/28	Memphis	12/4/1861	
White	James L.	Murray's		Pvt	7/1	Edina	10/24/1861	
White	Ira P.	A		Pvt	9/28	Memphis	12/4/1861	
White	John	G		Pvt	7/19	Alexandria	10/24/1861	
White	James	Murray's		Pvt	7/1	Edina	8/15/1861	
White	Wesley	G		Pvt	7/19	Alexandria	10/24/1861	
White	Daniel	M		Pvt	7/12	Edina	9/8/1861	No proof of service, disallowed
Whitehead	Francis	Moore's		Pvt	6/15	Wrightsville	10/24/1861	Rendered no service, to receive no pay
Wickell	William	F		Pvt	6/18	Alexandria	7/19/1861	
Wickham	James	K		Pvt	6/17	Luray	8/7/1861	
Wilber	Edward	F		Pvt	6/18	Alexandria	7/19/1861	
Wileman	James	B		Pvt	6/18	Memphis	10/24/1861	
Wiley	J. W.	M		Pvt	7/12	Edina	9/8/1861	
Wiley	Lewis J.	M		Pvt	7/12	Edina	9/8/1861	
Wiley	Elijah P.	M		Pvt	7/12	Edina	9/8/1861	
Williams	Louis	H		1Ser	6/15	Kahoka	10/26/1861	
Williams	James M.	L		Pvt	6/22	Sweet Home	8/15/1861	
Willington	H. T.	A		Pvt	9/28	Memphis	12/4/1861	Received pay in full in the 21st MO vols.
Wilnot	Rueben	O		Pvt	6/15	St. Francisville	8/11/1861	

Wilson	T. R.	O	Pvt	6/15	St. Francisville	8/11/1861	
Wilson	David	D	Pvt	6/20	Scotland Co.	9/20/1861	
Wilson	Enos	E	Pvt	7/15	Croton	8/20/1861	
Wilson	D. F.	O	Pvt	6/15	St. Francisville	8/11/1861	
Wilson	Albert	F	Pvt	6/18	Alexandria	7/19/1861	
Wilson	John	G	Pvt	7/19	Alexandria	10/24/1861	
Wingate	Absalom	O	Pvt	6/15	St. Francisville	8/11/1861	
Witt	Jeremiah	Murray's	Pvt	7/1	Edina	10/24/1861	
Wood	Samuel	F	Pvt	6/18	Alexandria	8/27/1861	
Wood	David H.	C	Pvt	6/17	Alexandria	8/17/1861	
Woodruff	William M.	K	Pvt	6/17	Luray	9/1/1861	
Woodruff	Mark	O	Pvt	6/15	St. Francisville	8/15/1861	Wounded at the Battle of Athens
Woodward	Daniel	M	Pvt	7/12	Edina	9/8/1861	
Wooley	Daniel M.	K	2Lieut	6/17	Luray	10/1/1861	
Wright	John	I	Pvt	6/16	Fairmount	7/7/1861	
Wright	William F.	G	Pvt	7/19	Alexandria	10/24/1861	
Wright	Lewis	M	Pvt	7/12	Edina	8/1/1861	
Wright	William E.	K	Pvt	6/17	Luray	8/5/1861	
Yeager	Samuel	K	Pvt	6/17	Luray	10/1/1861	
Zolinger	Rueben	Murray's	Pvt	7/1	Edina	10/24/1861	

Notes to Introduction

1. The temperature in nearby Keokuk, Iowa, on Friday, August 2, had risen to 100°F, for the first time in three years (*Keokuk Daily Gate City,* August 6, 1861). John Savage, a farmer from Salem, Iowa, who came to Athens after the battle with his hometown militia, kept a diary, noting uncommonly hot, dry weather in late July and early August (Alice Savage, *Excerpts from the Diary of John Savage* [N.p., 1980]; hereafter cited as Savage). A militia company from Coalport, Iowa, riding on August 4 for Athens in response to the threatened invasion of Iowa, had several of their horses give out from the heat (Charles J. Fulton, "The Coalport Home Guards," *Annals of Iowa* 3rd Series, 14 [October 1923]: 84; hereafter cited as Fulton).

2. The .54, .58, and .69 caliber slugs fired by muzzle-loading, military rifles of the time, named for co-developer Claude-Étienne Minié. The minie ball was a conical, soft lead bullet with a hollow base, smaller than the bore of the rifle, which allowed easy loading from the muzzle. When fired, the base would flare out to engage the rifling of the barrel. First developed in the 1840s, this was a tremendous improvement over spherical ball ammunition, which had to be patched to take advantage of rifling. The Model 1861 Springfield rifle (and other, similar military weapons of the time), could be loaded and fired several times a minute with great accuracy, a factor that would contribute to the success of the Union force at Athens. In Chapter 4, these weapons will often be referred to as "Minie Rifles" by observers of the battle.

3. J. W. Murphy, "Luray and Editor Murphy," *Clark County Courier,* September 19, 1913, hereafter cited as "Luray and Editor Murphy," in Jan Gross, *The Last Reunion: The Story of Clark County's Civil War Veterans, Book II* (N.p.: Jan Gross, 1991), 50; hereafter cited as *Last Reunion II.*

4. D. C. Beaman, "The Battle of Athens, Missouri," *Annals of Iowa* 3rd Series, 6 (January 1905): 591; hereafter cited as D. C. Beaman.

5. Rev. G. C. Beaman, "Battle at Athens, Missouri," *The Annals of Iowa,* 1st Series, 6 (April 1868): 136–139; hereafter cited as G. C. Beaman. I suspect, but have not determined, that G. C. and D. C. Beaman are related. Their accounts are complementary, but show no evidence of collaboration.

6. John Hiller, Letter to brother, August 5, 1861; hereafter cited as Hiller Letter, in Jan Gross and Patricia M. Mullenix, *The Last Reunion: The Story of Clark County's Civil War Veterans, Book I* (N.p.: Jan Gross and Pat Mullenix, 1990), 22–23; hereafter cited as *Last Reunion I.*

7. F. M. Tate, "The Farmington Company at Athens," *Keokuk Daily Gate City,* August 13, 1861; hereafter cited as F. M. Tate.

8. "The Incidents of the Battle," *Keokuk Daily Gate City,* August 6, 1861; hereafter cited as "The Incidents of the Battle."

9. See Dave Page, "A Fight For Missouri," *Civil War Times Illustrated* 34 (August 1995): 34. Page's article is largely a retelling of various standard accounts of the battle.

10. Bilby, Joseph. *Civil War Firearms: Their Historical Background, Tactical Use and Modern Collecting and Shooting* (Conshohocken, PA: Combined Books, 1996), 86; hereafter cited as Bilby.

11. Ibid., 74.

12. This spontaneous Home Guard charge anticipated such other famous instances of the rank and file taking charge of the battle as the Federal assault on Missionary Ridge, Tennessee, and, as recent scholarship indicates, the fabled charge of the 20th Maine down Little Roundtop at Gettysburg on the second day of battle.

13. James M. McPherson, *For Cause and Comrades: Why Men Fought in the Civil War* (New York: Oxford University Press, 1997), 8, 39–43.

14. Throughout his book cited in the previous note, McPherson addresses the salient role of ideological conviction in combat motivation. One of his findings is that a high proportion of soldiers in his sample expressing convictions as to why they were in the army, also participated in regiments frequently engaged. These men, themselves, suffered a disproportionately high rate of being wounded and killed.

15. "The Battle of Athens," *Clark County Gazette,* August 5, 1886, reprinted in Patricia M. Mullenix, *The Battle of Athens* (Kahoka, MO: Patricia M. Mullenix, 1991), 155; hereafter cited as Mullenix, *The Battle of Athens.*

16. "Archaeological Research: Battle of Athens State Park, Athens, Clark County, Missouri: Draft Report" (Kirksville, MO: Northeast Missouri Regional Planning Commission, 1986); hereafter cited as Boyd.

Notes to Chapter 1

1. The boundary between the extreme southeastern tip of Iowa and the northeast corner of Missouri, the Des Moines River would be a significant factor in the Battle of Athens.

2. "Expedition of Captain Sample's Company," *Keokuk Daily Gate City,* August 5, 1861, also in Ben F. Dixon, *The Battle of Athens: "Farthest North of the Civil War"* (San Diego, CA: Ben F. Dixon, 1960), reprinted in Mullenix, *The Battle of Athens,* 1; hereafter cited as *Farthest North.*

Once in the Croton Depot, the Keokuk men probably walked down Locust Street to where it intersected Front Street along the river. The Thome-Benning Mill stood across the Des Moines in Athens from this spot, and the Thome-Benning house above it, atop a bluff. Moore's headquarters were a couple of blocks further southwest, at a house owned by William McKee on Virginia Street.

3. Hiller Letter, 22–24. The letter is transcribed in Ben F. Dixon, *Martin Green's Boomerang* (San Diego: Family Historians, No. 15, The Benjamin Franklin Junior Historical Series, 1966) reprinted in Mullenix, *The Battle of Athens,* 70–72, hereafter cited as *Martin Green's Boomerang.* Dixon mistakenly transcribed "hovering" in the excerpt above as "moving." Hiller describes himself as Moore's "Judge Advocate." His obituary says that he was Moore's "Provost Marshall" ("Death of John Hiller,"

Kahoka Gazette Herald, November 26, 1899, in *Last Reunion, II,* 113).

The *Clark County Census Schedules,* June 1860, compiled by Isaac R. Fields of Waterloo, Missouri, include "the Hiller brothers, J. M., Hiram M., and Joseph H., merchants lately arrived from Pennsylvania…," in Ben F. Dixon, "The Battle of Athens: Athens, the Place," (newspaper article, July 4, 1941); hereafter cited as "Athens, the Place," in Mullenix, *The Battle of Athens,* 162.

4. John McKee's account of the battle, hereafter cited as "From John McKee," was published in an unnamed county newspaper, July 9, 1922, and appears in *Last Reunion I,* 25–26. John McKee was born "four miles east of Croton" in Iowa in 1842. In 1846 his father moved to a farm four miles south of Athens. He writes that "I attended school in Athens in 1860" and "know the ground around there like a book." His father was William McKee (John McKee obituary, *Clark County Courier* [July 18, 1924], in *Last Reunion II.* 89). David and William McKee are listed as farmers in the 1860 census schedules cited in the preceding note. David is the brother of William and uncle of John.

The Squire Harland referred is probably Aaron W. Harlan of Company E, the Croton Guards, Moore's Quartermaster Sergeant. Born in 1811, Harlan was one of the earliest settlers in the area, having been the first steamboat captain to navigate up the Des Moines to Keosauqua in 1837. He continued on with the 21st Missouri, but went on detached service as an undercover agent for the Department of Missouri in Tennessee in the fall of 1862, then was sent to Mississippi the following summer on a similar undertaking for Colonel Moore. Captured and exchanged on both occasions, Harlan decided to settle down and left the regiment for a clerk's position with the Superintendent of Freedmen in Memphis in December of 1863 (Leslie Anders, *The Twenty-First Missouri: From Home Guard to Union Regiment* [Westport, CT: Greenwood Press, 1975], 17–18, 114, 141, 154–155; hereafter cited as *Twenty-First Missouri*). A fixture at reunions of the 21st for years after the war, he recited a poem about the Battle of Athens at one of the gatherings in 1901 (*Martin Green's Boomerang,* 74–75). Aaron Harlan died in 1911 at the age of 100.

5. From a letter David Moore sent to George W. McCrary, incorporated by McCrary into a speech before the Missouri Commandery in 1892, later published as "The Battle of Athens," in *War Papers and Personal Reminiscences 1861–1865, Read Before the Commandery of the State of Missouri, Military Order of the Loyal Legion of the United States* (St. Louis: Becktold & Co., 1892), 171–172; hereafter cited as McCrary.

6. "The Incidents of the Battle." A "Special Correspondence," from Camp Carnegy, Canton, Lewis Co., Mo., August 6, 1861, in the *St. Louis Missouri Democrat,* August 10, 1861 (*Farthest North,* 8; hereafter cited as "Special Correspondence"), states that a messenger left Croton at 8:00 p.m. Both accounts state that Keokuk troops were ready to depart either "after 9 o' clock p.m." ("Special Correspondence") or "soon after 9 o' clock p.m." (*Gate City).* Given the hour and a half that it seems to have taken by train from Keokuk to Croton, it seems unlikely that men in a handcar could have made it in significantly less time, which also allowed for the Keokuk men to be summoned and assembled by 9:00 p.m. Therefore it seems more likely that 8:00 pm. is the *arrival* time in Keokuk and not the departure time from Croton.

This hypothesis is supported by the Rev. G. C. Beaman of Croton who writes that "on the 4th of August, the Sabbath, at four o'clock, P.M., the alarm was given, that fifteen hundred or two thousand 'Secesh' were actually on their way to Athens. Despatches [*sic*] were sent out by Col. Moore…" (G. C. Beaman, 137). If it took the train one and a half hours to make the trip between Croton and Keokuk, it seems likely that it would take men on a handcar at least twice as long.

Hiller may have been the sole messenger, as he implies in his letter (Hiller Letter, 22). The "Special Correspondence" specifies one messenger. The *Keokuk Daily Gate City* says "messengers." It seems unlikely that Moore would have entrusted this mission to only one man, but a handcar could not have accommodated very many messengers.

7. *Clark County Gazette,* August 5, 1886, in Mullenix, *The Battle of Athens,* 155. The Rev. G. C. Beaman mentions that "on the second of August, two messengers from Etna reported to Col. Moore, that four thousand 'Secesh' were near Etna, on their way to attack Athens" (G. C. Beaman, 137). Dixon cites Taylor Commission Records identifying Aristas Sackett, no doubt the above-mentioned father of Sam, as a deputy Home Guard organizer. Ben F. Dixon, *"Farthest North: 1861" The Man Behind the Men Behind the Guns* (San Diego, CA: Don Diego's Libreria, Benjamin Franklin Junior Historical Series, No. 21, 1969), reprinted in Mullenix, *The Battle of Athens,* 144; hereafter cited as *The Man Behind the Men.*

Another version of the story has Mrs. Sackett hiding a letter to Col. Moore in the clothing of her son and placing him and another boy on horses with a sack of corn on each. If they were stopped by the rebels (which they were), they were to say they were taking corn to the Athens mill. The Sackett's lived near Luray, which is about 16 miles from Athens. Considering the challenges of running 16 miles in bare feet, of the two stories, the latter seems more plausible ("Battle of Athens: That Exciting Engagement Graphically Described by H. Scott Howell," *Keokuk Daily Gate City,* December 27, 1895; hereafter cited as Howell).

8. It is unclear which creek this might be. The North Fabius River runs northwest-southeast just west of Memphis. The North Wyaconda runs parallel to it east of Memphis, about halfway to Kahoka. Other accounts locate Green's forces by August 4 on the Fox River running parallel to the North Fabius and North Wyaconda just east of Kahoka, another 14 miles or so east of the North Wyaconda.

Given the location of a few miles east of Memphis, it seems likely that Frederick and Charlotte drove directly into the rear of Green's column just northeast of Etna along the North Wyaconda River, or perhaps along a small creek emptying into it. If Green was indeed attempting to steal a march on Moore, attacking on the 5th instead of the 8th, then it seems probable that Green and Franklin's troops marched (or rode) at least from Etna on the 4th, which placed them in position for the encounter with Boone and Harrison.

9. Charles Frederick Boone, son of Frederick and Charlotte, observed that "Pa later said that by overheating it, he ruined one of the best horses he ever owned—and he owned some good ones in his day." Mrs. Albert Brown, "Civil War's Message to Garcia Changed the Battle of Athens," *Kahoka Gazette Herald,* August 17, 1951, in Mullenix, *The Battle of Athens,* 195–196. This article, which is the source of this

account of Frederick Boone's mission to warn Moore, appeared on the ninetieth anniversary of the battle, in which year Charles Frederick Boone was seventy-seven.

10. Charlotte, daughter of Jabez and Mary Harrison, was born in Virginia in 1841 and lived until 1923. Drucilla survived her. Around 1848, the Harrisons had migrated to northeast Missouri. Shortly thereafter, Mary died. Jabez moved his family to a farm near Luray and, in the autumn of 1849, married Susan Mills, widowed three years earlier when her husband was killed by lightning. Susan had immigrated from Kentucky when she was sixteen. C. F. Boone's account leaves the impression that Charlotte and Frederick were married at the time of their August 4 trip to Memphis and back. However, Charlotte's obituary gives their wedding date as September 2, 1861 (Charlotte Harrison Boone obituary, *Clark County Courier*, May 4, 1923, in *Last Reunion II*, 29). The Kahoka Daughters of Union Veterans Tent is named after Charlotte Harrison Boone.

11. *Twenty-First Missouri*, 28.

12. Hiller Letter, 22; "The Incidents of the Battle." Thirty years later, Moore wrote that the men under the "command of the gallant William W. Belknap," along with men under Sample and John W. Noble, arrived in about two hours from the time of his dispatch being sent. He observed that these reinforcements numbered "upwards of eighty men" (McCrary, 172).

13. *History of Lewis, Clark, Knox, and Scotland Counties, Missouri* (St. Louis,1887; reprint ed. Marceline, MO, 1981), 383; hereafter cited as *History of Lewis*. A *Chicago Tribune* correspondent identified only as "C," wrote that, "about 70 of the Keokuk militia went up to Croton…but would not pass over the river" ("C," "Northeast Missouri, Terrible Condition of Affairs, Correct History of the Athens Fight," *Chicago Tribune*, August 14, 1861; hereafter cited as "C").

Anders quotes the *Chicago Tribune* correspondent's words, "would not pass over the river," and then adds that the Keokuk captains "were afflicted with 'state's rights'" (*Twenty-First Missouri*, 28). While he does not cite his source for the latter, Anders may be quoting the *History of Lewis* (384), which states that once the battle began, not the night before, Belknap and Sample mustered their men but, "good Democratic lawyers as they were, they suddenly became strong respecters of State lines and did not choose to invade a neighboring sovereign State." This alleged motivation of the Keokuk troops for remaining on the Iowa side of the Des Moines is reiterated in a pamphlet on the battle distributed at Athens by the Missouri Department of Natural Resources, Division of State Parks. The contribution of the Iowa men during the battle is discussed below in Chapter 4.

In his 1892 letter, Moore makes no mention of recalcitrance on the part of the Iowa troops or of their commanders. After describing their arrival two hours from the time he sent his messengers to Keokuk, he observes simply that "many who here fired their first shots at an enemy, afterwards joined Iowa regiments and won immortal honor on many great battle fields for the Union and freedom" (McCrary, 172). It is uncharacteristic both of Moore's candor and long memory for him to refer to the "gallant William W. Belknap" (note 12 above; see also note 47 in Chapter 4 below for Moore's positive assessment of the Iowans' performance) if he had regarded Belknap as uncooperative at the time.

D. C. Beaman, Croton Depot Station Agent, orderly sergeant of Captain Farris's company, and no doubt a relative of Rev. G. C. Beaman, wrote in 1905 that, on the morning of the battle "neither (Sample) nor Belknap attempted to get their men in line or march them to the river in order. They were lying promiscuously about the depot, resting after a night's ride from Keokuk, and awaiting word from Colonel Moore, when the fight began much earlier than expected" (D. C. Beaman, 591).

14. "The Incidents of the Battle." "On the 1ˢᵗ of August, thirty-five tons of provisions came up on the cars of the Des Moines Valley R.R., for our army in Athens…Also, there were sent up two hundred stands of U.S. arms, and ammunition in proportion" (G. C. Beaman, 136–137). Guarding the military stores at Croton may have been how the Keokuk militia viewed their responsibilities in the matter.

15. "From John McKee," 25. "Old man Sullivan" is likely William C. Sullivan of Athens, aged 76. For more on the role of both William Sullivan and armaments in the battle, see Chapter 4 below.

16. Ibid.

Notes to Chapter Two

1. David Moore was born in July 3, 1817, in Columbiana County, Ohio. He moved to Wayne County, Ohio, in 1830, where he was apprenticed as a carpenter. In 1846 he served in the Mexican War with the Wooster Guards, of which he was the captain. In 1850, he moved with his wife Diademia and five children to Clark County, Missouri, where he farmed and later opened a general store in Wrightsville. After the war, Moore settled in Canton, Missouri. Diademia died in 1865 and Moore remarried the next year. He served two terms as Canton's mayor, then, in 1870, was elected to the state senate, leaving after four years. David Moore died in St. Louis July 19, 1893 (*Twenty-First Missouri*, 3–7, 257–258, 268; *History of Lewis*, 802–803).

2. Michael Fellman, *Inside War: The Guerrilla Conflict in Missouri During the American Civil War* (New York: Oxford University Press, 1989), 3.

3. Ibid.

4. Ibid., 6–7.

5. Kenneth Doud, *The Good Old Days: Clark County, Missouri* (Athens, MO: Kenneth Doud, 1963), 21; hereafter cited as Doud.

6. Fellman, 6.

7. The Des Moines County Anti-Slavery Society first convened in Burlington, in southeast Iowa, on March 27, 1844. A year later a fugitive slave from Missouri was freed by a United States Commissioner in Burlington and then sent to Canada by local residents—actions endorsed by the Iowa Governor (Philip D. Jordan, *Catfish Bend—River Town and County Seat* [Burlington, IA: Mississippi Valley Publishers, Craftsman Press, Inc., 1983], 115–117). A factor in Martin Green's planned invasion of Iowa was the bitterness slaveholders of northeast Missouri felt toward Iowans who generally failed to facilitate the return of runaway slaves. In 1860, Hiram Spruance, 10-year-old son of an Athens merchant, was suspected of telling slaves who were bringing grain to the Athens mill that they could cross the Des Moines River to

Iowa and gain their freedom (Fulton, 83).

8. Allan Nevins, *The Emergence of Lincoln,* vol. 1, *Douglas, Buchanan, and Party Chaos 1857–1859* (New York: Charles Scribner's Sons, 1950), 382.

9. Ibid., 364.

10. James McPherson, *Battle Cry of Freedom: The Civil War Era* (New York: Oxford University Press, 1988), 213–216.

11. Fellman, 269.

12. Ibid., 5. Situated mainly in a band across the north-central section of the state, with tobacco planters in the east, the "compromising nature" of the west-central hemp growers of Little Dixie was a function of economics. While their market for hemp was in the deeper southern states where it was used for bagging and binding cotton, the federal tariff on hemp which protected their market also alienated them from the "free trade" politics of their southern buyers.

13. Both Leslie Anders and Ben Dixon propose rather rapid conversions for Moore from Northern Democratic "Hickory" to Republican following Lincoln's election. Yet Anders concedes that there is virtually no evidence for "landmarks" of this putative journey. Barring evidence to the contrary, it is more probable that Moore did not precipitously abandon his Democratic compromising inclinations.

14. Allan Nevins, *The Emergence of Lincoln,* vol. 2, *Prologue to Civil War 1859–1861* (New York: Charles Scribner's Sons, 1950), 390–391.

15. Ibid., 408–409; McPherson, *Battle Cry of Freedom,* 256.

16. Thomas L. Snead. *The Fight For Missouri, From the Election of Lincoln to the Death of Lyon* (New York: Charles Scribner's Sons, 1886), 26.

17. Jackson was elected by a very small margin, the election itself being a cipher of most Missourians' desire to take the middle ground. In his gubernatorial campaign, Jackson dragged his feet in endorsing either Douglas or Breckinridge. If he endorsed Douglas, pro-slavery "Ultras" would desert him. If he endorsed Breckinridge, Democratic moderates would withdraw support. When Jackson finally endorsed Douglas, the Ultras put together an alternative gubernatorial ticket. Conservative Democrats, suspicious of his sincerity, backed Sample Orr on the Constitutional Union ticket. The Ultras' candidate, Hancock Jackson, ran a distant fourth, ahead only of the Republican nominee, James Gardenhire. Steven Rowan, trans., *Germans For a Free Missouri: Selections From the St. Louis Radical Press, 1857–1862,* Introduction and commentary by James Neal Primm (Columbia, MO: University of Missouri Press, 1983), 12–13; hereafter cited as Rowan.

18. Snead 25, 53.

19. Fellman, 5.

20. Snead, 66. The Germans of St. Louis were fiercely loyal to the Union. The February 4, 1861, *Anzeiger des Westens,* a St. Louis German newspaper, exhorted its readers never to "permit the slander to sully the pages of the history of this state: [that] *Missouri, too, betrayed its mother, the Union!"* (*Anzeiger des Westens,* February 4, 1861, in Rowan, 165). Many of these immigrants were "Forty-eighters," exiled revolutionaries from the failed German revolution of 1848. As their radical politics fueled Unconditional Unionism and abolitionism, these, combined with their ethnicity and foreign speech, made them objects of intense hatred of pro-secession

Missourians.

21. David C. Hinze and Karen Farnham, *The Battle of Carthage: Border War in Southwest Missouri, July 5, 1861* (Campbell, CA: Savas Publishing Company, 1997), 9; hereafter cited as Hinze.

22. Nevins, *Prologue to Civil War*, 392–393.

23. Ibid., 409. The Corwin Amendment, known as the "Ghost Amendment," has never been rescinded by Congress.

24. McPherson, *Battle Cry of Freedom*, 256–257.

25. Blair's brother, Montgomery, was Lincoln's Postmaster General.

26. Snead, 104–105, 109–110; Rowan, 13;

27. Snead, 125–126. Lyon, with a small contingent of troops from Kansas, was ordered to St. Louis to help defend the arsenal by President Buchanan and Gen. Winfield Scott on February 7—the day before the Confederacy was founded in Montgomery. While Nathaniel Lyon commanded the men or "garrison," of the St. Louis Arsenal, Brevet Major Peter V. Hagner, Lyon's superior, commanded the arsenal itself. Primm describes Hagner as "a less fervent Union man" than Lyon (Rowan, 166, note). Lyon struggled with Hagner in the next couple of months for control of the arsenal. The latter was finally removed to Fort Leavenworth, Kansas, on April 21, 1861, allowing Lyon to consolidate his authority.

28. An early handwritten copy of the document, possibly the original, listing the names of the original signers is reproduced in the opening pages of *Last Reunion, I*. The lack of punctuation in this excerpt reproduces that in the facsimile. This copy of the Highland School document used by the author includes a title, "Enrollment of Home Guards, March 1861, Highland School House." The piece of paper with this inscription appears to have become detached from the document and is reproduced at the bottom of one page. It seems likely that if this "title" had been part of the original document, then the date in March would have been included as well. This is supposition, but the wording seems to suggest that it is a later identification of the document. In fact, only this title connects the document with the Highland School in March 1861. The document is obviously a loyalty oath, and it has 161 names affixed to it. But the names are not signatures, because they are all written by one hand. They were obviously copied from another document or documents. Cross checking the names with the Hawkins Taylor roster, all of these who were later mustered into the 1st or 2nd Northeast Missouri Home Guard took their oaths in either Sweet Home or Alexandria. There is no evidence that the men whose names are attached to the document understood themselves as forming a home guard militia company. There is no mention of such in the oath, no indication of a vote for officers, or a designation of anyone as such—although some of the signers would become Home Guard recruiters in their own right, then serve under Moore once he was elected colonel. William Bishop, who did sign the document, would later be authorized by Lyon at St. Louis to enlist loyal men in northeast Missouri.

29. Snead, 150–151; Hinze, 26–27.

30. Snead, 151–152.

31. Ibid., 137, 157. The First Regiment of Missouri Volunteers, commanded by Frank Blair, was composed mostly of native-born Missourians and Irish immigrants.

The other three were made up of German immigrants. Lyon mustered in another six regiments in May, five of which became known as the United States Reserve Corps or Home Guard (Snead, 165–166).

32. Snead, 167–169.

33. This according to witness William T. Sherman (Rowan, 18). Both Sherman and Ulysses S. Grant were spectators in the crowd.

34 Snead, 173.

35. Harney's removal may have been precipitated by his meeting with Sterling Price in St. Louis on May 20. The two cut a one-sided deal—the Price-Harney Agreement—in which Harney, representing the federal government, acknowledged the role already accorded to Price by Jackson and the state legislature, that of major general in command of the Missouri State Guard. As such, Price agreed to keep order in Missouri and Harney promised not to make "military movements, which might…create excitement and jealousies." Jackson used this time to continue upgrading the Missouri militia (Hinze, 31–32).

36. McPherson, *Battle Cry of Freedom*, 274.

37. Ibid., 274–275.

38. Letter from C. L. Becker, *Keokuk Daily Gate City*, March 20, 1900.

39. Ibid. According to Becker:

> It was understood by nearly everybody that if he [Moore] had been elected captain of the Alexandria company, he would have with them gone into the confederate army, as well as his three sons, who afterwards fought in several battles on the opposite side from him. In fact, it was understood between him and his sons that they were to join the confederacy, although afterward denied.

These aspersions followed Moore throughout the war, into his postwar political career, and persist into the present. While it is true Moore's sons did fight for the other side, a fact which may have elicited a bit of extra effort for the Union on the part of the father, it is hard to imagine such a loyal soldier for the North choosing that path out of pique that he was not chosen to lead an apparently pro-secessionist militia, especially after Fort Sumter. Becker's article was reworked later as "Alexandria During the War," *Kahoka Gazette Herald*, August 18, 1911 (in *Last Reunion, I, 119*). There "Tuter" Johnson's nickname is given as "Puter." Both pieces show a strong southern partisanship, and there is no evidence apart from Becker's assertions that Moore originally intended to fight for the South.

40. From a newspaper article written by Timothy W. Holman, co-author with Nehemiah D. Starr of *The 21ˢᵗ Missouri Regiment, Infantry Veteran Volunteers* (Fort Madison, IA: Roberts & Roberts Printers, 1899), in 1900 and quoted by Ben Dixon in *The Man Behind the Men*, 132. This is supported in *History of Lewis* (378): "About the 20ᵗʰ of May, Col. Moore…received authority from Gen. Nathaniel Lyon…to recruit a company of men for Federal service."

Dixon speculates that Holman "had perhaps seen both the commission and the authority." According to Dixon, "other witnesses have confirmed Holman's statement by the testimony that Moore was, among all the leaders of home guard outfits raised before the Battle of Athens, the only one who actually held a commission," but

Dixon does not name the witnesses (*The Man Behind the Men,* 132).

41. Starr and Holman, *The 21ˢᵗ Missouri Regiment,* 6. Holman adds a parenthesis: "The above is a verbatim copy.—T. W. H." Starr and Holman's version is that quoted above because it seems likely that they were referring to an actual handbill or a transcript with equal primacy. Their spacing is also replicated above. Almost the same version appeared twelve years earlier in *History of Lewis,* 379. However, the latter version reads, "this county" instead of "the county," does not have a comma after "county," and does not have the same spacing.

42. *History of Lewis,* 379. Dixon writes that "In a rabid Secession community he was a rabid Unionist. The Knights of the Golden Circle had pinned a nightly notice for him to pull up stakes, on his front door… According to local tradition" Moore, "with his jack-knife…affixed a copy of his poster to the door of the rebel neighbor he suspected of having posted him!" (*Martin Green's Boomerang,* 50–51). In another place Dixon describes Moore's nocturnal visitors as members of the "Southern Legion" (*The Man Behind the Men,* 105).

43. Ben F. Dixon, "Battle on the Border: Athens, Missouri, August 5, 1861," *Annals of Iowa* 3ʳᵈ Series, 36 (Summer 1961): 4; hereafter cited as "Battle on the Border." Wrightsville was known as Union from then on. The Clark County village of Wrightsville/Union no longer exists.

44. Dixon, "The Battle of Athens: Pioneer Greens," (July 25, 1941), in Mullenix, *The Battle of Athens,* 177; hereafter cited as "Pioneer Greens." The senator was the brother of Martin Green. They were transplanted Virginians, arriving in Lewis County, Missouri, in 1836. They purchased a saw and grist mill on the Wyaconda River six miles northwest of Canton (around 30 miles south of Athens). There they farmed and operated the mill. Martin managed the latter while James studied law and was admitted to the bar. Martin became a county court judge and went on to become his county's assemblyman. James became a U.S. congressman in 1846. In 1855, while again a congressman, he was chosen by the Missouri legislature to finish the term in the U.S. Senate of David R. Atchison, who had resigned, subsequently gaining notoriety for leading Missouri "border ruffians" into Kansas. A pro-Secessionist, James Green was perhaps too radical for his constituency, and was not returned to the Senate in 1860. He pursued his Secessionist cause in the months following in northeast Missouri ("Pioneer Greens," 177).

According to *History of Lewis* (378), "A large number of Union men, strenuous anti-Secessionists, wanted the trouble settled without bloodshed. Another portion were wavering and irresolute, half-hearted and vacillating. All the while the Secessionists were bold and aggressive."

Not all Unionists failed to respond aggressively, however. According to Dixon, after Green's "kicked out like a dog" speech of April 29, "John Glover of Knox County walked up to" Green "and said: 'Senator, I am a Black Republican. How about trying to kick me out of the State?'" Dixon recounts in the same article that on June 12 a farmer wrote the editor of the *Missouri Democrat* urging "suspension from a piece of cross timber for Senator Green" ("Pioneer Greens," 177).

45. One should not infer from this a commitment on Moore's part to the federal program of suppressing the rebellion in other southern states.

46. Snead, 200.

47. *The Man Behind the Men,* 136, 139.

48. National Archives. Records of the Adjutant General's Office 1780's-1917. Record Group 94. 94.11 Other AGO Records 1861–74. Records of the commission on claims of officers and men in Departments of the West and the Missouri (Hawkins Taylor Commission), 1:138; hereafter cited as Hawkins Taylor Commission, see appendix. Anders places the number in Moore's company at 54 (*Twenty-First Missouri,* 12). Bishop's swearing in of Moore is not inconsistent with the tradition of Moore having received a commission "about the 20th of May." Moore may well have been commissioned to raise a company of Home Guards and to serve as their captain. Bishop carried a broader commission to swear in any and all in northeast Missouri whom he deemed loyal to the United States. Even if the tradition of Moore's commissioning was false, the fact would remain that Moore raised a company of 55 men by June 14 and that they took the oath of allegiance to the United States on the 15th, from which we might reasonably conclude that Moore first took action more or less around the time in May we have already suggested.

Notes to Chapter Three

1. *History of Lewis,* 379. William Jackson, organizer of the Kahoka Home Guards, was the great-great grandfather of the author. Motely, here, is usually given as Mattley. The Hawkins Taylor Commission identifies William McKee as a private. The author of *History of Lewis* may have misidentified David McKee as William. The Hawkins Taylor Commission lists Simon Pearce as a corporal, contains two Pierces, both privates, and does not mention a Story, a Fulton, or a Murrow. According to Dixon ("Battle on the Border," 8), Elias V. Wilson was chosen to command a force of 500 men at Edina, which included companies under Joseph Story, Nicholas Murrow and others. This regiment of Home Guards was dispersed by Green at Troublesome Creek (see note 34 below).

2. Hawkins Taylor Commission.

3. "C."

4. Ibid.

5. *Twenty-First Missouri,* 17.

6. *The Man Behind the Men,* 140. In the days following the July 4 election, Moore's opponents spread their dissension with talk of how the colonel's loyalties might be suspect in as much as his wife was said to favor secession and two of his sons had gone off to join the other side. And hadn't Moore sought rank in a Secessionist militia outfit in Alexandria? (*Twenty-First Missouri,* 23).

7. *Twenty-First Missouri,* 17.

8. "C."

9. The account of this day comes both from *Twenty-First Missouri* (16–17) and from a newspaper article by J. W. Murphy, who was present, but was only four years old at the time. Murphy spoke on September 19, 1928, at the Old Settler's Meeting, Kahoka, Missouri ("Address by J. W. Murphy at Old Settler's Meeting," *Kahoka*

Gazette-Herald, September 28, 1928, in *Last Reunion, I,* 27–31; hereafter cited as "Address by J. W. Murphy"). He claims to have sensed not only jubilation but feelings of "doubt and dismay that had taken hold on the minds of the people present." He writes that "it was a critical time in the history of the state…good citizens were anxious and uneasy." Both Anders and Murphy concur that the drilling occurred in the morning. Murphy adds that it occurred on the south half of the square, a detail with the ring of authenticity. Both agree that Hackney was the drill master. Both agree that music opened the afternoon. Murphy mentions "Showalter's band" and Anders the Roseberry drum and bugle corps. Both specify that speeches occurred next. Murphy's paper is primarily about young Resor's speech, which he places before those of the Home Guard officers. Anders does not mention Resor's speech. Murphy makes no mention of the election of field officers.

The author has followed Murphy's chronology, suspecting that young Resor may well have been a "draw" on the program and that, if he orated for two hours, then he may well have gone first or have been deferred to by the older men. Of course, the chronology may well have been otherwise. In a 1913 article, Murphy wrote that Resor was his uncle ("Luray and Editor Murphy," 50–51).

10. Anders states that the delegation was sent around July 10 and that Spellman returned from St. Louis on July 17, 1861, having gotten Bishop to arrange for 250 rifles and other materiel to be shipped to Croton (*Twenty-First Missouri,* 23). Dixon contends, perhaps based on information from Bishop's papers, these arms were requisitioned from the St. Louis Arsenal and arrived in Alexandria on July 15, 1861 (*The Man Behind the Men,* 140). These were most likely .69 caliber flintlocks such as the US Model 1816, altered to percussion, as this type represented the majority of shoulder arms stored at the St, Louis Arsenal prior to the Civil War (United States War Department, *The War of the Rebellion: A Compilation of the Official Records of the Union and Confederate Armies,* 70 vols. in 128 [Washington, D. C. 1880–1901], Series 3, vol. 1:1; hereafter cited as *O. R.*)

In a letter of which Anders may have been unaware, David McKee recalls a different date of departure. He writes that "about the 20th same month (July), was appointed one of a committee of three to proceed to St. Louis for arms and Subsistence." McKee describes how he recruited for Bishop's cavalry, authorized by Lyon, and became an officer (Letter from David McKee to James B. Fry, Provost Marshall Genl., December 7, 1863, St. Louis, Missouri, in *Last Reunion, II,* 67–68). McKee became Major of the 7th Missouri Cavalry when Bishop's Blackhawk Cavalry was consolidated with other independent cavalry companies on February 27, 1863. He resigned his commission that August due to failing health. McKee died in Kahoka of cancer in 1896 ("Major David McKee At Rest," *Clark County Courier,* March 18, 1896, in *Last Reunion, II,* 69). William McKee became a Captain in this regiment. For further background on the McKees, see Chapter 1 above.

11. In 1900, a State Guard veteran described Martin Green's army as "more of a flocking together than an organized army of men." It was basically an undisciplined mob:

A more motley aggregation of white men and boys than accompanied General Green

> on that occasion was probably never collected together on this earth. They ranged in age probably from twelve to seventy-five or eighty years old. The mixture of apparel and appearance was something wonderful to behold. Some were barefooted, many in their shirt sleeves only, and a few without headgear of any kind. Nearly all had horses, but many had no saddles, and some did not even have bridles, but guided their horses with plain rope halters.

Letter from I. M. Walters, *Keokuk Daily Gate City,* March 23, 1900; hereafter cited as I. M. Walters.

Martin Green's involvement with the Missouri State Guard came about as follows: On the same day that the Home Guard was consolidating in Kahoka, July 4, 1861, a scuffle on the dock at Canton, Missouri (a little less than thirty-five miles southeast on the Mississippi River), between northern and southern sympathizers led to blows between Captain John Howell of the Canton Home Guard and one Charles Soward, son of Richard Soward, proprietor of the Soward House in Canton. There had long been ill feeling between the older Soward and Howell, and within a few hours of the incident on the dock, Richard Soward had killed Howell with a double barreled shotgun. Soward was arrested, and the Home Guard's weapons had to be locked up to prevent further bloodshed. That night Colonel H. M. Woodyard rowed a skiff to Quincy, Illinois, where he requested a battalion of troops be sent to Canton to restore order. The next morning, Colonel John M. Palmer and the 14th Illinois Volunteers arrived from Qunicy and occupied the town. Senator James Green escaped to Monticello, but was subsequently captured and paroled. Martin Green, approaching Canton that morning and "carrying on his arm a basket of cherries for a friend in town," learned of the presence of Unionist troops and turned around. He headed directly for the Secessionist camp at Horseshoe Bend, where, within a few days he was elected colonel of the regiment forming there (*History of Lewis,* 76–81).

12. Anders *Twenty-First Missouri,* 23–24; *Martin Green's Boomerang,* 52; "Battle on the Border," 7.

13. *Twenty-First Missouri,* 23. Anders does not cite his source for this quotation. The implication is that this was taken from an original document and that Moore was a terrible speller.

14. This account of the Kahoka period of the 1st Northeast Missouri Home Guard is drawn from *Twenty-First Missouri,* 23–24, "C," and *History of Lewis,* 380–381. The last source gives the Warsaw Greys' number as twenty; Anders simply says that the Greys, "a small company of infantry," came; and "C," the *Chicago Tribune* correspondent, gives their number as fifty. The author of *History of Lewis* puts in quotation marks that the Greys came "'to the help of the Lord against the mighty'" (380). It is unclear whether this is that author's spontaneous embroidering with scripture, or whether he is quoting a contemporary source.

A piece entitled "Affairs in Clark County," signed "Justicia," which appeared in the *St. Louis Tri-Weekly Missouri Republican,* on August 16, 1861, gives a pro-State Guard perspective on the events leading up to the Battle of Athens, beginning with July 21, 1861, and provides an interesting parallel to "C's" account of more or less the same period. Justicia's account confirms that Moore was joined at "Cahokia" by "a company from Illinois and one from Iowa." ("Justicia," "Affairs in Clark County," *St. Louis Tri-Weekly Missouri Republican,* August 16, 1861, in *Farthest North,* 31; hereafter cited as "Justicia").

15. "From John McKee," 25.

16. "Justicia," 31.

17. *Twenty-First Missouri,* 24. The statement is ascribed here to "Farris," presumably Joseph T. Farris, Captain, Co. E., 1st Northeast Missouri Home Guard. Farris, formerly a Des Moines riverboat pilot and the first man to run a steamboat up the Des Moines as far as Ft. Dodge, Iowa, was another who eventually ran afoul of Moore. He followed Moore into Federal service in the 21st Missouri. In August 1862 fifteen men of his company mutinied. At least part of the motivation seemed to be their belief that they were to, or wanted only to, serve in northeast Missouri. In December of that year Farris also refused an order and was arrested. Farris resigned from the 21st but went on to be a captain in Iowa's Southern Border Brigade in early 1863. In 1864 he became Captain in the 60th U.S.C.T (*Twenty-First Missouri,* 90; 117–118). Farris lived until 1924 (Joe Farris obituary, *Clark County Courier,* February 20, 1924, in *Last Reunion II,* 96).

18. *History of Lewis,* 380.

19. *Martin Green's Boomerang,* 61. Dixon states that this information came from Washburn's company order book, but he does not say where or when he transcribed it. While Washburn places the Etna skirmish on July 21, 1861, the author of *History of Lewis* (380) dates it on July 22. Dixon's source in *Martin Green's Boomerang* identifies Washburn as Captain of Company H. The Hawkins Taylor Commission says Washburn led Company I.

20. *Martin Green's Boomerang,* 61; Anders, *Twenty-First Missouri,* 24–25; Cyrus Bussey, "The Battle of Athens, Missouri," *Annals of Iowa* 3rd Series, 5 (July 1901): 82; hereafter cited as Bussey. It is presumably the skirmish at Conkle's farm to which Justicia refers when he reports that "the next morning (Monday, 22), in the vicinity of Chambersburg, a detachment forty strong, attacked a body of State troops numbering the same." The distance from Luray in a straight line north to Chambersburg was approximately eight miles. It can be easily seen how one writer might place the skirmish as "north of Luray," as Anders does, and another "in the vicinity of Chambersburg," as Justicia does. Washburn wrote simply, "Marched back to Luray and marched to Conkel's farm—there had a skirmish" (*Martin Green's Boomerang,* 61). The location of Nick Conkle's farm is given by Anders as being in the bottoms of the Little Fox River. Justicia continues by writing that "the States Rights men were not expecting an attack, and could only muster fifteen or sixteen men to repel it. These, however, were enough, and after about five minutes fighting, the protectors retreated, with the loss of three killed and one wounded, according to their own confession, while not one of the State forces was hurt" ("Justicia," 31–32; it is not clear just which side is being identified here as "the protectors").

21. *Twenty-First Missouri,* 25. Doud (22) observes that since "there were far more" southern sympathizers "in the Athens vicinity than pro-Unionists, they, of course, suffered the most." He names W. H. Spurgeon and one Stafford, both of whom operated drygoods stores, George Gray, who operated a packing plant, B. Rebo, a groceryman, Judge Baker, and Jane Gray, as persons whose businesses or homes were

appropriated for use by the Home Guard. However, Doud notes that Joe Benning, "an avowed southerner," was not disturbed.

22. This incident was recalled by George Gray's daughter, Hannah, 28 years old at the time (Margarette Dreyer Cheney, Unpublished Gray Family genealogy, 1953, courtesy of Roger Boyd, Battle of Athens State Historic Site; hereafter tied as Cheney).

23. "Justicia," 32. Similar allegations were made against Green's State Guard by "C," the *Chicago Tribune* correspondent (see the excerpt above at the beginning of this chapter).

24. *Twenty-First Missouri,* 25. According to the 1860 Federal Slave Schedule for Missouri, Sarah Gray, widow of Athens pioneer Isaac Gray, owned two female slaves, no mention of a male. Barney may have been a free black, may have been acquired after 1860, or may simply have been left off the census. William Gray, son of Isaac and Sarah, married Jane Phillips in about 1853, when she was 16. He built a small frame house for them next to his father's two story log house on the southeast edge of Athens near the Des Moines River. William died sometime in the next seven years, and Jane Gray, age 23, was counted as a member of her mother-in-law's household on the 1860 U.S. Census (Isaac had died in 1857). Sarah Gray died in March 1861, leaving 24 year-old Jane in charge of the Isaac Gray farm. It's not known whether ownership of the slaves was passed from Sarah to Jane, but it must have appeared so. In 1868 Jane married her late husband's cousin, George W. Gray, son of George Gray, Isaac's brother. They eventually had two children (Cheney). At the turn of the century, she was known in the community as Aunt Jane Gray, famous for her maple syrup (Boyd, 40). Kenneth Doud, who later lived in the Jane Gray house, recalled that Jane had three negro slaves, Tom and Violet and their daughter Betty (or Betsy) ("As I Recollect: The Reminiscences of Kenneth I. Doud, as Told to His Son Richard in 1972," unpublished manuscript, courtesy of Roger Boyd, Battle of Athens State Historic Site).

25. *Twenty-First Missouri,* 25–26.

26. Joseph and Susan Benning, first cousins, moved to Missouri from near Athens, Kentucky, in 1834. Joseph's uncles, Isaac and George Gray, followed a year later, along with another uncle and his daughter. The Bennings and Grays laid out the town of Athens, Missouri. Joseph Benning bought into fellow-Kentuckian Arthur Thome's grist, saw, and carding mill along the river, and established a hog-slaughtering operation not far from it. When the rampaging river wrecked Thome's mill and his son-in-law did the same to his finances, Thome sold his home to Benning to pay his debts. Built by Thome in 1843 and architecturally reminiscent of the larger house that his family left behind in Kentucky, it was situated up the hill from the mill, affording residents a fine view of the Des Moines and Iowa beyond.

It is likely that the Thomes and Bennings did not see eye-to-eye politically. Thome had freed his slaves in Kentucky, reputedly influenced by his son who was converted to abolitionism in his northern boarding school. When the Kentucky legislature passed a statute criminalizing manumission, the Thomes left the state. Susan Benning was an outspoken Confederate partisan and when Moore's Home Guard occupied Athens, her husband confined her to the house lest she get them into trouble. Moore was undoubtedly aware of their politics and would have considered any "peace" meeting at the Bennings suspect. Lucretia S. Craw, "Athens and the Southerns," in *Last Reunion, II,* 58–60; hereafter cited as Craw; Dixon, "They Fought in the Battle of Athens," in Mullenix, *The Battle of Athens,* 207.

27. *History of Lewis,* 381–382. Captain Baker is identified as one of the leaders of the delegation in this account. Apparently he was one of the Athenians Moore considered Secessionist since his house was occupied. Green's artillery would be placed near his house during the battle.

28. Ibid., 381. This source states that "Moore allowed his men to return to their homes to cultivate their crops and to provide for their families. Although he could not hold them for a moment against their will, they always asked for a furlough and none departed without leave and usually returned on time. They took 'turns' in going home and not more than half were absent at one time, the other half being kept on duty for emergencies" (380). In an introductory letter of June 6, 1861, preceding one from Lyon to Bishop dated June 10, 1861, authorizing Bishop to raise Home Guards in northeast Missouri, Major H. A. Conant wrote to Bishop stipulating that the "enlisted men…keep up a thorough organization for discipline & drill *at the same time to attend to their usual vocations* (*The Man Behind the Men,* 138; italics added). Obviously this order was given earlier. One would expect that it would be enforced relative to the current possibility of attack.

29. "C."

30. On the other hand, consider that the establishment of the Athens encampment would have been Moore's first opportunity to arm his troops with the 250 muskets that had been sent from St. Louis. Perhaps if Moore had had more weapons to distribute he would have kept more of his soldiers in camp. Naturally those receiving the weapons would have devoted time to familiarizing themselves with the equipment. Years later, the daughter of a farmer who had brought his grain to the Athens mill the first weekend in August 1861, recalled seeing Home Guard soldiers engaged in target practice in the hollow above the mill (Roger Boyd, telephone interviews, August 2007).

31. *History of Lewis* records that "immediately after" the failure of the meeting at Bennings, "Col. Green was earnestly solicited by certain citizens in and about Athens, who were in sympathy with the cause of secession to come to that point and drive Col. Moore and his forces away or capture them, stating that the Union soldiers were destroying their property, etc." The author notes that "while Col. Green was willing to comply with their request, Lieut.-Col. Joseph C. Porter and Maj. Benjamin W. Shacklett, both objected to it." Nevertheless, "about the 1st of August Green moved from his camp at Edina to attack the Federal camp at Athens" (382).

32. *Martin Green's Boomerang,* 68–69.

33. It is possible that this document was also used to restate the specific message of the delegation.

34. *Twenty-First Missouri,* 26; *Martin Green's Boomerang,* 53.

35. "Expedition of Capt. Sample's Company," *Keokuk Daily Gate City,* August 5, 1861. This account complements and more or less corroborates that of the *Chicago Tribune* correspondent.

36. Richard S. Shue, *Morning at Willoughby Run: July 1, 1863* (Gettysburg, PA: Thomas Publications, 1995), 127. The words are those of Corporal Robert Beecham, 2nd Wisconsin, concerning the charge of the Iron Brigade into Herbst's woods at Gettysburg on the morning of July 1, 1863.

37. G. C. Beaman, 136–137.

38. *Twenty-First Missouri,* 11–12, 27; Bussey, 82–83.

39. After leaving 135 rifles with Captain James Best and Lieutenant William Harle, 40 rifles with D. K. Turk, and 60 rifles with Joseph Bayless at Croton, Bussey dropped off 100 rifles with Captain Oliver H. P. Scott in Farmington. He traveled on to Summit (present day Mount Zion), Iowa, where he left 200 guns for Captain Mayne and for Henry C. Caldwell of Keosauqua. From there he traveled to Ottumwa and hauled the remaining weapons overland to Bloomington, where they were distributed to Captain Henry H. Trimble and other militia leaders (Bussey, 84–85). The reference to "Springfield muskets" comes from Anders (*Twenty-First Missouri,* 27), whose source for this information is not known. Bussey himself does not specify the make or model of the arms. For further discussion on the type of arms Bussey might have distributed, see note 61 in Chapter 4.

40. "When I reported at camp that night old man Sullivan told me to get my old double barrel shot gun…fortunately some muskets had arrived from Keokuk and I was given one of those." ("From John McKee," 25).

41. *History of Lewis,* 379. Moore's words in this excerpt echo those to Bishop in a letter of June 6, 1861, from Major H. A. Conant. This was an authorization from Nathaniel Lyon for Bishop to muster Home Guard units in northeast Missouri. Conant wrote, that General Lyon "is at this time unable to promise you any arms but you must arm yourselves with the indiscriminate arms in the hands of your people until such time as you can be better provided." *The Man Behind the Men,* 138.

42. *Twenty-First Missouri,* 15. The insertion of "good" was presumably done by Anders. Further evidence of the paucity of arms available to average citizens in this area is found in a Keokuk newspaper account two days after the battle which reports that Union men were hurrying to Croton from various locales and that "they came with just such arms as they could pick up, and some had only hatchets, big knives, and clubs" ("The Battle at Athens," *Keokuk Daily Gate City,* August 7, 1861). As word of Martin Green's threatened invasion of Iowa spread north throughout the anti-slavery communities of southeastern Iowa, personal firearms and hunting weapons were requisitioned from far and wide to arm ad hoc militia groups. See O. A. Garretson, "The Battle of Athens," *Palimpsest* 8 (April 1927): 140–141.

43. McCrary, 172.

Notes to Chapter Four

1. "From John McKee," 25.

2. My sources for the location of homes and businesses in Athens are the findings of Roger Boyd's archaeological study of 1986, plus more recent discoveries, upon which Matt Kantola's map of the town (page 57) is based, and the descriptions of the

town in Doud, 31ff. In 1861 Athens, Missouri, was a thriving market town of 800 to 1000 inhabitants. Unfortunately, the battle marked the beginning of its decline. Many of the businesses on both sides of the river's edge were swept away in a flood in 1866, but in other respects, Athens seemed to be recovering from the devastation of the war. Then in the 1880s, the town suffered an economic blow from which it would not recover. Politics and lingering resentments from the war determined that the Chicago, Santa Fe & California Railroad (today known as the BNSF Railway) that was to be built through northern Missouri to connect Chicago and Kansas City would go through the new town of Revere, bypassing Athens. Gradually, the people and their buildings (at least those not built of brick) moved to Kahoka or Revere. At the turn of the century Athens was little more than a village. By the 1930s, it had become a ghost town, with only a handful of residents (Boyd, 105–120).

3. Boyd, 19. Boyd's archaeological study of this area led him to conclude that the Benning slaughterhouse and Gray packing house were probably one and the same (Boyd, 127).

4. "Soon after daylight, a number of Keokuk men were over at Athens for breakfast…" ("The Incidents of the Battle"). The "Special Correspondence from Camp Carnegy," also observes that Keokuk men were in camp on the morning of the 5th, but does not specify that they were having breakfast ("Special Correspondence," 8). John Noble wrote, in 1900, that while watching the Missouri shore from the maple grove below Croton with the men of the Keokuk Rifles, he and some of his comrades noticed the Jane Gray house across the river, and supposed that they might be able to cross over and ask for some coffee from the occupants. Noble was not attached to any organized militia, but he and some others in his situation elected Israel Anderson their captain. (Letter from John Noble, *Keokuk Daily Gate City*, January 28, 1900; hereafter cited as John Noble). Anderson would later become captain of Company C, 3rd Iowa Cavalry, with Noble as his First Lieutenant. Eventually, Noble would rise to command of the 3rd Iowa Cavalry and be brevetted a Brigadier General. Another source identifies the hungry Iowans as Farmington militiamen (see note 32 below).

5. *Twenty-First Missouri*, 28; "From John McKee," 25. John Hiller, in a letter to his brother that day, writes that "a little after daylight this morning the picket guard rushed in reporting the rapid advance of a large force" (Hiller Letter, 22). In his transcription, Dixon omits the word "rapid" (*Martin Green's Boomerang*, 70).

6. "From John McKee," 25. McKee writes that "Captain Payn of St. Francisville took command." McKee mentions that his father, William McKee, had taken command of their company after Hull's defection in Kahoka. If so, this must have been temporary, as McKee is not identified in the Hawkins Taylor Commission documents as a captain. Payne, mustered by Bishop on June 10, is listed as Captain of Company N.

Payne's patrol was probably very close to, if not actually bestriding, Baker Street, likely named for former County Judge William Baker. If they mounted in their camp, say in the middle of the block across from the school bordered by Elm and Turner Streets, they would have ridden only some 280 yards. Baker's house was among those in Athens occupied by the Home Guard (*Twenty-First Missouri*, 25). A Captain Baker is identified as one of the leaders of the peace delegation meeting held at

Joseph Benning's house. It is assumed here that Judge William Baker and Captain Baker are one and the same. John Hiller records later in his letter that Baker was with the State Guard at Athens and was taken prisoner that day (Hiller Letter, 24). Dr. Thomas H. Harlan, assumably pro-secession, had been captured "while attempting to flee," when Moore first entered Athens ("Skirmishing in Clark County, Mo.," *The Valley Whig,* July 29, 1861).

7. "From John McKee," 25. McKee mentions only one gun. Other sources, as will be seen below, record that Captain James Kneisley's battery consisted of two or three cannon. It was not general practice for infantry commanders to have their artillery precede them. In the event of an engagement with the enemy, these guns would be useless as the infantrymen charged around and in front of them. If a successful charge was made against them without infantry support, they would be overrun and captured.

8. Ibid. *History of Lewis* (383) corroborates McKee's account: "About sunrise Green's advance guard attacked and drove in Moore's mounted pickets under Capt. William McKee and Dr. Oliver B. Payne." This account cites an actual attack by the State Guard as the reason for Payne's pickets returning to their lines, which John McKee does not, and therefore gives a more significant role to Payne's men than McKee does: "The Federals resisted long enough to give a thorough alarm and enable Moore to get his men into line." Neither McKee nor the *History of Lewis* mention, as Anders does, forward pickets under Lt. Harle.

9. McCrary, 172.

10. Moore gives the precise number as 333 (McCrary, 172). In line were the companies of Captains Best, Jackson, Roseberry, Washburn, Small, Mattley, Hackney, and Lt. Harle (Leslie Anders, "'Farthest North': The Historian and the Battle of Athens," *Missouri Historical Review* 69 [January 1975]: 159; hereafter cited as "Historian and the Battle"). Newspaper accounts in the days following the battle are in general agreement as to the numbers engaged on each side. The number of Home Guard is given as 300, 350, 400, or 400–500; the number of State Guard is given as 500, 800, 1,000–1,200, 1,400–1,500, 1,500, 1,800, or 2,000 (*Farthest North,* 2–36). Of Moore's initial four hundred or so, about thirty-five had been sent across to Croton under the command of Captain Joe Farris of the Croton Guards. There they guarded both prisoners (probably suspected or actual Secessionists Moore had rooted out of Athens), and the 35 tons of arms and materiel (*History of Lewis,* 384; *Twenty-First Missouri,* 27–28).

The *Keokuk Daily Gate City,* reports that "James McCarty, a wounded rebel, said that…he knew there were only 800 engaged in the attack on Athens. Other prisoners thought there were 1,200 to 1,500" ("Great Excitement," *Keokuk Daily Gate City,* August 6, 1861; hereafter cited as "Great Excitement"). The *Hannibal Messenger,* August 9, 1861, notes that "not all of [Green's] 1,800 men reached the actual line of battle," as they were strung out from Chambersburg to Athens. The article adds, however, that when the battle began, "the entire column participated heartily in the action" ("The Battle of Athens—Full Particulars," *Hannibal Messenger,* August 9, 1861, in *Farthest North,* 22; hereafter cited as "Full Particulars"). Justicia concurs with this, although estimating the State Guard numbers far more conservatively: "On last Monday (the 5th), Col. Green, with about 500, marched over from Edina, and attacked the Federals in Athens. Through some misunderstanding, the State forces did not all get into action—not more than two hundred of them getting in sight of the enemy." As will be seen, Justicia's rationale for the State Guard retreat from Athens is also a "misunderstanding" ("Justicia," 32).

11. Hiller Letter, 22. The author is unaware of the exact location of Armstrong's "blown down" storeroom at this writing. McKee writes that "Colonel Moore had formed his line of infantry 320 strong, at the brick kiln, one fourth mile from where the enemy was drawn up" ("From John McKee," 25). It is not known to which brick kiln McKee refers; Athens had more than one (Boyd, 45). The only archaeological evidence of a brick kiln in the area places it slightly west of the Athens school and McKee's original bivouac area, which would be two blocks closer to the State Guard than the position described by Hiller (Roger Boyd, telephone interviews, August 2007). Tradition follows Hiller's placement of the defensive line along Spring Street, probably because the Hiller letter was written the day of the battle and is more precise, while McKee's story was written 60 years later. McKee continues: "Our company took a position behind that of Colonel Moore," which would have been anywhere northeast of Elm Street. While imprecise as to the location of Moore's mounted troops, McKee's account suggests the tactic that Moore kept his cavalry in reserve for deployment where needed as the battle developed.

12. Hiller Letter, 22. According to Dixon, the improvised canister had been cut up the night before the battle at a Chambersburg blacksmith shop owned by an "Old Man Botkin" (*Martin Green's Boomerang*, 77). The anvil used in the process was on display at Kenneth Doud's battlefield "museum" in the 1960s, and is owned today by the Battle of Athens State Historic Site. I. M Walters, who had been with Green's right flank, recalled in 1900 that the shrapnel was improvised on the spot during the battle after the solid shot had been used up, that the solid shot had been forged from scrap iron at Chambersburg by a "blacksmith by the name of McDowell, of Marion county," perhaps a soldier in the State Guard (I. M. Walters). One such relic, an oblong solid shot hammered together from scrap metal and partially rounded on a grind stone, was picked up behind Croton years later and is on display at the Santa Fe Depot Museum in Fort Madison, Iowa (Roger Boyd, telephone interviews, August 2007). John McKee (25) writes that the State Guard artillery began with solid shot, then switched to their improvised canister rounds. Walters claims that they switched to scrap iron after they ran out of solid shot.

13. Hiller Letter, 22. In Dixon's transcription (*Martin Green's Boomerang*, 70), "gunner" is given as "gunners." Justicia agrees with Hiller: "The cannons were badly managed—in every instance overshooting—and consequently did no execution" ("Justicia," 32). According to Moore "nearly all the enemy's cannon shot flew over our heads" (McCrary, 172). Rev. G. C. Beaman writes that "their cannonading did no injury, all the balls passing some four feet over the heads of our men…" (G. C. Beaman, 138–139). I. M. Walters asserts that that the pieces of scrap iron fired by Kneisley's cannon "accomplished nothing, except the benefit of the scare they caused by the noise they made on the roofs of houses as they scattered about." Part of the folklore of the battle that Ben Dixon remembered from his youth was that, of James

Kneisley's two Hannibal cannons, "one of 'em couldn't shoot, and the other didn't hit anything" (*Martin Green's Boomerang,* 80).

On the other hand, *History of Lewis* (384) tells that the canister was fired "with some effect," although the writer does not elaborate on what this "effect" could be. And at least one recorded injury was caused by cannon shrapnel (see note 23).

14. "Their cannon was planted on the hill near Capt. Baker's house" (Hiller Letter, 22). *History of Lewis,* states that Kneisley's cannon fired down the "main street"— i.e., Thome Street (384). Ben Dixon's map of the battle shows the rebel battery on the southwest corner of the block west of Virginia Street, between Righter and Baker Streets (*The Man Behind the Men,* 89). This position seems the most likely given the hole fired through the Benning House. However, Anders states that Kneisley parked his battery on "cemetery ridge commanding the road to Alexandria," overlooking the cornfield ("Historian and the Battle," 159–160). It seems unlikely Kneisley would have moved his battery during the fight to this position, given the circuitous route required to do so. Anders does not cite his source for this statement and is the only source known to the author to position Kneisley on Cemetery Hill.

According to Dixon, both the six and nine-pound guns were poured at the Cleaver and Mitchell Foundry of Hannibal, Missouri. The nine-pounder "was poured for Capt. Wm. B. Drescher's Marion Artillery Company at Palmyra. When it disbanded, the gun was given to J. W. Kneisley at Hannibal for his battery…organized on May 21st." He adds that Kneisley already had the six-pounder. The foundry was taken by U.S. Reserves on June 11, 1861. (*Martin Green's Boomerang,* 77). The weights given here refer to the shot of various diameters, with proportional weights, corresponding to the diameters of the bores of the cannon barrels

15. *Martin Green's Boomerang,* 77. It is a part of Athens lore that one of Kneisley's cannon was made from a piece of wood and that it exploded on the first shot, but there are no contemporary accounts verifying this. There are a number of contemporary references to "imitation cannon." The *Gate City* (August 6, 1861) reports: "The rebels had one nine-pounder, one six-pounder and one log cannon." The *Chicago Tribune* reporter writes "the rebels had three pieces—one an eight pounder…the other two pieces were imitation cannon, made out of the cylinders of old steam engines" ("C"). Another *Tribune* reporter, who signed his article as "X," specifies "three (rebel) cannon, two of them brass and the third bored out of a log!" ("The Battle at Athens, Mo.," *Chicago Tribune,* August 8, 1861). The 1887 *History of Lewis* says of Green's artillery: "A company from Marion brought two iron cannon, a six and a nine pounder…a steam pipe was improvised into a sort of swivel or mountain howitzer" (82).

The most complete account of the wooden cannon comes from A. P. Lowry, writing 40 years after the battle. Lowry was a soldier in the 6th Iowa and part of the group that came up from Keokuk after the battle was over. After crossing the river, his group

> marched up near the corn field, deployed as skirmishers, and advanced to the top of the hill, passing as we went, the log cannon…It was made of a sycamore tree, had two or three strips of iron lengthwise, and about five iron bands around it. Has a six inch bore and was mounted on the hind wheels of a cart or wagon. It stood on the

> bluff back of town and was fired but once, and exploded…We put it in the car with
> us and took it to Keokuk with us, and when we left there soon after, it stood in front
> of our headquarters.

(A. P. Lowery, "Iowa Battle at Athens, Mo.," *Iowa State Register,* March 23, 1902;
hereafter cited as A. P. Lowry).

16. Craw, 58. The author can attest to the cannon shot, having seen the cupboard
in the 1960s, standing in the same spot where it had been struck, the upper left
corner taken away by the solid shot. The ball crashed through the wall about three-
quarters up the right front door of the house, to the left of the door, splintering the
molding around it, through the rear wall of the house and out over the bluff, either
into the river or, more likely, given its trajectory, into Croton on the opposite bank
of the Des Moines. Susan Benning refused to have the holes in her walls repaired,
leaving them as graphic testimony to the havoc the hated Yankees had wrought in
her neighborhood. The holes remain in the restored Thome-Benning House today.
According to Croton station agent D. C. Beaman, "(one) shot went over the heads of
General Belknap and myself soon after we got to the depot. It whistled like a shell,
the whistling being made by a sand hole in it, and struck in the hill on my father's
farm back of Croton…" Beaman recovered this ball and later presented it to the
Iowa State Historical Department, along with a rebel flag someone (possibly Beaman himself) had picked up on the battlefield after the battle (D. C. Beaman, 593).
G. C. Beaman wrote that "a tree in my yard was cut off by a cannon ball" (G. C.
Beaman, 139). John Noble recalled that "the balls from the enemy's cannon…flew
quite across the river and struck the hillsides behind us…Many cannon balls however, falling short, struck in the river and splashed up great fountains of water" (John
Noble). The battle rapidly spawned its share of tall tales, perhaps some with roots
in facts. For example, "old Ike Bills used to brag that he caught a wagonload of can-
nonballs while crossing the river from Athens to Croton during the battle" (*Martin
Green's Boomerang, 56*).

17. Doud, 25. Doud writes that "Everybody…went to their cellars, or, if they
didn't have one, to their neighbor's cellar." Colonel Moore recalled in 1892 that "the
women and children of the village were sent to a big mill under a steep bluff, where
they were sheltered from the fire of the enemy…" (McCrary, 172–173).

18. Hiller Letter, 24. "The nine children of Charlotte Milliken (1799–1851) and
William Hiller, Jr. (1796–1851) of Greene County, Pennsylvania all migrated to
northeastern Missouri and southeastern Iowa after their parents died. They were:
Harriet (1823–1893), John (1825–1899), James (1827–1862), Margaret (?–1894),
William (1832–1905), Hiram Milliken (1834–1895), George (? –1904), Amelia
(1838–?), and Royal (1842–1914)." Hiller Family Papers, 1785–1993 (3856), Western Historical Manuscript Collection-Columbia (Missouri), "Biographical Sketch,"
http://whmc.umsystem.edu/invent/3856.html. Royal and Harriet were John Hiller's
brother and sister; Billy and Alexander may have been Harriet's children.

19. Doud, 32.

20. G. C. Beaman, 137. Henry H. Wright of the 6th Iowa, who was present in
Croton, wrote later: "The scene at the Croton station was calculated to chill the
blood in the veins of stout-hearted men in the ranks of the military. Men, women

and children, crazed with fear and excitement, running about crying and pleading for help to reach safety from the awful roar of the cannon and small arms" (H. H. Wright, "The Battle of Athens Again," *Annals of Iowa* 3rd Series, 7 [April 1905]: 70; hereafter cited as Wright). Wright was a private in the 6th Iowa and later wrote a history of the regiment.

21. *Twenty-First Missouri,* 25. One cannon was finally sent on the day of the battle. Word of the State Guard attack reached Keokuk early on August 5, and soon after 8:00 a.m. three companies of Colonel John A. McDowell's 6th Iowa Infantry left on flat cars for Croton ("Great Excitement;" A. P. Lowery). When two hours later handcar messengers reached Keokuk with the rumor that "some 2000 rebels had attacked the Athens camp and driven the Union men over to Croton and the rebels themselves were actually crossing the river," the proverbial fur really began to fly. "Citizens rampaging round town, companies going it on the double quick, and so on. Some five companies of the 5th and three or four companies of the 6th were soon at the depot. A brass six pounder was hauled down there" ("Great Excitement").

22. Jasper Blines, "Reunion of the Twenty-First Missouri," *Clark County Courier,* September 24, 1920, in *Last Reunion I,* 124; hereafter cited as Blines.

23. Letter from John C. Moore, *Keokuk Daily Gate City,* March 21, 1900 (hereafter cited as John C. Moore); Hiller Letter, 22. Dixon, in his transcription (*Martin Green's Boomerang,* 70) renders Hiller's statement: "Our boys stood fine. Remarkably for raw soldiers. And returned a volley of musket balls." What Dixon took for an "n" appears almost certainly to be an "r" to this writer. The *Gate City* reports: "The Colonel…ordered his men to reserve their fire until the enemy (all mounted) were close upon them. This was done, and the Union men fired volley after volley with the steadiness and regularity of veteran soldiers" ("The Battle of Athens," *Keokuk Daily Gate City,* August 7, 1861). This account appears to be wrong in claiming that the attacking center of Green's line was mounted—there is ample evidence that they were fighting dismounted. It is possible that Green mounted an initial cavalry attack on Moore's center, as Moore seems to have done on Green's right in the cornfield. However, one would expect such to be mentioned in Home Guard accounts. More than likely, Green's troops fought as dismounted cavalry and the *Gate City* account mistakenly implies a cavalry charge. The *Hannibal Messenger* repeats the assertion ("Full Particulars," 17).

The timing, and sometimes the sequence, of events in the battle is extraordinarily difficult to determine. How long was it before Moore gave the order for his men to return fire? Did he order it, or did some begin to return fire spontaneously? It seems prudent that Moore would have his men lie down under cannon fire. But for how long? When it became clear that Kneisley's artillerists were overshooting, was the next antidote to jitteriness for the Home Guards the return of fire? At what point and why did the cannonade cease? D. C. Beaman (593) recalls that the rebel gunners "fired only five solid shot—all they had—and a few loads of scrap iron." In Doud's reconstruction of the battle (from the recollections of his father who was a child at the time, and interviews with other eyewitnesses), Kneisley's "six-pounder jammed at the third shot and some say the barrel split…the old nine-pounder shot wild. Must have got 7 or 8 charges of shot out of it" (Doud, 25). I. M. Walters remembers only one cannon being fired and that only eight or ten times because of a lack of gun powder. (In fact, Walters claims that Green's only purpose in coming to Athens was to cross the Des Moines there and approach Keokuk from the northwest in order to raid a powder magazine in the latter city; that he understood David Moore was actually in Canton.) Justicia writes that "the cannon getting out of repair, the commander ordered them off the field" ("Justicia," 33). The Hannibal foundry that cast the guns also cast 100 rounds of solid shot for each (Roger Boyd, telephone interviews, August 2007), but the preponderance of evidence suggests that regular artillery ammunition was not available in any great quantity at Athens.

24. Hiller Letter, 22–23.

25. Green's strategy may have been to occupy Moore's center with artillery fire while surprise attacking both flanks. The Home Guard, in the face of an advance by Green's center, would be boxed in, and either slaughtered, or forced to surrender (especially if he was able to flank, i.e., get behind, them) or flee. Part of the folklore of the battle, probably made up by Dixon, is a council of war held by Green and his officers the night before the battle, where this very strategy is laid out (*Martin Green's Boomerang*, 54–55).

26. "From John McKee," 25. While the impression McKee gives of being surrounded very quickly is likely accurate, it may be somewhat exaggerated, especially his remembered responses, better to justify the retreat of his company. However, the Rev. G. C. Beaman writes of the same coordinated attack: "…the enemy began the engagement, firing a cannon shot as the signal gun. In two minutes after, their right and left wings commenced firing" (G. C. Beaman, 137).

27. McCrary, 172.

28. *Twenty-First Missouri*, 29. Incidentally, James Best's younger brother Joseph, a private in the 1st Northeast Missouri Home Guard, later colonel of the 21st Missouri, married Moore's daughter, Frances, after the war.

29. *Twenty-First Missouri*, 29.

30. Hiller Letter, 22.

31. Elijah Loring Starr obituary, *Clark County Courier* (April 20, 1923), in *Last Reunion I*, 87. Sample and Belknap also had pickets out the night of August 4 and the early morning hours of August 5.

32. McCrary, 172; Hiller Letter, 23; "Historian and the Battle," 159. Eight or ten men of Captain Oliver H. P. Scott's Farmington militia (which had been armed with 100 U.S. rifled muskets on August 2 by Cyrus Bussey and called to Croton August 4 by Moore) had crossed early Monday morning to breakfast with friends in Athens and confer with Moore. "As these men were returning to join their company, having arrived at the ford a short distance below town, the right flank of the enemy numbering some three hundred suddenly emerged from the corn in which they were concealed, and at a distance of not more than thirty yards poured a heavy volley of shot at them." The Farmington men fired back all the ammunition they had before retreating across the river (F. M. Tate).

According to D. C. Beaman, the rebel flanking force was "probably fifty in number…" (D. C. Beaman, 591). Rev. G. C. Beaman gives the number of State Guard in the cornfield as two hundred. He maintains as well that these men were lying for some time in the cornfield, having been "sent…through the brush, between Moore's pickets, on the main road back and down the river…" This movement occurred "during the night of the 4th of August…" (G. C. Beaman, 137). While the reverend's timing of this movement is vague, taken literally it means that these men were in place before midnight of the 4th and lay hidden some five to six hours at least. He writes also that

> all the Union men laid on their arms during the night, expecting an attack, but did not discover the right and left wings of the enemy in the corn and bushes. As daylight dawned, and as the night pickets on the main road back were just taken in, and before the day pickets were out to the extreme lines…the enemy rushed in on the main road, planted their cannon on the bluff just above and back of town.

This could be taken to mean that Moore had pickets on his front, but not on his left and right flanks.

Ten-year-old, Oliver Morrison, who accompanied his State Guard uncle, Andrew Morrison, to Athens, told his neighbor, J. W. Murphy, years later that the State Guard center arrived in Athens only about an hour or an hour and a half before the battle began, around 4:00 a.m., which does not contradict Beaman ("Address by J. W. Murphy," 30).

Both Beamans refer to Moore's "outposts." D. C. states that, at the opening gun, "Colonel Moore's men were mostly in line on the hill at Athens, but small outposts were near the river above and below the town to meet a flank attack by the rebels should one be made." D. C. continues to describe the rout of "the union outpost" in the area of the Gray house at the cornfield, followed shortly by "a union reinforcement from Colonel Moore" of this outpost, or what was left of it. According to D. C. Beaman, then, the initial State Guard fire from the cornfield was directed toward this "small outpost," which broke and was soon replaced by "reinforcement" from Moore (D. C. Beaman, 591–592). The Rev. G. C. Beaman (138) writes that the State Guard in the corn "attacked our picket guards and forty men sent from Farmington to aid us," but does not speak of reinforcement from Moore. If both Beamans are correct, then it seems likely that this Farmington contingent mentioned by G. C. is the same "small outpost" mentioned by D. C. F. M. Tate, quoted above, writes that the eight or ten fired upon on the Missouri side by Shacklett were not an outpost put in position by Moore, but were simply in the process of returning to Croton from a visit to Athens. On the other hand, John Noble recalls that before the battle he had seen "along this slope descending before us [on the Missouri side—author], Colonel Moore had placed a company behind fences and some light obstructions to guard his flank."

Doud tells of his father's experience, as a child, of being stopped by a Union guard at the Old Stone Bridge over Stallion Branch, which would have been Moore's right flank, but this was after the battle (Doud, 24).

33. Tate. The August 6 account in the *Gate City* ("Incidents of the Battle") states that: "In crossing the river Mr. Dickey, of Farmington, was badly wounded, Constable Hendrickson got a buck shot in his leg, John Bruce (of the firm McCrary & Bruce) and J. W. Noble, esq. were slightly grazed," implying that all four were

wounded retreating across the river. F. M. Tate writes that the retreating Iowa troops were Farmington militia and that only two of them (Joseph Dickey and Russell Smith) were wounded. John Noble writes that he was with the group that came up from Keokuk the previous evening, that he had crossed the river in search of coffee, but that he received his wound, a bruise on his arm caused by a spent ball, once he had returned to the Iowa side. It is not known what units Hendrickson and Bruce belonged to or if they were wading the river or shooting from the Iowa side when they were hit. However, "McCrary & Bruce" was a Keokuk law firm, which makes it likely that Mr. Bruce was with the Rifles or Rangers.

34. D. C. Beaman, 592. Beaman contends that it was "impossible for us to wade the river, and any attempt to fight in line would have been disadvantageous," probably because by the time the Rifles and Rangers were in position, Shacklett's Guardsmen were already firing at the Farmington men. For a discussion of the supposed hesitancy of the Keokuk men, see note 13 in Chapter One above.

35. Ibid., 591–592. The distance between the two maple groves was probably more than 200 yards, an easy range for the military weapons of the Iowa militiamen, but not so for the shotguns and squirrel rifles of the State Guard. This arms differential would become a factor elsewhere on the battlefield as well.

36. "The Incidents of the Battle;" Hiller Letter, 23; John Noble. Hiller specifies that the rebel troops were in the "old log house," Noble says they were firing from "a little white house." Recall that Jane Gray's first husband had built a small frame house on the Isaac Gray property very near his father's original two story log house (see note 24 in Chapter 3). It is assumed that the log house was still standing at the time of the battle and the State Guard troops occupied both structures. Only the smaller, frame house remains today.

37. Hiller Letter, 23. This is not the flag pictured on the cover of this book. The Treatment Report by the conservators of the Iowa Battle Flag Project does not mention bullet holes. While Hiller does not identify the troops which "stampeded," it will become clear both from the context of what follows in his letter, and from a reference to colors carried on the retreat by the *History of Lewis* (see following note), that it is almost without a doubt Spellman's retreat to which he refers.

Chicago Tribune correspondent "C" claims that the retreat was actually led by Lt.-Col. Callihan, commander of Moore's left flank. He writes that "in the very beginning of the action, Lieut. Col. Callahan [*sic*], who commanded a company of cavalry, retired with his company across the river…" Justicia concurs that Callihan did not remain long to do battle, writing that "at the first fire…the Rev. Lieut. Col. Callahan [*sic*] (a Methodist Protestant Minister of this county), gave the order to retreat, gallantly leading the flying column across the Des Moines" ("Justicia," 33) The *Chicago Tribune* correspondent does not spare Callihan, adding that "it is said that this gallant officer, who claims to be a graduate of West Point, never stopped until he reached Montrose on the Mississippi River." If what "is said" concerning the length of Callihan's retreat, according to this reporter, is accurate, then he and his men rode approximately 15 miles east "as the crow flies" from Croton. The reporter continues, writing that "through the country over which he and a few of his comrades passed, they spread the report that the Unionists were cut all to pieces, and the Secessionists were advancing into Iowa. The consequence was that the wildest panic seized the people—some flew to arms, some to the bush". The *Gate City* reports that "in the very beginning of the action about 40 Union Cavalry, commanded by Lieut.-Col. Callahan [*sic*], ingloriously fell back, and fled across the Des Moines to Croton" ("The Battle at Athens," *Keokuk Daily Gate City,* August 7, 1861). The article states that another 75 to 100 infantry followed Callihan out of confusion, but that many recrossed the river "to skirmish each on his own hook," showing "that they were no cowards."

The editor of the *Gate City* writes that at about 10 o'clock of the night of the battle two friends came into his office "with sad and anxious faces," relating that Lt.-Col. Callihan had told them that "Col. Moore was a traitor, and his regiment demoralized, surrounded and captured, and that Croton was undoubtedly taken." The editor was able to reassure his friends that the day had turned out quite differently, to their great relief ("A Successful Retreat," *Keokuk Daily Gate City,* August 7, 1861).

38. *History of Lewis,* 385. This source does not mention the flag being riddled, only that Spellman brought it off.

39. McCrary, 172. While the *Chicago Tribune* reporter faults Callihan primarily, Hiller and both Beamans fail to mention either Callihan or Spellman (although G. C. mentions a retreat to Montrose); and Moore, thirty-one years after the fact, clearly faults Spellman, identifying those who retreated as "his company," and makes no reference to Callihan. Moore may have been recalling his problems with Spellman in July of 1861 (see *Twenty-First Missouri,* 23). The *History of Lewis* fails also to mention Callihan. Aaron Harlan in his 1901 poem on the battle attributes the retreat to Callihan (*Martin Green's Boomerang,* 75). Dixon claimed in 1941 that the *Chicago Tribune* reporter was mistaken in identifying Callihan as the initiator of the flight across the Des Moines, stating this correspondent had "perpetrated a rather serious injustice of the Callihan family" (Dixon, "The Battle of Athens: Bibliography," in Mullenix, *The Battle of Athens,* 163–164). In 1951 Dixon wrote that Captain Spellman's hat was shot away at the same time he saw the Iowa militiamen retreating, whereupon he shouted "Come on, men!…we'll never stop 'em," and joined the stampede (Ben F. Dixon, "Battle Report," in Mullenix *The Battle of Athens,* 197; also "Battle on the Border," 10). However, by 1966, Dixon had changed his views and was attributing primary responsibility for the retreat to Callihan. Now it was Callihan who had been startled by having his hat shot away and who supposedly shouted as he fled "Come on, men! …we'll never stop 'em!" (*Martin Green's Boomerang,* 56–57). Anders, perhaps following Dixon, ascribes the quote and the retreat to Callihan who, he later writes, ended up as Chaplain of the 119th Illinois (*Twenty-First Missouri,* 29, 119). The State of Missouri's pamphlet on the battle also attributes the quote to Callihan.

40. *Twenty-First Missouri,* 31; Edith Wasson McElroy, *Years of Valor* (Des Moines, IA: Iowa Civil War Centennial Commission, 1969), 172. McElroy writes that "this house was presented by the Sprouse family to the Iowa Society for the Preservation of Historic Landmarks as a permanent monument to the battle." It is not known whether this was William Sprouse's house at the time of the battle (which might explain why he was taken there) or if it was acquired by the Sprouse family after

the battle. According to the Hawkins Taylor Commission, Sprouse was in Co K, not in Spellman's Co C. (William Sullivan, killed on Athens hill, was in Co K as well.) However, his being taken to an aid station in Croton suggests that he was injured somewhere near Croton. In April 1962, when her son was a Civil War enthusiast eight years of age, the author's mother transcribed the text of a plaque that was affixed to the house where Sprouse died. The plaque reads in part: "This house was used as a 'Field Hospital' during the battle of Athens, Missouri…William Sprouse died in the house from wounds suffered in the battle…" The house was torn down sometime between 1969 and 1986.

41. G. C. Beaman, 138..

42. *History of Lewis,* 384–385. Spellman's cavalry and Small's infantry are usually cited in the same breath as comprising Moore's left wing. They are contrasted in that Spellman's troop, probably led by Callihan, broke and ran while Small stood fast and won the day in the cornfield. It is impossible to determine precisely the sequence and timing of these events short of better evidence. However, it seems likely that the Farmington men preparing to ford the river to return to Croton and Israel Anderson's band, including John Noble, were the first to be fired on by Shacklett. By the time Spellman and Small were approaching their position on Moore's left, Shacklett was receiving fire from the Iowa militiamen on the Iowa side. Spellman's men, being mounted, arrived on the scene before Small's men, and were led across the river by the panicked Callihan. D. C. Beaman (591) recalls seeing "the routed union outpost…retreating, some across the river and some back on to the Athens hill." If, as it seems, he was watching a good sized group of Home Guard scattering, then these were probably Spellman's men, and possibly some of Small's (Beaman does not specify cavalry or infantry), or perhaps the men Noble had seen positioned "behind fences and…slight obstructions."

The writer of the *History of Lewis* could not resist commenting in a footnote on Ellsberry Small's proportions. From the perspective of 1887, he observed that "there is nothing in a name, for he weighed 350 pounds, or thereabouts, although he was of but average height. He was a staunch and brave Unionist, and did good service for the cause. Considering the recklessness with which he exposed himself at Athens, and his elephantine proportions, it is a great marvel that he was not killed" (*History of Lewis,* 385). Small went onto serve as a private in the 21st Missouri.

43. *History of Lewis,* 385.

44. McCrary, 172.

45. Hiller Letter, 23. Whether Hiller was part of the rout, or crossed the Des Moines explicitly to try to stem its tide, is unclear. In his letter, Hiller says that he held the position of Judge Advocate under Moore, which would make him a member of Moore's officer staff. And the fact that he was dispatched to Keokuk the evening of August 4 to request reinforcements suggests that he held a position of leadership in Moore's regiment. He may have been sent across to Croton specifically by Moore to rally retreating troops, although if this were the case, it seems likely that Hiller would have mentioned it in his letter.

Years later, John Hiller would maintain that the retreat across the Des Moines was made under the misapprehension that a retreat had been ordered, which suggests that he was, in fact, part of Callihan's rout ("Battle of Athens," *Keokuk Constitution-Democrat,* August 6, 1889).

46. "C."

47. D. C. Beaman, 592. Beaman seems to imply here that the fire from the Iowa side would have been insufficient to thwart the State Guard in the corn. And he states later in his article that "we never knew what damage we did, but as…the rebels soon…[got] behind the maple trees it is not likely that many were killed or wounded. They returned our fire for a while but did us no damage, as a two-foot maple tree makes pretty good breastwork."

Justicia, on the other hand, ascribes most of the damage sustained by Shacklett's men to the Iowans on the other side of the river, diminishing the fighting prowess of his fellow "Federal" Missourians. His only concession to the latter is superior numbers: "It is conceded by all that the Federals on the Missouri side of the Des Moines greatly outnumbered the State troops engaged. While on the Iowa side of the river, there was a large body, and these inflicted almost all the damage the attacking party sustained, their minie rifles shooting across the river with ease" ("Justicia," 33).

G. C. Beaman (138) also gives complete credit to the Keokuk men and the Croton Guards, firing from the Iowa side, for the ultimate routing of the State Guard from the corn (although he does mention a "crossfire"). The *Keokuk Daily Gate City* reports on August 6, that during the time the Iowa troops were struggling with Shacklett "say an hour and a half, Col. Moore and his four or five hundred men were engaged with the enemy's center and left wing, and gallantly repulsed and routed them." On August 7, the paper paints the same scenario: "it appears that when the attack was made upon him, [Moore] deployed a small force to engage the enemy's left wing…The Col. himself headed his main force." The implication is that Moore gave no thought to his left flank. Therefore, naturally "Col. Moore, in his report to Col. Worthington, gives great credit to the Keokuk boys for holding the enemy's right wing in check, and finally driving them back" ("The Battle at Athens," *Keokuk Daily Gate City,* August 7, 1861). (William H. Worthington was colonel of the 5th Iowa Volunteers and in overall command of the Iowa troops in Keokuk. Ben Dixon notes in *Farthest North* [37], that this report "was either lost, destroyed or is still in hiding.") And according to Tate: "The repulse of this portion of the enemy's forces is entirely due to those troops stationed on this side of the river, and the little squad who engaged them on the opposite shore."

Hiller, G. C. Beaman, Tate, and the *Keokuk Daily Gate City* neglect to mention the role of Small and his men in stopping and routing the State Guard in the cornfield. Credit is no doubt due to the Iowa troops, but it is unlikely that the Rifles and Rangers and Farmington militia firing from the Iowa side of the river, even supported by Hiller and his rallied Home Guardsmen, were solely responsible for the retreat of Shacklett's entire force from the cornfield.

48. Hiller Letter, 23.

49. "The Incidents of the Battle." An Athens historian of later years was Kenneth Doud, whom the author had the pleasure of meeting as a boy. Doud lived in Jane Gray's small frame house and delighted in pointing out the many balls embedded in its various exterior sides as testimony to its having stood in a crossfire. The house

was sided in later years, then covered with metal sheathing to protect it pending restoration.

The *Keokuk Daily Gate City* goes on to claim that once Shacklett's men evacuated the house, "as we are informed, the Rangers and Rifles crossed over to Gray's house, drove the rebels out of the corn, and routed them with loss of several rebel lives," a claim not supported by any other contemporary sources (however, see next note). The *Gate City's* praise of the Rifles and Rangers is leavened slightly in the next day's issue, when it is noted: "…if the Rangers and the Rifles had co-operated in military style, instead of being left to fight Indian fashion, each man on his own hook, they could undoubtedly have taken a large number of prisoners and many more horses" ("The Battle at Athens," *Keokuk Daily Gate City,* August 7, 1861). If fighting "Indian fashion" is taken to mean fighting from behind trees, this would tend to contradict the previous day's claim that the Keokuk militia had recrossed the river and driven the rebels out of the cornfield. If the Keokuk men advanced across the river to the Missouri side as the *Gate City* account of August 6 states, they did so once Shacklett's right was retreating.

In 1901, Cyrus Bussey claimed that "before ten o'clock" on the day of the battle he was in Croton and formed up "several hundred men, including the companies of Capts. Sample and Belknap and companies of the 6th Iowa Infantry," then

> Without a moment's hesitation these companies moved forward, into the river and up the bank on the other side, sending a heavy fire into the ranks of the enemy. These reinforcements were evidently wholly unexpected. The effect was to completely demoralize the rebels, who rapidly retreated, leaving thirty-five or forty men killed or wounded (Bussey, 86).

According to Bussey, among those in the assault was John W. Noble. But as noted previously, Noble remained on the Iowa side and received his minor wound from a spent ball. More plausible is Henry Wright's recollection that three companies of the 6th Iowa Infantry were sent across the Des Moines by Colonel John A. McDowell after the battle had ended to aid in the pursuit of Green (Wright, 70). A. P. Lowery supports this.

Anders dismisses Bussey's and other claims after the fact that the 5th and 6th Iowa regiments had any great influence on the outcome of the battle ("The Historian and the Battle," 166–168).

50. "C." The *Tribune* reporter may have gotten his information from the *Gate City,* which reported that many of the infantry "who were probably confused by Callahan's movements…returned to the skirmish" ("The Battle at Athens," *Keokuk Daily Gate City,* August 7, 1861).

51. "Historian and the Battle," 162.

52. According to the Reverend Beaman, it took about half an hour from the time a crossfire was established on the State Guard to the time at which they "fled for dear life" from the cornfield (G. C. Beaman, 138). John Noble writes of a duel between one Barnesconi of his group and a rebel firing from Jane Gray's frame house. "When Barnesconi would fire, he would step out and fire upon us. Barnesconi finally got another of our men to fire in his stead, and when the reb stepped out, Barnesconi

brought him down." John Moore, son of Colonel Moore, was dispatched by his mother before dawn on the morning of the battle to check on the welfare of his older brother, William, a lieutenant under Green. John arrived after the battle was over via the river road (Water Street) and "saw young Thompson lying dead at the edge of a cornfield…" (John C. Moore). I. M. Walters adds a State Guardsman named Ewalt to the list of the dead in the cornfield.

53. The author traversed the area around Stallion Branch in the summers of 1993 and 1994. In 1993, a year famous for flooding in Iowa, the creek was running strong. In 1994 it was bone dry, and he walked its bed almost to the Des Moines River.

54. *History of Lewis,* 384. The *History of Lewis* identifies Cox as a Captain. The Hawkins Taylor Commission documents list him as a 2nd sergeant of Company F. See *Twenty-First Missouri,* 15–16, for background on Hackney and Cox.

The Rev. G. C. Beaman estimates the number of the State Guard at Stallion Branch at one hundred and claims that, like Shacklett's men, they had been put in place the night before the battle. According to the Reverend, Green's left wing was to have been guided by one "Moreland of Athens," but this guide was taken prisoner by the Home Guard, "which frustrated that wing, as they were ignorant of the rough ground in that direction." It is not known when exactly Duell and Kimbrough lost their guide, but it must have been at some point after they had at least partially taken their position, as otherwise there might have been no threat to the Home Guard right (G. C. Beaman, 137–138).

55. The map in the Battle of Athens pamphlet, prepared by the State of Missouri, locates Hackney's troops on what appears to be the bank of the creek.

56. "From John McKee," 25–26. It is difficult to tell whether Payne and McKee's cavalry retreat preceded or succeeded Moore refusing and advancing his right under Hackney and Cox to meet Duell and Kimbrough at Stallion Branch. If this "flight," in Moore's language, followed Duell and Kimbrough's advance, then it seems hard to avoid the conclusion that Payne and his men studiously avoided reinforcing the Home Guard right on the Missouri side at this point. If their retreat preceded Hackney and Cox's advance, then perhaps it is possible that they were unaware of the reinforcements along Stallion Branch.

57. Hiller Letter, 23. The letter is transcribed in *Martin Green's Boomerang,* 71, where Dixon reads "hill" instead of "run." The word in the author's copy of the facsimile of the original letter appears to be the latter. Kenneth Doud places Benning's slaughterhouse "near the west end of town" where "the road crossed the creek, on what was known as the 'Old Stone Bridge'." Doud indicates that both of these landmarks were near the mill below the Joseph Benning house (Doud, 24).

58. "When the Johnnies Ran," *Clark County Courier,* August 11, 1911, in *Last Reunion I,* 20; hereafter cited as "When the Johnnies Ran." The unnamed writer of this article establishes his credibility by stating that he "has talked with many survivors of the battle of Athens." The article covers specifically the recollections of J. T. Norris.

59. J. W. Murphy mentions this State Guard breastwork in an address at the Old Settler's Meeting, Kahoka, Missouri, in September 1928. Murphy quotes his neighbor in Burlington, Iowa, Oliver Morrison, who was ten years old at the time of the

battle. Morrison's family lived at Luray, Missouri, and his uncle, Andrew Morrison, was a State Guardsman. Murphy recounts what his neighbor had told him, that he, Oliver, camped with his uncle and the State Guard at the Thompson farm the night of August 4, 1861, and moved out toward Athens with the rest of the Guard, about midnight. Morrison recalled that they arrived on the outskirts at about 4:00 a.m., tied their horses in a nearby timber, and began constructing the breastworks of fence rails ("Address by J. W. Murphy," 30). Murphy, in another piece ("Luray and Editor Murphy," 50) written for a reunion of the 21st Missouri, states that he was a young boy at the time, living on his father's farm two miles south of Ashton, but does not claim to have witnessed the battle himself. J. W. Murphy was the editor of a newspaper in northeast Missouri 1913. By 1928 he had moved to Burlington, Iowa, some seventy-five miles north.

In a 1919 article, Murphy recounts an 1880 visit to the battlefield and speaks of "the rail fence behind which the Confederate forces were massed" as having been removed (J. W. Murphy, "Editor Murphy Writes of Athens," *Kahoka Gazette Herald*, March 14, 1919, in Gross, *Last Reunion II,* 53; hereafter cited as "Editor Murphy Writes of Athens"). Battle of Athens Site Administrator Roger Boyd says that tradition places a breastwork from the battle on Elm Street where it crosses Virginia (Roger Boyd, telephone interviews, August 2007). This is considerably far forward of Kneisley's position on Baker Street, and basically right at John McKee's cavalry camp. For this reason and the fact that the structure was of a more permanent nature, having been made of earth, the berm that persisted to the end of the 19th century was more likely part of Moore defences. Any barricade erected by the State Guard would have been more temporary and unlikely to last, even until 1880.

60. "Address by J. W. Murphy," 30. Tests conducted by the army in the 1850's determined that the .58 caliber minie ball fired from a rifle-musket could penetrate four inches of soft pine at 1,000 yards (Bilby, 87–88).

61. "Address by J. W. Murphy," 30. J. T. Norris also remembered fighting with the knowledge that the State Guardsmen's "squirrel rifles and corn knives wouldn't reach as far as the Federal guns" ("When the Johnnies Ran," 20). Moore acknowledged the differential: "They were armed with shot guns and squirrel rifles, which were no match for our improved muskets" (McCrary, 173). Moore's testimony weighs heavily here because presumably it would have been more in his interest to claim that tactics, not technology, accounted mainly for his victory.

Prior to the middle of July, David Moore's army was probably no better armed than Green's. Recall that sometime after July 17 Moore received 250 stands of arms through Colonel Bishop (see note 10 in Chapter 3 above). Then, on August 2 Cyrus Bussey had distributed more than 500 rifles (counting those given to the Keokuk and Farmington militias) that he had commandeered in Keokuk. A. P. Lowry of the 6th Iowa wrote in 1902 that his company (Co I) was armed with smoothbore flintlocks (probably US Model 1816s) converted to percussion, muzzleloaders which fired "buck and ball" (a cartridge consisting of a .69 caliber round ball topped with three buckshot). But, according to F. M. Tate, the Keokuk militiamen in the Iowa maple grove were armed with "Yaeger rifles and muskets." In a lengthy 1895 newspaper account of the Keokuk Rifles's participation at Athens, H. Scott Howell wrote: "our arms were a short, heavy gun with a large bore, called Yaegers…" (Howell). John Noble, writing in 1900, recalled that before leaving for Croton on August 4, he had armed himself with a "Mississippi Yaeger rifle."

Noble may have been referring to US Model 1841 rifle, a .54 caliber caplock so named for its use by Jefferson Davis's Mississippi regiment during the Mexican War. "Yaeger" (or *Jäger,* German for "hunter") describes a sort of short-barreled, heavy German hunting rifle. The name was attached to the 1841 rifle possibly because of its shorter overall length of 48 ¾ inches (as opposed to approximately 58 inches for both the Model 1816 and the Model 1861 Springfield rifles). Some of the 1841s were rebored to .58 caliber prior to the Civil War (Bilby, 53). Cyrus Bussey does not specify the model or caliber of the weapons he took in Keokuk, beyond saying that they came directly from Washington, DC, and they were the same caliber as the ammunition Frémont had given him on July 30. If the Keokuk (and probably also the Farmington) militia was armed with Model 1841 rifles (either rebored to .58 caliber or not), one might infer from this that all weapons distributed by Bussey were of this description. It is unlikely that Moore's weapons were of any newer manufacture, as there was an extreme shortage of the very newest models (the 1861 Springfield) at the beginning of the war, and the rifles Bussey seized were meant to be used by Dodge for training, then left to arm the citizens of western Iowa once Dodge's infantry departed for the war (Bussey, 91). Moore's reference to "improved muskets" might imply older US models that had been converted or rebored, like the US Model 1816 or Model 1841. Bussey might have distributed smoothbore conversions, but all indications are that these weapons were rifled.

Most all sources agree that Martin Green's men were armed with whatever they could find: flintlocks, small caliber sporting weapons, shotguns, pistols, hatchets, corn knives, and clubs, and they were very short of ammunition (I. M. Walters). *History of Lewis* (82) describes the arming of Green's men at Horseshoe Bend:

> The men were all mounted and armed with hunting rifles, shot-guns and revolvers. Provisions and provender were obtained from friends in the country. Ammunition was taken wherever it could be found; the stores at Williamstown and Monticello were stripped of their powder, lead and caps, which were sometimes paid for and sometimes not.

This was the situation for Missouri rebels in general in 1861 (Bilby, 29). Hinze and Farnham concur, writing that the "countryside produced little more than useless antiques, shotguns and squirrel rifles. Most of the Missouri militiamen assembled unarmed, sporting only high spirits and…bold confidence…" (Hinze, 32).

Local U.S. authorities were determined to keep any weapons out of the hands of the disloyal. The following notice appeared at intervals during the summer of 1861 in the *Keokuk Daily Gate City*:

> War! War! War!
> All persons keeping or having for sale any or all kinds of Munitions of War, such as Guns, Pistols, Revolvers, and all kinds of Ammunition, are required not to sell to any person without an order from the undersigned. This order must be strictly complied with, under penalty of forfeiting all articles mentioned, in their possession. John Stannus, Surveyor of the Port, Keokuk, July 13, '61.

This is possibly the same "John Stannus of Keokuk, [who] has a horse won by his rifle" (Untitled battlefield report, *Keokuk Daily Gate City,* August 6, 1861.)

62. *Twenty-First Missouri,* 31; *The Man Behind the Men,* 90; "Luray and Editor Murphy," 50. Anders mistakenly identifies Sullivan as an "elderly onlooker," but he was a Home Guard soldier, as filled with martial élan as any teenager in Moore's army. He was involved in the distribution of Bussey's muskets at Athens ("From John McKee," 25), and according to the *Keokuk Daily Gate City,* "he was shot while eagerly and bravely pursuing the enemy in advance of his friends ("More Incidents," August 7, 1861; the paper had erroneously reported on August 6 that Sullivan had been "taken prisoner and *murdered*"). Murphy confuses Sullivan with William Sprouse, who was mortally wounded and taken to Croton where he died. Jabez Harrison was J. W. Murphy's uncle. He mentions that another uncle, W. P. Murphy, later enlisted, but does not specify his regiment or branch of service, only that he rode "Old Frank" to the service, this thanks to the fact that Harrison's widow, Susan, followed Green's army into Knox county and insisted that they return the horse ("Luray and Editor Murphy," 50). John C. Moore saw Sullivan's body after the battle and noted that he had been shot in the forehead.

63. "When the Johnnies Ran," 20. Presumably this exaggerated report is of the initial success of Shacklett's men pouring fire down on Spellman's hapless Home Guardsmen stampeding across the Des Moines with "colors flying."

64. Ibid.

65. Ibid. This cry occurred, according to "a man who was with the Federals," when "the Johnnies began charging…" Norris did not regard this as a full-blown charge because, after stating that he and his comrades might as well have been shooting into the air once they realized the range of the Federal muskets, he states that "of course, in the circumstances, the thing for us to have done would have been to charge the enemy…" He continues by stating that "there were plenty of us to have overwhelmed him, brass buttons and all." This may well have been possible if Norris and his comrades could have closed the distance between the Home Guard center and themselves.

Norris's last comment makes one wonder if the Home Guard had been supplied with regulation uniforms as well as muskets. Anders contends that David McKee and Spellman's delegation to St. Louis was sent to arrange not only for muskets but also "for rations and clothing to come later by rail to Croton" (*Twenty-First Missouri,* 23). If so, and if it came, it seems a fair assumption that this "clothing" might have been regulation Federal uniforms, or at least some parts thereof. Doud writes that his father, in being detained by the Home Guards after the battle, encountered "a man in nondescript trousers, blue coat with large brass buttons and battered head gear known as a forage cap," and later "other men in parts of uniform…" (Doud, 24). When John Moore reached the battlefield in mid-morning, he noticed "many hundreds of Iowa soldiers, all in uniform" in Athens, "taking breakfast." These were probably the regular volunteers of the 5th and 6th Iowa. Archaeological digs on the battlefield have yielded a number of brass buttons in the area of the McKee House (Roger Boyd, telephone interviews, August 2007).

John Noble, not a member of any organized militia group, fashioned his own uniform before leaving for Croton:

> I had attended a fancy dress ball (or party) at Col. John Sullivan's in the character of a Dutchman, and there had worn a hickory shirt, knickerbockers, with belt and a red cap...I found...they suited the case exactly. I put on my uniform, leaving off the cap and adopting a soft hat in lieu. My wooden shoes "wooden" do, and I put on heavy boots...

According to H. Scott Howell: "The uniform of the City Rifles was made of gray cloth with black braid trimmings and cap to match..." (Howell).

66. "When the Johnnies Ran," 20.

67. McCrary, 173. The bayonet is often denigrated as an insignificant combat weapon in Civil War literature. Yet, later bayonet charges in the war against seasoned troops proved true Jasper Blines' description of Moore's order to "Charge Bayonets" as "an emergency appeal which inspires the attacked with amazement and horror, and the young and untrained of Green's companies were seized with fear and were panic stricken" (Blines, 124).

68. "The Battle at Athens," *Keokuk Daily Gate City,* August 7, 1861. The *History of Lewis* (385) states:

> ...the advancing [State Guard] line halted, stood a moment irresolute and weak, and then wavered. It was the turning point in the fight, Green saw it, and sought to rally and force his men again into action. Moore saw it, and with all of his extraordinary volume of voice, called out loud enough for every man on both side to hear him, even above the roar of the conflict: 'Forward! charge bayonets!' With a shout, the Unionists sprang away to the front, up the hill, over all the irregularities of the ground, unimpeded and unresisted."

The author clearly views Moore's timing as crucial: "Five minutes more and Green would have rallied his men, they would have caught their 'second wind,' and who could tell what the result would have been" (*History of Lewis,* 385).

69. D. C. Beaman, 592–593. The various stories surrounding Moore's sons at the Battle of Athens fall mostly in the category of tall tales, but cannot be ignored for the fact that at least one of his sons, 20-year-old William, *did* join Martin Green's army and that this contributed to the animosity and suspicion that some of his political foes harbored for David Moore. Ben Dixon wrote in 1969: "it is difficult...to substantiate the story that three of Col. Moore's boys fought in Green's army at Athens; or that two of them, John and Gene, started the Rebel stampede" (*The Man Behind the Men,* 114). But this did not keep Dixon from filling an earlier book with all sorts of fancied scenes featuring the Moore sons before and during the battle (*Martin Green's Boomerang,* 49–50, 54–55, 57, 80).

Before the outbreak of war, David and son William Moore had organized rival companies of militia in their village of Wrightsville (later known as Union, thanks to David Moore). "Every Saturday morning each company—one for the Union and the other for the South—would march about the square and execute all sorts of military maneuvers. The people were dreading that every day something would occur that might precipitate an encounter, because feeling was running high" ("When the Johnnies Ran," 20). There is no way of knowing, but the animosity between the two groups couldn't have been running too high at this point, or neither would have tolerated the other's presence. And it has been established that David Moore's Unconditional Unionism was not cemented until sometime after the attack on Fort Sumter. At some point in the early summer, his sons went off to join the State Guard (*Twenty-First Missouri*, 23).

If the oldest son William had brought a company of Wrightsville boys with him, it stands to reason he would have been made its commander. And a Captain William Moore was listed in the order of battle on Green's right wing at Athens ("Full Particulars," 22). Dixon places the younger two sons here and even credits one with having shot off Lt.-Col. Callihan's (or was it Captain Spellman's?) hat. When they heard their father shout "Forward! Charge! Bayonets!" they looked at one another and said: "Did you hear that…that's Pappy…an' he's mad as a hornet!…Less git outa here!" (*Martin Green's Boomerang,* 57–58). Although Moore's "Give the Rebels hell, boys! Charge!" was said to have been heard "above the din of battle" ("The Battle at Athens," *Keokuk Daily Gate City,* August 7, 1861), it is hard to imagine it could be heard down in the Gray cornfield. Roger Boyd believes the Moore sons must have been fighting with Green's center in order to have heard their father's voice (Roger Boyd, telephone interviews, August 2007). John C. Moore, David's third son and 15 years old in 1861, wrote a letter to the *Keokuk Daily Gate City* in 1900 in which he denied fighting at the Battle of Athens. He said his older brother William was a lieutenant under Green, but that there was another "Will Moore" commanding on Green's right. He makes no mention of his brother Eugene.

William Moore met with his father in Keokuk in April 1862, where the latter was recuperating from losing a leg at the Battle of Shiloh, and vowed to quit the State Guard. The father pledged to pay the son's expenses to study medicine in Ohio. The latter went west to practice his profession and died around the turn of the century. Eugene became a successful newspaperman in Memphis and Palmyra, Missouri, and Toledo, Ohio. John became prosecutor of Scotland County, moved west and became mayor of Enid, Oklahoma, where he died in 1919 (*Twenty-First Missouri*, 78, 268).

70. I. M. Walters.

71. "When the Johnnies Ran," 20. Norris makes no mention of a Home Guard charge, bayonet or other. The only reason for the mad retreat he offers is his and his comrades' realization that they were outgunned by the Home Guards (as discussed above). This seems sufficient motivation for a withdrawal, even a fighting withdrawal, but it hardly seems sufficient to account for the scene Norris describes. Young Oliver Morrison's narration to J. W. Murphy parallels Norris, that "the Confederates soon found that Moore's men had a great advantage in weapons, so they decided to quit" ("Address by J. W. Murphy," 30–31). As a result of his men breaking into the unordered charge, Moore stated that "the enemy fled in every direction from the field" (McCrary, 173).

According to Kenneth Doud, the Home Guard was formed by Moore into a "V" formation, with the point of the "V" directed at Green's center. Whether Doud was extrapolating from other battles (e.g., the 6th Wisconsin charged the unfinished railroad cut the first day at Gettysburg in this formation), or whether this is a detail of the Home Guard charge he actually heard from witnesses, cannot be determined from his account (Doud, 25).

Jeffrey Wert claims that the 6th Wisconsin's formation was unintentional in that the flank companies did not hear the order to charge. Consequently, those in the center of the regiment along the Chambersburg Pike went over a fence first, those on the flanks following once they saw the charge underway. It is entirely possible that Moore's formation, if per Doud, resulted from similar lack of hearing (Jeffrey Wert, *A Brotherhood of Value: The Common Soldiers of the Stonewall Brigade, C.S.A., and the Iron Brigade, U.S.A.* [New York: Touchstone/Simon & Schuster, 1999], 256).

Jasper Blines wrote that "Moore's logic was to break their center. He said that was the real military logic of the crisis and the only way to win" (Blines, 124).

72. When the Johnnies Ran," 20. Justicia (33) writes that Kneisley's withdrawal instigated the general stampede: "It is said that retreat was caused by a misunderstanding of orders: the cannon getting out of repair, the commander ordered them off the field; at this the whole centre gave way, thinking the order to retreat was given, then the upper division [Duell and Kimbrough—author] and lastly the one below the town [Shacklett—author]." Justicia writes also that only 200 or 500 State Guards were actually in action, and this due to a misunderstanding as well (32).

73. "When the Johnnies Ran," 20. Norris is mistaken in remembering that no prisoners were taken on the retreat. John Hiller (23) states specifically that "15 or 20" prisoners were captured at this point in the battle.

One of the tall tales engendered by the retreat was that of Martin Green astride a Missouri mule which kept balking. Green, after berating the mule with such backhanded jibes as, "Mule, you don't know how to run! You ought to be in Dave Moore's army!" was said to have finally abandoned his steed, giving it a healthy kick with the words, "Get out of the way, you long-eared Yank, and let somebody run who can!" (*Martin Green's Boomerang*, 59).

Contrary to his image in this tale, which Dixon ascribes to Yankee humor, Martin Green became a brigadier general, fighting at Iuka, Corinth, Port Gibson, and Vicksburg. At Corinth he led his men in a charge which resulted the next day in taking some inner works of the Federal defenses. Commanding a sector of the Vicksburg defenses, he was wounded on June 25, 1863, and, while reconnoitering a Union position on the 27th, was shot through the head and killed instantly. Norris and the *History of Lewis* note that many of his men who retreated at Athens served valiantly on future battlefields.

74. Some later accounts imply that it was Moore's charge on the center which occasioned the collapse of the State Guard flanks (see, e.g., *The Man Behind the Men*, 114). This may be due to desire to credit Moore, particularly, and his charge with turning the tide of the battle. There is some evidence suggesting that the retreat of Green's flanks may have preceded Moore's charge (see next note). Tactically, one might wonder why Moore would advance his center as far as he did if he was uncertain whether Green's right or left was to his rear and capable of sweeping in behind him. Thus his own recollection that he ordered his right and left to stand fast makes eminent sense. One wonders whether this order reflects reports that they were, in-

deed, standing fast; if not, information that Green's right and left were retreating.

75. *History of Lewis,* 385–386. One of Shacklett's men wrote years later that the State Guard right pulled back around Cemetery Hill out of the range of rifle fire from the Iowa side, but went no further, having not been informed of Green's retreat.

> …the wonder is that [we were] not annihilated… Shortly afterwards some of Green's men appeared at the edge of the timber and hallooed to us loudly that General Green had retreated. No second announcement was needed. We retreated across the corner of the field to the timber and was soon with the main force again, retreating westward with them. (I. M. Walters)

76. Hiller Letter, 23.

77. "From John McKee," 26.

78. Hiller Letter, 23.

79. *History of Lewis,* 388.

80. John Hiller writes: "we took several prisoners and horses probably 15 or 20 of the latter and guns blankets ammunition etc." (Hiller Letter, 23). Other captured items mentioned in newspaper reports immediately following the battle include "trophies," two rebel (or "secession") flags, "5 wagon-loads of supplies, and a quantity of arms." One source adds to the previous list, "the mock cannon" (see note 15 above). David Moore remembered the "fruits of victory" as including "many prisoners, 450 horses, saddles and bridles complete, hundreds of arms, and a wagon load of long knives with which they expected to fight the infantry" (McCrary, 173). The Rev. G. C. Beaman lists "sixty-three horses, three or four wagon loads of provisions, some few guns, one keg of powder, and sundry small weapons" (G. C. Beaman, 139).

81. *History of Lewis,* 388. The location of Green's camp at this point is given by this source as "Short's well." The *History of Lewis* goes on to add that "the cannon used at Athens afterward formed a part of Capt. Kneisley's 'black battery,' and did service at Shelbina, Lexington, Pea Ridge and elsewhere." According to J. W. Murphy, Colonel Shacklett's son claimed after the war that the State Guards sunk the guns in a pond on the Harr farm four miles west of Athens, later recovering them by night from their temporary watery grave ("Luray and Editor Murphy," 50).

82. G. C. Beaman, 139.

83. "More Incidents," *Keokuk Daily Gate City,* August 7, 1861.

Notes to Chapter Five

1. Hiller Letter, 24. The "Hon Wm Moreland" Hiller mentions may be the same Moreland who was to have guided the State Guard left wing (see note 54 in Chapter 4).

John Hiller did not remain with David Moore; whether this was a consequence of his having left the fight on the Missouri side or not is unknown to the author. His obituary states that he was provost marshal with the 1st Northeast Missouri Home Guard, but resigned and joined the 2nd Missouri Cavalry, "serving as acting Captain and as such was commander of the post at New Madrid, Mo., for a time." He returned to Athens after the war and became postmaster; he then became "Government Storekeeper and Guager [*sic*]." Dividing his later years between Kahoka and Vernon, Indiana, where his brother-in-law lived, he died in Vernon and was returned to Kahoka for burial. His obituary concludes that "he was a man of generous impulses and had many friends in the community" ("Death of John Hiller," *Kahoka Gazette-Herald,* November 26, 1899, in *Last Reunion II,* 113).

Hiram Milliken Hiller, according to his brother John, "was not in the fight having gone to Elders the night before" (Hiller Letter, 23–24). A William Elder, Sr., along with his son, William, Jr., were members of Hackney's "Athens" company (F). In a document of June 21, 1861, Hackney, Cox, Hull, David McKee, and others asked that he "be stricken from" the "rolls, for…secretly making disloyal speeches" (Hawkins Taylor Commission documents, cited in *The Man Behind the Men,* 146). The author has not determined whether this is the same Elder family.

Dixon wrote in 1962, that Hiram Hiller headed up one wing of the "neutralist" or "peace committee," the other wing of which met at the Bennings on July 25, 1861. Hiller's wing went to St. Louis first to see Frémont. It was then to go to Jefferson City to see the governor, in the hope that both would withdraw troops from north of the Missouri River. Frémont did not give them an audience, and Hiller returned to Athens, writes Dixon, "just in time to unlimber his trusty squirrel rifle and take a few pot shots at some of Martin Green's fleeing heroes" ("They Fought in the Battle of Athens," in Mullenix, *The Battle of Athens,* 206–207). Apparently Dixon, who published his transcription of John Hiller's letter in 1966, was unaware of what John wrote about Hiram not being at the battle, or did not pick up on this detail, when he wrote his article of 1962.

What is the significance of Hiram Hiller visiting a possibly disloyal family the night before the battle? More to the point, what was David Moore's attitude toward Hiram's participation in the peace delegation? If the *Chicago Tribune* correspondent's interpretation is correct, that the effect of the peace delegation was to encourage defections from Moore's Athens camp prior to the battle, then there was significant sympathy among the Home Guard rank and file for the mission of these peace committees (see note 29 and the corresponding text in Chapter 3 above).

According to J. W. Murphy, "loyal meetings were held in both Grant and Sweethome townships" in early 1861 "where and when men were enrolled in the Home Guards" (the Highland School meeting in March, described in Chapter 3, was doubtless one of these meetings). "The Home Guards, enlisted in this county, became the nucleus of Colonel Moore's army…Hiram M. Hiller…organized these Home Guard meetings and apparently…was the soul of the Union movement in Clark county…" ("Address by J. W. Murphy," 31).

If both Murphy and Dixon are correct, is Hiller's being the "soul of the Union movement" and fighting at Athens consistent with his being a member of the peace delegation to St. Louis? Hiller went on to fight and command in Federal service. His commitment to the Union was the last word. Perhaps he was a Unionist who attempted to prevent, almost to the last minute, what his brother described as "our neighbors…engaged against us," but in the final analysis was willing to wage war to save the nation.

Hiram did not remain with Moore either. In 1863 he became colonel of the 2nd

Missouri Cavalry, the regiment in which his brother served as acting captain. Hiram "served with gallantry and distinction throughout the war." He and his wife kept their residence in Athens until after the war when they moved to nearby Waterloo, Missouri, to farm. They moved to Kahoka in 1872. There, on August 14, 1895, he was the victim of what his obituary called "the most distressing accident of a local nature that this paper has ever been called upon to chronicle." The colonel had seen fit to crawl under instead of go around a stalled freight train in town. The train started up while he was under it, crushing his left leg from knee to ankle and mangling his left arm. His leg was amputated, but he died the same day ("Col. H. M. Hiller Injured by the Cars, Resulting in His Death," *Kahoka Gazette-Herald*, April 14, 1895, in *Last Reunion II*, 114).

The colonel's old white war horse was also a celebrity in Kahoka. Having served faithfully during the war, the old horse was put out to pasture on a farm on the Fox River a couple of miles north of Kahoka. On July 4, 1872, the old horse apparently heard the strains of martial music from a band and galloped all the way into the town square where the festivities were underway (Ben F. Dixon, "Colonel Hiller's War Horse," *Clark County Courier*, February 27, 1942, in *Last Reunion II*, 115).

2. Justicia (34) writes:

> After the repulse of the State Troops, the Home Guard displayed more vandalism than ever…Small scouting parties ranged all over the country taking up loose horses on the prairie, and driving off stock. In the town they destroyed gardens and took possession of private houses: they broke open Judge Baker's house and appropriated everything in it, taking meat, flour, groceries, bedding, silver spoons, and even ladies' wearing apparel. The same is true of the house of Mathias Scott and others. In the surrounding country they seized horses, wagons, provisions, and in fact everything they wanted, without even giving their worthless I.O.U.'s in exchange.

3. *Twenty-First Missouri*, 31. In addition to appropriating his store for a hospital, the Home Guard refused to let Spurgeon's merchandise be moved out for several days, according to Justicia (34).

Newspaper accounts immediately following the battle gave the number of Home Guard wounded as anywhere from 6 to 18, and that of the State Guard from 7 to 75. Rev. G. C. Beaman, writing in 1868, gave the Home Guard loss as 23 wounded, State Guard 60 or 70 wounded (G. C. Beaman, 139).

History of Lewis provides the following sketch of William Aylward:

> Dr. William Aylward lived about nine miles northeast of Memphis [Missouri], and was farming and selling goods when the war broke out. He was assistant surgeon of Col. Moore's command while it lay at Athens…He was a staunch Union man, and a great hater of those who sympathized with the Southern cause…On the Sunday [July 13, 1862] previous to the fight near Pierce's Mill, Col. [Joseph] Porter marched into Memphis with two or three hundred men, and occupied the place over night. He then arrested Dr. Alyward…That night Dr. Aylward was killed and left lying in a field…(521).

The revenge killing of Aylward led to considerable condemnation of Col. Porter's command in the pro-Union Missouri newspapers. For more information on Alyward see Joseph A. Mudd, *With Porter in North Missouri* (Washington, DC, 1909. Reprint. Iowa City, IA: Press of the Camp Pope Bookshop, 1992), 65–75.

4. Most papers reprinted the roster originally given in the *Keokuk Daily Gate City,* August 6, 1861.

5. *Twenty-First Missouri,* 31. In October, Mattley and the men of his company would refuse the movement toward federalization, stating that their war was in Missouri. Moore arrested Mattley who resigned shortly thereafter (41). Fuller is listed as "Porter Fuller" in the list of wounded in the *Keokuk Daily Gate City* of August 6, 1861.

6. "From John McKee," 26; John C. Moore.

7. Hiller Letter, 23–24. The spelling in this excerpt, as in all of Hiller's, has not been corrected. "Secession" may be a nickname for Jim McArtor. The *Keokuk Daily Gate City* lists a James McCarty among the injured rebels. This may be the same individual as Hiller's Jim McArtor, as both Hiller and the paper specify a non-mortal hip wound ("The Rebel Loss at Athens," *Keokuk Daily Gate City,* August 6, 1861). However, families of both names lived in Clark County (*History of Lewis,* 932–933).

8. Hawkins Taylor Commission. Newspaper accounts immediately following the battle give the number of Home Guard dead as anywhere from 2 to 12. G. C. Beaman correctly notes three battle deaths and one mortal wounding (G. C. Beaman, 139).

9. "The Rebel Loss at Athens," *Keokuk Daily Gate City,* August 6, 1861. The *Gate City* reported initially that "the number of rebels killed and mortally wounded is doubtless over 25. Six or eight were found on the field, and the rebels who brought in the flag of truce, in the afternoon, admitted they had carried off 14 dead and many more were wounded and missing."

10. "More Incidents," *Keokuk Daily Gate City,* August 7, 1861. Other newspaper accounts immediately following the battle put the number of State Guard dead as low as 2 and as high as 43. Justicia, who consistently reports higher Home Guard and lower State Guard numbers than other accounts, writes that "the loss of the State forces were two killed and eight or ten wounded—one of the wounded may die."

Since there are other reports, reputedly made by State Guardsmen, enlisted men and officers, giving substantially higher numbers of State Guard dead, it seems at least likely that Justicia is deflating the State Guard casualties and inflating those of the Home Guards for propaganda's sake. This is not to claim that pro-Home Guard sources did not engage in distortions as well. Justicia claims also that the State Guard party carrying the flag of truce was "was arrested by…Colonel Moore, and detained for several days. They brought with them two captains they wished to exchange, Col. Moore promised to give two privates in exchange for them. This promise he did not keep, but finally, he released two boys." There is no other account known to the author claiming that two Home Guard Captains were captured by the State Guard. It is unclear in the last sentence of this excerpt from Justicia as to whether the "two boys" ultimately released by Moore were those promised in exchange for the prisoners brought in by the State Guard party with a flag of truce, or whether these two are of that party themselves which had been "detained for several days;" the former seems more likely from the context ("Justicia," 33–34).

Another account of the battle in the Justicia vein was published in the St. Louis *Daily Bulletin*:

> We have been furnished the following letter, written by a gentleman at Athens, giving an entirely different account of the battle at that place. The gentleman who furnishes the letter endorses the reliability of the writer:
> "Col. Martin Green (brother of ex-Senator Green), at the head of 450 men, who had been organized under the military bill, attacked Col. Moore, whose force numbered 650, and drove them across the Des Moines river, where Moore was reinforced from Keosauqua and other towns above. Green attacked them a second time and drove them before him, until Col. Moore was reinforced again, when after a hard fight, Green retreated, carrying off their two pieces of artillery, wounded, etc. Green had to fight in all from two to three thousand men, yet his boys fought with all the coolness of veterans, and drove them back in every hand to hand fight.
> "Among the state troops who were killed, eight in all, were some of the best men. The following names are all that I have obtained: Jos. Ewalt, Eli Butler, Mr. Moore, Mr. Williams, Young Bowles, all living in this neighborhood.
> "There is no doubt but the Federals lost from 200 to 300 men, in killed and wounded.
> "The country is thoroughly aroused and the masses are very indignant at the intermeddling with their rights by the people of Illinois and Iowa, who, at the instance and information of every intermeddling, cowardly Black Republicans, send their armed hordes to rob and murder our best citizens.
> [Signed] A. B. O."

(Reprinted as "A Secesh Account of the Battle of Athens," *Keokuk Daily Gate City*, August 15, 1861.)

Leaving aside the exaggerated numbers, it is understandable that a civilian, possibly observing the battle from the relative safety of Croton, could witness three separate Home Guard retreats, the recrossing of the river near the dam by Payne and Hiller, and the advance of the 6th Iowa in midmorning and come up with this description of the battle.

11. "Luray and Editor Murphy," 50–51. Fifteen years later Murphy identifies his source as W. H. Shacklett, probably the same person ("Address by J. W. Murphy," 30–31). According to the *History of Lewis* (1211), Benjamin Shacklett had four living sons at the time of the Civil War: Eli, Jacob, William F. and Ben G.

12. "Address by J. W. Murphy," 31.

13. The village of Ashton, halfway between Kahoka and Luray, was laid out in 1883 (*History of Lewis*, 362).

14. "Luray and Editor Murphy," 50. Since the Wyaconda River is that to which Murphy's father went, we may assume that it was the closest water source. The Wyaconda runs more or less parallel to the Des Moines and is some fifteen miles southwest of Athens.

15. Wright, 70.

16. "Following Up the Enemy," *Keokuk Daily Gate City*, August 6, 1861; "Military Movements," *Keokuk Daily Gate City*, August 7, 1861. It is interesting to note that General John Pope, overall commander of Federal troops in Missouri north of the city of St. Louis, had already ordered an invasion of northeast Missouri on

August 2, for the purpose of dispersing "all bands of armed Secessionists." Bussey's 3rd Iowa Cavalry was to head for Memphis, eventually rendezvousing with the 5th and 6th Iowa Infantry regiments at Edina, which in turn were to march from Keokuk by way of Waterloo and from Canton by way of Monticello, respectively. Events at Athens had changed these plans, however (*O. R.*, Series 1, vol. 3:421–422).

17 "Battle on the Border," 12–13.

18 "Reported Disturbance in Athens," *Keokuk Daily Gate City*, August 8, 1861; "Another Alarm," *Keokuk Daily Gate City*, August 27, 1861.

19. Hiller Letter, 24.

Notes to Appendix

1. *O. R.*, Series 3, 1:67.

2. *The Man Behind the Men*, 139.

3. H. R. 148, 37th Congress, 2nd Session (1861–63), *A Century of Lawmaking for a New Nation: U.S. Congressional Documents and Debates, 1774–1875*, http://memory.loc.gov/ammem/amlaw/.

4. *O. R.*, Series 3, 3:1138; U.S. Congress. *Senate Executive Journal.* 38th Congress, March 16, 1863, *A Century of Lawmaking for a New Nation: U.S. Congressional Documents and Debates, 1774–1875*, http://memory.loc.gov/ammem/amlaw/.

5. Ben F. Dixon, "They Fought in the Battle of Athens, August 5, 1861," *Last Reunion, I*, 14.

6. Benjamin F. Gue, *History of Iowa From the Earliest Times to the Beginning of the Twentieth Century*, 4 vols. (New York: The Century History Company, 1903), 4:259.

Bibliography.

Books, Pamphlets, Articles

Anders, Leslie, "'Farthest North': The Historian and the Battle of Athens." *Missouri Historical Review* 69 (January 1975): 147–168.

__________. *The Twenty-First Missouri: From Home Guard to Union Regiment.* Westport, CT: Greenwood Press, 1975.

Beaman, D. C., "The Battle of Athens, Missouri." *Annals of Iowa* 3rd Series, 6 (January 1905): 590–593.

Beaman, Rev. G. C., "Battle at Athens, Missouri." *Annals of Iowa* 1st Series, 6 (April 1868): 136–139.

Bilby, Joseph. *Civil War Firearms: Their Historical Background, Tactical Use and Modern Collecting and Shooting.* Conshohocken, PA: Combined Books, 1996.

Bussey, Cyrus. "The Battle of Athens, Missouri." *Annals of Iowa* 3rd Series, 5 (July 1901): 81–92.

Craw, Lucretia S., "Athens and the Southerns," in Gross, *The Last Reunion: The Story of Clark County's Civil War Veterans, Book II,* 58–60. N.p.: Jan Gross, 1991.

Dixon, Ben F. "Battle on the Border: Athens, Missouri, August 5, 1861." *Annals of Iowa* 3rd Series, 36 (Summer 1961): 1–15.

__________. "The Battle of Athens: Athens, the Place," in Mullenix, *The Battle of Athens,* 160–162. N.p.: Patricia McWhortor Mullenix, 1991.

__________. "The Battle of Athens: Bibliography," in Mullenix, *The Battle of Athens,* 162–164. Kahoka, MO: Patricia McWhortor Mullenix, 1991.

__________. *The Battle of Athens: "Farthest North of the Civil War."* San Diego, CA: Ben F. Dixon, 1960. Reprinted in Mullenix, *The Battle of Athens,* 1–38. Kahoka, MO: Patricia McWhortor Mullenix, 1991.

__________. "The Battle of Athens: More About Moore," in Gross and Mullenix, *The Last Reunion: The Story of Clark County's Civil War Veterans, Book I,* 33–

34. N.p.: Jan Gross and Pat Mullenix, 1990.

__________. "The Battle of Athens: Pioneer Greens," in Mullenix, *The Battle of Athens,* 176–178. Kahoka, MO: Patricia McWhortor Mullenix, 1991.

__________. "Battle Report," in Mullenix, *The Battle of Athens,* 197. Kahoka, MO: Patricia McWhortor Mullenix, 1991.

__________. "Eightieth Anniversary of the Battle of Athens," in Mullinix, *The Battle of Athens,* 159–160. Kahoka, MO: Patricia McWhortor Mullenix, 1991.

__________. *"Farthest North: 1861" The Man Behind the Men Behind the Guns.* San Diego, CA: Don Diego's Libreria, Ben Franklin Junior Historical Series, No. 21, 1969. Reprinted in Mullenix, *The Battle of Athens,* 89–148. Kahoka, MO: Patricia McWhortor Mullenix, 1991.

__________. "Jim and Martin Green," in Mullenix, *The Battle of Athens,* 192. Kahoka, MO: Patricia McWhortor Mullenix, 1991.

__________. *Martin Green's Boomerang.* San Diego, CA: Family Historians, No. 15, The Ben Franklin Junior Historical Series, 1966. Reprinted in Mullenix, *The Battle of Athens,* 39–88. Kahoka, MO: Patricia McWhortor Mullenix, 1991.

__________. "They Fought in the Battle of Athens," in Mullenix, *The Battle of Athens,* 206–208. Kahoka, MO: Patricia McWhortor Mullenix, 1991.

Doud, Kenneth. *The Good Old Days: Clark County, Missouri.* Athens, MO: Kenneth Doud, 1963.

Fellman, Michael. *Inside War: The Guerrilla Conflict in Missouri During the American Civil War.* New York: Oxford University Press, 1989.

Fulton, Charles J. "The Coalport Home Guards." *Annals of Iowa* 3rd Series, 14 (October 1923): 82–94.

Garretson, O. A. "The Battle of Athens." *Palimpsest* 8 (April 1927): 138-149.

Gross, Jan. *The Last Reunion: The Story of Clark County's Civil War Veterans, Book II.* N.p.: Jan Gross, 1991.

Gross, Jan and Mullenix, Patricia M. *The Last Reunion: The Story of Clark County's Civil War Veterans, Book I.* N.p.: Jan Gross and Pat Mullenix, 1990.

Gue, Benjamin F. *History of Iowa From the Earliest Times to the Beginning of the Twentieth Century.* 4 vols. New York: The Century History Company, 1903.

Hinze, David C. and Farnham, Karen. *The Battle of Carthage: Border War in Southwest Missouri, July 5, 1861.* Campbell, CA: Savas Publishing Company, 1997.

Hiller, John M., Letter to brother, August 5, 1861. In Gross and Mullenix, *The Last Reunion: The Story of Clark County's Civil War Veterans, Book I,* 22–24. N.p.: Jan Gross and Pat Mullenix, 1990.

History of Lewis, Clark, Knox and Scotland Counties, Missouri. St. Louis, Chicago: The Goodspeed Publishing Co., 1887. Reprint. Marceline, MO: Walsworth Publishing Co., 1981.

Jordan, Philip D. *Catfish Bend—River Town and County Seat.* Burlington, IA: Mississippi Valley Publishers, Craftsman Press, Inc., 1983.

McCrary, George W. "The Battle of Athens." In *War Papers and Personal Reminiscences 1861-1865, Read Before the Commandery of the State of Missouri, Military Order of the Loyal Legion of the United States,* 169–176. St. Louis: Becktold & Co., 1892.

McElroy, Edith Wasson. *Years of Valor.* Des Moines, IA: Iowa Civil War Centennial Commission, 1969.

McKee, David. Letter from David McKee to James B. Fry, Provost Marshall General. December 7, 1863, St. Louis, Missouri, in Gross, *The Last Reunion: The Story of Clark County's Civil War Veterans, Book II,* 67–68. N.p.: Jan Gross, 1991.

McPherson, James M. *Battle Cry of Freedom: The Civil War Era.* New York: Oxford University Press, 1988.

__________. *For Cause and Comrades: Why Men Fought in the Civil War.* New York: Oxford University Press, 1997.

Mudd, Joseph A. *With Porter in North Missouri: A Chapter in the History of the War Between the States.* Washington, DC: The National Publishing Company, 1909. Reprint. Iowa City, IA: Press of the Camp Pope Bookshop, 1992.

Mullenix, Patricia M. *Athens' Memories: From Battlefield to Missouri State Historic Site,* in Mullenix, *The Battle of Athens,* 149–234. N.p.: Patricia McWhortor Mullenix, 1991.

Mullenix, Patricia M. *The Battle of Athens.* N.p.: Patricia McWhortor Mullenix, 1991.

Nevins, Allan. *The Emergence of Lincoln.* Vol. 1, *Douglas, Buchanan, and Party Chaos 1857–1859.* New York: Charles Scribner's Sons, 1950.

__________. *The Emergence of Lincoln.* Vol. 2, *Prologue to Civil War 1859–1861.* New York: Charles Scribner's Sons, 1950.

Page, David. "A Fight For Missouri." *Civil War Times Illustrated* 34 (August 1995): 34-38.

Rowan, Steven, trans. *Germans For a Free Missouri: Selections From the St. Louis Radical Press, 1857-1862.* Introduction and commentary by James Neal Primm. Columbia, MO: University of Missouri Press, 1983.

Savage, Alice. *Excerpts Form the Diary of John Savage.* N.p., 1980.

Shue, Richard S. *Morning at Willoughby Run: July 1, 1863.* Gettysburg, PA: Thomas Publications, 1995.

Snead, Thomas L. *The Fight for Missouri: From the Election of Lincoln to the Death of Lyon.* New York: Charles Scribner's Sons, 1886.

Starr, Nehemiah D. and Holman, Timothy W. *The 21st Missouri Regiment Infantry Veteran Volunteers. Historical Memoranda.* Fort Madison, IA: Roberts & Roberts, Printers, 1899.

Wert, Jeffrey. *A Brotherhood of Value: The Common Soldiers of the Stonewall Brigade, C.S.A., and the Iron Brigade, U.S.A.* New York: Touchstone/Simon & Schuster, 1999.

Wright, H. H. "The Battle of Athens Again." *Annals of Iowa* 3rd Series, 7 (April 1905): 70.

Government Sources

Library of Congress. *A Century of Lawmaking for a New Nation: U.S. Congressional Documents and Debates, 1774-1875.* http://memory.loc.gov/ammem/amlaw/.

National Archives. Records of the Adjutant General's Office 1780's-1917. Record Group 94. 94.11 Other AGO Records 1861-74. Records of the commission on claims of officers and men in Departments of the West and the Missouri (Hawkins Taylor Commission).

United States War Department. *The War of the Rebellion: A Compilation of the Official Records of the Union and Confederate Armies,* 70 vols. in 128. Washington, D.C.: US Government Printing Office, 1880-1901. Reprint. Harrisburg, PA: National Historical Society, 1980.

Newspaper Sources

Chicago Tribune

"C." "Northeast Missouri, Terrible Condition of Affairs, Correct History of the Athens Fight." *Chicago Tribune.* August 14, 1861.

"X." "The Battle at Athens, Mo." *Chicago Tribune.* August 8, 1861.

Clark County Courier

Blines, Jasper. "Reunion of the Twenty-First Missouri," *Clark County Courier.* September 24, 1920, in Gross and Mullenix, *The Last Reunion: The Story of Clark County's Civil War Veterans, Book I,* 124–125. N.p.: Jan Gross and Pat Mullenix, 1990.

Charlotte Harrison Boone obituary. *Clark County Courier.* May 4, 1923, in Gross, *The Last Reunion: The Story of Clark County's Civil War Veterans, Book II,* 29. N.p.: Jan Gross, 1991.

Dixon, Ben F. "The Battle of Athens: Martin Green, Rebel," *Clark County Courier.* September 26, 1941, in Gross and Mullenix, *The Last Reunion: The Story of Clark County's Civil War Veterans, Book I,* 35–36. N.p.: Jan Gross and Pat Mullenix, 1990.

__________. "Colonel Hiller's War Horse." *Clark County Courier.* February 27, 1942, in Gross, *The Last Reunion: The Story of Clark County's Civil War Veterans, Book II,* 115. N.p.: Jan Gross, 1991.

Elijah Loring Starr obituary. *Clark County Courier.* April 20, 1923, in Gross and Mullenix, *The Last Reunion: The Story of Clark County's Civil War Veterans, Book I,* 87. N.p.: Jan Gross and Pat Mullenix, 1990.

J. H. Oldenhage obituary. *Clark County Courier.* July 10, 1914, in Gross, *The Last Reunion: The Story of Clark County's Civil War Veterans, Book II,* 117. N.p.: Jan Gross, 1991.

Joe Farris obituary. *Clark County Courier.* February 20, 1924, in Gross, *The Last Reunion: The Story of Clark County's Civil War Veterans, Book II,* 96–97. N.p.: Jan Gross, 1991.

John T. McKee obituary. *Clark County Courier.* July 18, 1924, in Gross, *The Last Reunion: The Story of Clark County's Civil War Veterans, Book II,* 89. N.p.: Jan

Gross, 1991.

"Major David McKee at Rest. After Months of Untold Suffering the Brave Spirit is Released." *Clark County Courier*. March 18, 1896, in Gross, *The Last Reunion: The Story of Clark County's Civil War Veterans, Book II*, 69. N.p.: Jan Gross, 1991.

Murphy, J. W. "Luray and Editor Murphy." *Clark County Courier*. September 19, 1913, in Gross, *The Last Reunion: The Story of Clark County's Civil War Veterans, Book II*, 50–51. N.p.: Jan Gross, 1991.

"Reunion of the Twenty-First Missouri." *Clark County Courier*. September 24, 1920, in Gross and Mullenix, *The Last Reunion: The Story of Clark County's Civil War Veterans, Book I*, 124–125. N.p.: Jan Gross and Pat Mullenix, 1990.

"When the Johnnies Ran." *Clark County Courier*. August 11, 1911, in Gross and Mullenix, *The Last Reunion: The Story of Clark County's Civil War Veterans, Book I*, 20–21. N.p.: Jan Gross and Pat Mullenix, 1990.

Clark County Gazette

"The Battle of Athens." Letter from David Moore, July 24, 1886. *Clark County Gazette*. August 5, 1886, in Mullenix, *The Battle of Athens*, 155. N.p.: Patricia McWhortor Mullenix, 1991.

Hannibal Messenger

"The Battle Of Athens—Full Particulars." *Hannibal Messenger*. August 9, 1861, in Mullenix, *The Battle of Athens*, 16–18. N.p.: Patricia McWhortor Mullenix, 1991.

Iowa State Register

A. P. Lowery, "Iowa Battle at Athens, Mo." *Iowa State Register*. March 23, 1902.

Kahoka Gazette-Herald

Becker, C. L., "Alexandria During the War." *Kahoka Gazette-Herald*. August 18, 1911, in Gross and Mullenix, *The Last Reunion: The Story of Clark County's Civil War Veterans, Book I*, 119–120. N.p.: Jan Gross and Pat Mullenix, 1990.

Brown, Mrs. Albert. "Civil War's Message to Garcia Changed The Battle of Athens." *Kahoka Gazette-Herald*. August 17, 1951, in Mullenix, *The Battle of Athens*, 195-196. Kahoka, MO: Patricia McWhortor Mullenix, 1991.

"Col. H. M. Hiller Injured by the Cars, Resulting in His Death." *Kahoka Gazette-Herald*. April 14, 1895, in Gross, *The Last Reunion: The Story of Clark County's Civil War Veterans, Book II*, 114–115. N.p.: Jan Gross, 1991.

"Death of John Hiller." *Kahoka Gazette-Herald*. November 26, 1899, in Gross, *The Last Reunion: The Story of Clark County's Civil War Veterans, Book II*, 113. N.p.: Jan Gross, 1991.

Murphy, J. W. "Address by J. W. Murphy at Old Settler's Meeting." *Kahoka Gazette-Herald*. September 28, 1928, in Gross, and Mullenix, *The Last Reunion: The Story of Clark County's Civil War Veterans, Book I*, 27–31. N.p.: Jan Gross and Pat Mullenix, 1990.

Murphy, J. W., "Editor Murphy Writes of Athens." *Kahoka Gazette-Herald*. March 14, 1919, in Gross, *The Last Reunion: The Story of Clark County's Civil War Veterans, Book II*, 53. N.p.: Jan Gross, 1991.

Keokuk Constitution-Democrat

"Battle of Athens." *Keokuk Constitution-Democrat*. August 6, 1889.

Keokuk Daily Gate City

"The Battle at Athens." *Keokuk Daily Gate City*. August 7, 1861.

"Battle of Athens: That Exciting Engagement Graphically Described by H. Scott Howell." *Keokuk Daily Gate City*. December 27, 1895.

"Expedition Of Captain Sample's Company." *Keokuk Daily Gate City*. August 5, 1861.

"Following Up the Enemy." *Keokuk Daily Gate City*. August 6, 1861.

"General Noble's Speech at Athens." *Keokuk Daily Gate City*. August 5, 1900.

"Great Excitement." *Keokuk Daily Gate City*. August 6, 1861.

"The Incidents of the Battle." *Keokuk Daily Gate City*. August 6, 1861.

Letter from C. L. Becker. Part of the series "Historical Notes by C. P. Birge Upon Events in Clark County in 1861." *Keokuk Daily Gate City*, March 20, 1900.

Letter from I. M. Walters. Part of the series "Historical Notes by C. P. Birge Upon Events in Clark County in 1861." *Keokuk Daily Gate City*. March 23, 1900.

Letter from John C. Moore. Part of the series "Historical Notes by C. P. Birge Upon Events in Clark County in 1861." *Keokuk Daily Gate City.* March 21, 1900.

Letter from John Noble. Part of the series "Historical Notes by C. P. Birge Upon Events in Clark County in 1861." *Keokuk Daily Gate City.* January 28, 1900.

"Military Movements." *Keokuk Daily Gate City.* August 7, 1861.

"More Incidents." *Keokuk Daily Gate City.* August 7, 1861.

"The Rebel Loss at Athens." *Keokuk Daily Gate City.* August 6, 1861.

"A Secesh Account of the Battle of Athens." *Keokuk Daily Gate City.* August 15, 1861.

"A Successful Retreat." *Keokuk Daily Gate City,* August 7, 1861.

Untitled battlefield report. *Keokuk Daily Gate City.* August 6, 1861.

Tate, F. M. "The Farmington Company at Athens." *Keokuk Daily Gate City.* August 13, 1861.

St. Louis Missouri Democrat

"The Fight at Athens, Missouri." *St. Louis Missouri Democrat.* August 9, 1861, in Mullenix, *The Battle of Athens,* 13–15. N.p.: Patricia McWhortor Mullenix, 1991.

"The Fight in Clark Co., Mo." *St. Louis Missouri Democrat.* August 9, 1861, in Mullenix, *The Battle of Athens,* 11–12. N.p.: Patricia McWhortor Mullenix, 1991.

"From Camp Carnegy, Canton, Mo., Special Correspondence, August 6, 1861." *St. Louis Missouri Democrat.* August 10, 1861, in Mullenix, *The Battle of Athens,* 8-10. N.p.: Patricia McWhortor Mullenix, 1991.

St. Louis Tri-Weekly Missouri Republican

"The Battle of Athens." *St. Louis Tri-Weekly Missouri Republican.* August 8, 1861, in Mullenix, *The Battle of Athens,* 4. N.p.: Patricia McWhortor Mullenix, 1991.

"Justicia," "Affairs in Clark County," *St. Louis Tri-Weekly Missouri Republican.* August 16, 1861, in Mullenix, *The Battle of Athens,* 31–34. N.p.: Patricia McWhortor Mullenix, 1991.

Unspecified

"From John McKee." Unnamed county newspaper, July 9, 1922, in Gross and Mullenix, *The Last Reunion: The Story of Clark County's Civil War Veterans, Book I,* 25–26. N.p.: Jan Gross and Pat Mullenix, 1990.

The Valley Whig (Keokuk)

"Skirmishing in Clark County, Mo." *The Valley Whig.* July 29, 1861.

Unpublished Sources

Boyd, Roger. "Archaeological Research: Battle of Athens State Park, Athens, Clark County, Missouri: Draft Report." Kirksville, MO: Northeast Missouri Regional Planning Commission, 1986.

Cheney, Margarette Dreyer. Unpublished Gray Family Genealogy. 1953.

Doud, Richard. "As I Recollect: The Reminiscences of Kenneth I. Doud, as Told to His Son Richard in 1972." (Unpublished manuscript).

Murphy, Steve. "The Battle of Athens, Clark County, Missouri, August 5, 1861." (Unpublished manuscript, July 1995).